Credits

Authors
Paul Tondeur
Jeff Winder

Reviewers
Trevor Burton
Stuart Caunt
Patrick Rushton

Acquisition Editor
James Lumsden

Development Editor
Darshana D. Shinde

Technical Editor
Gaurav Datar

Indexer
Rekha Nair

Editorial Team Leader
Gagandeep Singh

Project Team Leader
Priya Mukherji

Project Coordinator
Zainab Bagasrawala

Proofreader
Camille Guy

Graphic Coordinator
Nilesh Mohite

Production Coordinator
Aparna Bhagat

Cover Work
Aparna Bhagat

About the Authors

Jeff Winder is an independent Flash developer living and working in Amsterdam, the Netherlands. He discovered Flash and ActionScript in 2003, mainly creating timeline animation, but was soon gripped by non-timeline coding. He has a special interest in new technologies that are related to Flash, especially open source projects such as WiiFlash, FLARToolKit, and Papervision3D. Jeff acquired an MSc in Social Psychology at the University of Amsterdam. He is also a passionate musician, playing guitar and drums. Since 2006, Jeff has been self employed and working for leading agencies. You can contact him at `http://www.jeffwinder.nl`.

 Jeff wrote chapters 1, 3, 5, 6, 10, 11, and 12.

I am not sure whether I should thank my close friends and family for their warm support, or apologize, for not being there for a while. Anyway, I deeply appreciate your patience and understanding, so to everyone who kept asking how the book was coming along—thank you!

I would also like to thank Paul. Writing this book together has been a rewarding experience.

Paul Tondeur is as an Internet entrepreneur who lives and works in Amsterdam, the Netherlands.

He started as a freelance PHP and Flash developer during his study of multimedia technology in 2003. After successfully completing his study, he was asked to become the CTO of a Dutch online marketing agency in 2004. At this company, he developed a strong interest for 3D and got the chance to get professionally involved as the technical lead for serious Second Life projects. However, Second Life was too limited to fulfill his needs to create accessible interactive multiplayer 3D content on the Web, and this is when he found out about Papervision3D during the early days. Because of his passion for the Flash platform, this was love at first sight.

At the beginning of 2009, Paul decided he had to take more advantage of his technical skills as an Internet entrepreneur. Currently he helps other companies as a Unity, Papervision3D, Red5, and mobile streaming consultant. Together with a team of people around him, he is also involved in creating a browser-based MMO, incorporating the usage of Red5, Unity, Flash, and Papervision3D. You can contact him at http://www.paultondeur.com.

 Paul is the initiator of this book and wrote chapters 2, 4, 7, 8, 9, and 13.

I would like to thank my family and friends who have been enormously patient and supportive while I was working on this book and had no time for social life. Especially my girlfriend — Marloes — has been of great support. She kept me inspired and motivated when I was working around the clock to finish this challenging task. Last, but not least I want to thank Jeff for being such an encouraging partner to write this book with.

We both would like to thank the following people or groups of people. First of all, this book would never have been possible without the knowledge shared by the Papervision3D community, which we experienced as open and enthusiastic. The many blogs and tutorials have been an important source of information, along with all the questions and answers on the mailing list.

We also would like to express our gratitude towards the reviewers, proofreaders, editors and modelers. The meticulous inspection of the manuscript by the reviewers—Stuart, Trevor, and Patrick—has been of great value. The cooperation with the editors at Packt Publishing —James, Darshana, Zainab, and Gaurav—has been inspiring and satisfying.

We very much appreciate the answers that the Papervision3D team gave us when we had some questions left. Finally, a special thanks to Janneke de Koning and Job Steggink, who created and animated the 3D model used in the book.

About the Reviewers

Trevor Burton lives in the North of England and currently works as a Senior Software Engineer at Infrared5. He works primarily in Actionscript and Java, and has been working with Flash since Flash 4. He has also worked with Papervision3D since it was released as an open source project in 2006 and has a wealth of experience developing Flash games, from banner adver-games to multi-million pound online gambling applications. In his spare time, he experiments with multiuser and human-computer interaction (http://www.flashmonkey.org).

Stuart Caunt's interest in 3D computer graphics started a long time ago, sometime around the release of Tron in 1982. His interest in 3D modeling lead to him obtaining a Ph.D. in astrophysics and from there the development of parallel-processing models of magnetized fluidflows.

After leaving research he became a software engineer at a research institute in France. From the development of OpenGL 3D data visualization tools, he has pursued other projects of his own in the domain of 3D computer graphics. Most recently this has been web-oriented and he has published a popular series of tutorials at http://blog.tartiflop.com for both Papervision3D and Away3D.

Patrick Rushton is a user-experience designer living in Amsterdam. He works as Interaction Director at communications agency Dynamic Zone, where he uses Flash to create brand-building online experiences that combine interactivity, motion graphics, gaming, and 3D. He blogs about web design, music, 3D modeling, and interactive television on his web site http://www.patrickrushton.com.

Table of Contents

Preface

This book is about Papervision3D, an open source engine that brings 3D to the Flash Player. Papervision3D is an easy-to-use library written in ActionScript 3.0 that allows developers to create 3D in Flash. Papervision3D lets you build real-time 3D, giving you the tools to create exciting and interactive 3D experiences. From simple banners to advanced online campaigns and from creative portfolios to shooter or racing games, the possibilities are numerous. Because it runs in Flash, you can easily put it on the web, or make it available as installable AIR application.

Getting started with Papervision3D can be quite a challenge due to several initial steps that need to be taken such as downloading the source, installing new tools, and unfamiliarity with custom classes. This book shows you how to download Papervision3D and how to make it work in Flash, Flex Builder, and Flash Builder. A short and down-to-earth introduction to working with classes is included and in a walk-through you will build your first application. From here on, we take a closer look at the engine, discussing a broad range of topics. We will examine how to work with built-in 3D objects, use cameras, and apply materials. Many examples and demos are included, illustrating how to animate cameras, objects and light, and load custom-made models. To add more realism to your objects, you will learn how to add special effects and shaders. After reading this book, you will also know how to optimize the performance and quality of your projects.

This book covers the basics, but is by no means only for beginners. The thorough explanation of the engine and the numerous tricks and tips make it a valuable resource for every Papervision3D user.

What this book covers

Chapter 1 – Setting Up is a step-by-step introduction on how to configure Flash CS3, Flash CS4, Flex Builder, or Flash Builder for creating Papervision3D projects. Several ways of downloading the Papervision3D source code are discussed and you will publish an example project to make sure you have configured your authoring tool correctly to get along with this book.

Chapter 2 – Building Your First Application will guide you through the steps that lead to building your first Papervision3D application. If you are new to working with classes and object-oriented programming, a brief introduction will help you on your way. Once this topic has been covered, the chapter continues by explaining what a scene in Papervision3D is made of and how to build a basic application.

Chapter 3 – Primitives covers primitives, which are basic building blocks for Papervision3D applications. It shows how to create a plane, sphere, cylinder, cone, cube, paper plane, and an arrow. An explanation about how vertices and triangles form a 3D object is included.

Chapter 4 – Materials examines how to use the available Papervision3D materials and properties such as interactivity, smoothing, animation, and tiling. You will build a 3D carrousel, made of materials that are discussed throughout this chapter.

Chapter 5 – Cameras explains how to affect the way you see objects in 3D space by altering the settings of the camera. Some of these settings originate in real-world cameras such as focus, zoom, and field of view. Other settings are common in 3D, but don't have an equivalent in the real world. All available camera types will be discussed. By the end of this chapter, you will know how to work with a target camera, free camera, debug camera, and spring camera.

Chapter 6 – Moving Things Around discusses how to animate your 3D objects and camera by moving or rotating them. You will not only learn how to manually animate objects on enter frame but will also be shown how to use Tweener — a tweening engine that makes it very easy to animate your objects and add all kinds of easing.

Chapter 7 – Shading introduces the presence of light in order to add several levels of shade to 3D objects. All available shading types will be discussed, from very lightweight flat shading, to better looking but heavier shading types such as Gouraud shading, cell shading, Phong shading, bump maps, and environment maps.

Chapter 8 — External Models is about working with models and animated models that have been created in external programs. A handy list of advice is included that can be used by modelers who are in need of creating a model for use in Papervision3D. The workflow between a few modeling tools and Papervision3D is explained in detail. You will learn how to export models from Autodesk 3ds Max, Maya, SketchUp, and Blender. Several models will be imported into Papervision3D such as the Utah teapot and an animated mill.

Chapter 9 — Z-Sorting covers how Papervision3D draws its renders to the viewport and the issues with determining which object should be drawn first. Several strategies to solve these issues are discussed such as viewport layers and quad tree rendering. Examples that are made with an external 3D model will be used to demonstrate these solutions.

Chapter 10 — Particles discusses the lightweight particle object, which is a 2D graphic that always faces the camera. The concept of a particle is discussed in detail and we will walk through several examples that demonstrate how you create particle materials, particle fields, emitters, and billboards. We will take a look at Flint, which is an external particle system that provides easy ways to emit particles.

Chapter 11 — Filters and Effects covers how you can add all kinds of filters and effects to your renders. Adding glows, shadows, blurs, blend modes and alphas are demonstrated in detail, as well as effects like fire, fog and reflection. We will create an illusion of depth of field by applying several levels of blurs to objects, depending on their distance to the camera.

Chapter 12 — 3D Vector Drawing and Text covers vector-based shapes in 3D space. They can either be lines, shapes, built-in vector text, or vector text generated by an external typography tool.

Chapter 13 — Optimizing Performance discusses how to speed up the performance of your Papervision3D applications. An introduction on what performance exactly is will be given, followed by a broad range of tips and tricks that guarantee the best possible performance.

While reading through chapters you might come across the following icon: [Ex.]. The icon will be combined with the name of an example. The name in between the icons refers to two things — to the full working example in the code bundle and to an appendix in the code bundle. For example, if you see something like [Ex.] Text3DExample, this indicates that the code for Text3DExample is available as a working project that can be found in the code download.

What you need for this book

To get along with this book, you need to have Flash CS3, Flash CS4, Flex Builder 3, or Flash Builder 4 installed. All examples run on Mac, Windows, and Linux. Where needed, the book demonstrates how to set up things under Windows and Mac only.

You should also be able to make the examples work with FDT, Flash Develop, and previous Flex Builder versions, although these have not been tested and might require some extra work.

The code and examples in the book have been tested for Papervision3D 2.1 revision 920. Read in Chapter 1 how and where you can download this version.

Who this book is for

This book is aimed at Flash and 3D developers who want to get started with creating interactive 3D experiences in Flash, and for those who have already worked with Papervision3D, but want to extend their knowledge and understanding. The book assumes that you have some experience with ActionScript 3.0, but you do not have to be familiar with classes and OOP, an introduction on these topics is included.

Conventions

In this book, you will find a number of styles of text that distinguish between different kinds of information. Here are some examples of these styles, and an explanation of their meaning.

Code words in text are shown as follows: Next, we need to define the `modelLoaded()` method.

A block of code will be set as follows:

```
var sprite:Sprite = new Sprite();
addChild(sprite);
```

When we wish to draw your attention to a particular part of a code block, the relevant lines or items will be shown in bold:

```
var sprite:Sprite = new Sprite();
sprite.x = 100;
sprite.y = 100;
addChild(sprite);
```

New **terms** and **important words** are shown in bold. Words that you see on the screen, in menus or dialog boxes for example, appear in our text like this: "clicking the **Next** button moves you to the next screen".

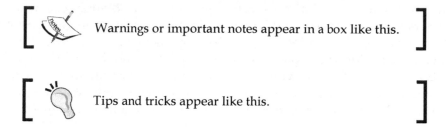

Warnings or important notes appear in a box like this.

Tips and tricks appear like this.

Reader feedback

Feedback from our readers is always welcome. Let us know what you think about this book—what you liked or may have disliked. Reader feedback is important for us to develop titles that you really get the most out of.

To send us general feedback, simply drop an email to feedback@packtpub.com, and mention the book title in the subject of your message.

If there is a book that you need and would like to see us publish, please send us a note in the **SUGGEST A TITLE** form on www.packtpub.com or email suggest@packtpub.com.

If there is a topic that you have expertise in and you are interested in either writing or contributing to a book, see our author guide on www.packtpub.com/authors.

Customer support

Now that you are the proud owner of a Packt book, we have a number of things to help you to get the most from your purchase.

Downloading the example code for the book

Visit http://www.packtpub.com/files/code/5722_Code.zip to directly download the example code.

The downloadable files contain instructions on how to use them.

Errata

Although we have taken every care to ensure the accuracy of our contents, mistakes do happen. If you find a mistake in one of our books—maybe a mistake in text or code—we would be grateful if you would report this to us. By doing so, you can save other readers from frustration, and help us to improve subsequent versions of this book. If you find any errata, please report them by visiting http://www.packtpub. com/support, selecting your book, clicking on the let us know link, and entering the details of your errata. Once your errata are verified, your submission will be accepted and the errata added to any list of existing errata. Any existing errata can be viewed by selecting your title from http://www.packtpub.com/support.

Piracy

Piracy of copyright material on the Internet is an ongoing problem across all media. At Packt, we take the protection of our copyright and licenses very seriously. If you come across any illegal copies of our works in any form on the Internet, please provide us with the location address or website name immediately so that we can pursue a remedy.

Please contact us at copyright@packtpub.com with a link to the suspected pirated material.

We appreciate your help in protecting our authors, and our ability to bring you valuable content.

Questions

You can contact us at questions@packtpub.com if you are having a problem with any aspect of the book, and we will do our best to address it.

1
Setting Up

Getting an open source project such as Papervision3D up and running can be daunting if you don't know where to start. In this chapter, we will walk through the process of setting up your development environment step by step. You will learn how to download, install, and configure everything you need to create Papervision3D applications.

This chapter covers the following:

- Three ways to download Papervision3D
- Configuring your authoring tool to make the code work
- Running some examples
- Using the documentation

When we call Papervision3D an open source 3D engine for the Flash platform, what exactly does "engine" stand for?

Basically, Papervision3D is made up of a set of folders with a certain structure. These folders comprise of custom ActionScript classes that provide a well-laid-out architecture, which allows you to create 3D content in Flash. There is nothing like a `.exe` or `.app` file that you can download. There's no file that you can double-click and install. However, by downloading these set of folders and by including them in your ActionScript project, you can access them the same way you would access the Flash API or the custom classes that you may have written yourself.

For example, if you are familiar with ActionScript 3.0 you have probably heard of the `DisplayObject` class. `MovieClip`, `Sprite`, and `Button` are all display object classes. Analogous to this class, there is a class within the Papervision3D library called `DisplayObject3D` with its own variables, methods, and properties. Therefore, after downloading and installing these set of folders, you'll be able to access `DisplayObject3D`'s variables, methods, and properties just like you would access them in a regular built-in class such as `DisplayObject`.

To illustrate, let's compare some code, based on the Flash API to the code written with the Papervision3D library. The next two lines may look familiar as they instantiate the Flash `DisplayObject` class and add the instance to the stage:

```
var myObject:DisplayObject = new DisplayObject();
stage.addChild(myObject);
```

Now, take a look at the following two lines that hold some Papervision3D code:

```
var myObject3D:DisplayObject3D = new DisplayObject3D();
scene3D.addChild(myObject3D);
```

This time the Papervision3D `DisplayObject3D` class is instantiated and the instance is added to a 3D scene. You can clearly see the similarity between the 2D Flash code and the Papervision3D code. More on 3D scenes will be discussed in Chapter 2. The Papervision3D API has many methods and properties that resemble their 2D equivalents. Methods such as `addChild()` and `removeChild()` have been added to Papervision3D, in order to stay as close as possible to the Flash API and its display list.

Let's take a look at how we can download the library of Papervision3D classes, also known as the **source code**.

Downloading Papervision3D

Papervision3D is hosted by Google Code. You can find the **Project Home** at:
`http://code.google.com/p/papervision3d/`

This page serves as an important resource with lots of references to examples, tutorials, and documentation. But for now we are interested in the source code. We could visit the page and go to **Source | Browse** and download all the files one by one manually, but that would be a lot of work. Apart from that, the other ways to get our hands on the code are as follows:

- Download the code through **Subversion**—a version control system
- Download a **ZIP** file
- Download an **SWC** file

There are some important differences however. The SWC file contains **compiled** code whereas downloading the code in the ZIP or using Subversion will give you **non-compiled** code. Before we take a closer look at the ZIP file, the SWC file, and what Subversion is, let's see what compiled and non-compiled code are all about.

Difference between compiled and non-compiled source code

Downloading the non-compiled source means that you will get the folders and classes, just as they are without them being compiled in any format. You can actually open the classes and read the code. This can be extremely helpful in the process of learning. Taking a look at what's inside a class is a good way to improve your programming skills. You could even experiment and modify the source classes; however, we will not do this throughout the course of the book. Although modifying code in an external library may sometimes be tempting. A better practice is to leave the code as it is and find other ways to modify or extend it. A disadvantage of altering the source is that the modification may get overwritten and lost the moment you download a newer version of the source code.

The non-compiled code will work for Flex Builder, Flash Builder, Flash CS3, and Flash CS4.

The SWC, however, contains source code that has already been compiled. Compare this with publishing a Flash movie. The moment you publish, your code gets *compiled* into an SWF. In this case, the classes are hidden, so you cannot see and open them anymore.

 Note that the SWC will not work for Flash CS3.

It is now clear that Subversion and the ZIP file will give you non-compiled code, and the SWC contains compiled code. By taking a closer look at these three options we'll make it easier to decide which one to choose.

What is Subversion?

Subversion, also known as **SVN**, is an open source version control system. It allows developers, or teams of developers, to upload and download current and historical versions of the project they're working on.

Suppose a team of developers is working on the same project, like the Papervision3D team. If one of the developers makes a change to the project and uploads, or **commits** it, SVN incorporates the change into a new version of the project. At the same time SVN, being a version control system, saves the previous versions. In other words, you can always retrieve older versions from the server. Many open source projects use SVN because it makes working on the same project by multiple developers less tedious.

You may wonder why this is important to us. If you think of SVN as the location where all the versions of a project are stored, then it is also the place where we can find and download the latest version of the project. For developers who prefer to work with the latest features, the need to keep the code up-to-date is inherent to Papervision3D being an open source project. It is constantly developing and changing.

So, how do you download the latest version of a project to your computer using SVN? You need an **SVN client**. This is a software program that you install on your computer. The client will serve as the tool to download the latest revision of the source code.

What's inside the ZIP?

The ZIP file contains non-compiled source code. There is one difference with the source code on the SVN server though. Where the SVN server always contains the most recent revision, the ZIP file tends to be more or less outdated. This makes sense, as the SVN source code is the most recent code you'll ever see as a user. It's up to the members of a project to continuously release an updated ZIP. For several reasons, this does not always happen, resulting in a ZIP that may be outdated. However, the code in the ZIP file may be better tested and thus more stable compared to the SVN code. Due to the constant changes that are being made to an open source project, the code on the SVN server may contain new features or even bugs, which could result in breaking the code in your project(s) the moment you download a new revision.

And what's inside the SWC?

Think of an SWC as a library of classes that already have been compiled. If you incorporate the Papervision3D SWC into your project, you have access to all the Papervision3D classes, but you won't be able to actually see and open them.

We've just seen that the code in the ZIP file may not always be up-to-date with the code on the SVN server. The same goes for the SWC. But we have also seen that the ZIP file may be more stable than the SVN code and this is also true for the SWC.

Choosing between the SWC, the ZIP, and the SVN

If there are three ways of getting the source code, which way should you go?

Clearly, the process of downloading the SWC or the ZIP is easier than downloading through SVN, as you don't have to install an SVN client. However, once you've set up your SVN client, the updating process is nicely integrated into your system and you will always be able to get the latest revision. It's up to you to decide what is important to you.

We've discussed several pros and cons of working with compiled and non-compiled source. Let's create an overview by putting them in a diagram.

	SWC (compiled)	ZIP (non-compiled)	SVN (non compiled)
Flash CS3	-	+	+
Flash CS4	+	+	+
Flex Builder 3	+	+	+
Flash Builder 4	+	+	+
Probably stable	+	+	-
Up-to-date	-	-	+

Hopefully, by now you have enough information to decide whether you want to work with the SWC, the ZIP, or SVN.

This book doesn't pretend to favor one way over the other as all three have their pros and cons. Therefore, deciding which way to go is mainly a matter of personal preferences and needs. However, the examples of this book are based on Papervision3D 2.1, revision 920. If you want to be sure that all the example work, then it's best to go for the ZIP or the SWC, which contain this revision. The sections on downloading the ZIP and the SWC will show you where to get it.

If you prefer to work with SVN, you should realize that newer versions may lead to compatibility problems with the examples, for instance resulting in compile errors. If you download a version that leads to compile errors or other problems, you can always fall back on the tested source code in the ZIP or SWC with revision 920.

The next sections will cover all three options, starting with SVN.

Downloading the non-compiled source using SVN

We'll first go over downloading and installing an SVN client that is appropriate for your system (especially Windows and Mac OS X) and then use the client to download the non-compiled source code. If you choose to work with the ZIP or the SWC, you can skip this section and continue reading *Downloading the non-compiled source using the ZIP* or *Downloading the compiled source*.

There are a whole bunch of SVN clients available on the Internet. We will first choose a client for Windows, then for Mac OS X.

On Windows

We will use **TortoiseSVN** as the SVN client for Windows. We will download and install this program and then use it to download the Papervison3D source code.

1. Go to http://tortoisesvn.net/downloads.

2. Download the latest installer. The Setup Wizard will take you through the process of installing. You don't have to change the default settings.

3. Restart your PC after you've finished the installation.

 A frequently asked question is whether you should download and install Subversion next to TortoiseSVN. The answer is NO. Subversion is included in TortoiseSVN.

Now that you have installed an SVN client, let's use it to download the Papervison3D source code.

4. Create a new folder somewhere on your computer. You can call it whatever you want. In this book, we'll call it papervision3d_source. It's the folder that will contain the Papervision3D source code.

5. Right-click on this folder. You'll notice that your context menu now has some extra options involving TortoiseSVN.

6. Select **SVN Checkout...**.

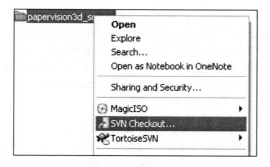

7. A window pops up asking for the **URL of repository**. Fill in:
    `http://papervision3d.googlecode.com/svn/trunk/as3/trunk`

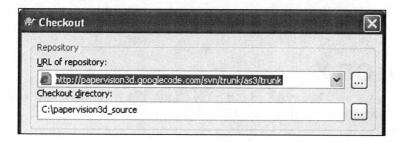

 The structure and names of the folders on the SVN server may vary over time. If the address above is not valid, please visit Papervision3D's Google Code page or the errata page that accompanies this book.

8. Then click **OK**. TortoiseSVN will start downloading the source files from the SVN server.

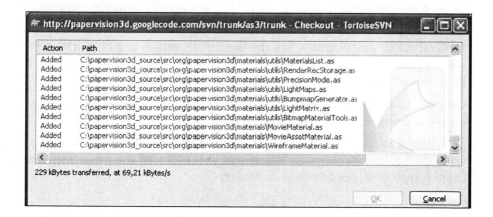

9. When the download is complete click **OK** again.

The download may take a while to complete due to the size of the files included. The Papervision3D team added not only the source code to the SVN server, but also examples and documentation for the project. When the download has completed, open the papervision3d_source folder and take a quick look at what's inside. You will see quite an amount of folders and files. These are the folders and files you have just downloaded.

Every now and then you may want to download the latest version of the source code to keep the code up-to-date. Similar to your first checkout, go to the papervision3d_ source folder and right-click on it. But this time select **TortoiseSVN | Update**. The latest revision on the SVN server will now get incorporated in your local working copy.

Next, we will configure the authoring tool of your choice so that we can actually use the code. You can continue reading *Configuring your authoring tool for Papervison3D*.

On Mac OS X

For Mac OS X, we will use **svnX** as our SVN client. We will download and install this program and then use it to download the Papervison3D source code.

If you visit the download page of svnX at http://www.lachoseinteractive. net/en/community/subversion/svnx/download/, it will tell you that there are two requirements for using svnX. It assumes you have Mac OS X 10.4 or higher and you'll need *a working install of Subversion*. Although there are several others available, the svnX download page links to a working install that was made by Martin Ott. So, let's get this one first.

1. Go to http://homepage.mac.com/martinott/.

2. Download the My Subversion-#.#.# package (the version numbers may vary over time). This is a ZIP file.

3. Open the ZIP and double-click the file inside, which is a PKG file. A window will appear that will guide you through the process of installing. When Mac's Easy Install has finished, we can download svnX.

4. Go back to the svnX download page at http://www.lachoseinteractive. net/en/community/subversion/svnx/download/.

5. Download svnX. This time you will download a DMG file. Double-clicking it will open a new Finder window where you will find the svnX.app. Drag or copy it into your Applications folder.

Now that we have successfully installed svnX as our SVN client, we're ready to download the Papervision3D source code.

1. Create a new folder somewhere on your computer. You can call it whatever you want, but in this book we'll call it `papervision3d_source`. This is the folder that will contain the Papervision3D source code.

2. Launch svnX by double-clicking `svnX.app` in your `Applications` folder.

3. Go to **Window** and select **Repositories**. The **Repositories** window displays the list of projects that you have downloaded. It's still empty, but we're about to add Papervision3D.

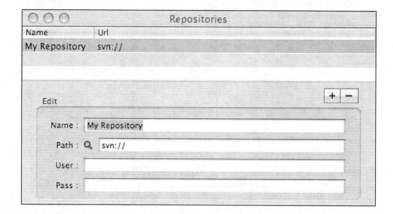

4. Add a new project either by selecting the default repository or by clicking the **+** icon. You can fill in anything for **Name** but in our example we will use `Papervision3D`. You can leave the fields **User** and **Pass** blank.

5. Type or paste the following URL into the **Path** field:
   `http://papervision3d.googlecode.com/svn/trunk/as3/trunk`

The structure and names of the folders on the SVN server may vary over time. If the address above is not valid, svnX will display an error message: **Not a valid URL**. If so, please visit the errata page that accompanies this book.

6. Double-click on the project you've just added. A new pop up window appears with details of the project. You can see a list of commits done by the Papervision3D team members. Every list item represents a revision and you can tell who uploaded the change and when it was uploaded. There is also a log message, written by the developer who committed the change(s), with some basic information about what has been changed.

7. If not yet selected, select the revision at the top of the list.

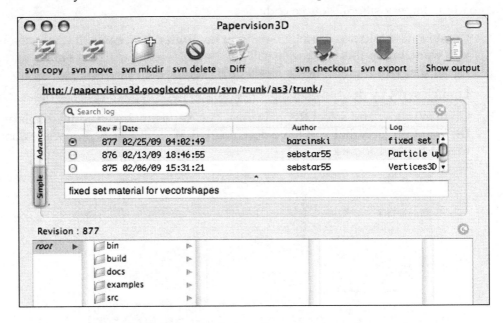

8. Click on the **SVN CHECKOUT** button and browse to the `papervision3d_source` folder you've just created.

9. Select it and click **Open**. By doing this, svnX will start downloading the files from the server into this folder.

10. At the same time, a new window will pop up. This is the **Working Copies** window.

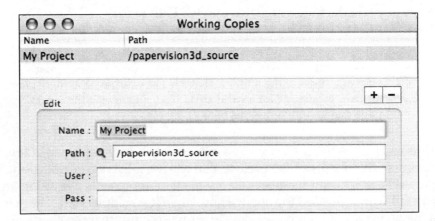

11. Change the default **Name** into something more appropriate such as `Papervision3D`.

The download may take a while to complete, due to the size of the files included. The Papervision3D team added not only the source code to the SVN server, but also examples and documentation for the project. When the download is complete, open the `papervision3d_source` folder and take a quick look at what's inside. These are the folders and files you have just downloaded.

If you want to download the latest version of the source code to keep the code up-to-date, open svnX and go to **Window | Working Copies.** Double-click the working copy of Papervision3D and a new window will appear. Click the green **Update** button to replace the local copy in your `papervision3d_source` folder with the latest revision on the SVN server.

Next, we will configure the authoring tool of your choice, so that we can actually use the code. Continue reading *Configuring your authoring tool for Papervision3D*.

Downloading the non-compiled source in the ZIP file

The ZIP file holds non-compiled source code. You can find it on the Google Code pages of Papervision3D. As discussed before, the examples in this book are based on Papervision3D 2.1, revision 920. We will download this version to make sure that all the examples work. The next steps demonstrate how to get the ZIP with this revision.

1. Create a new folder somewhere on your computer. You can give it any name, but in this book we'll call it `papervision3d_source`. Inside this folder, create a new folder and call it `src`.
2. Go to `http://code.google.com/p/papervision3d/downloads/list`.
3. Look for the ZIP file, which has the following summary: **Papervision3D 2.1.920.zip** (for use with "Papervision3D Essentials" book).
4. Download the ZIP file, and save it anywhere on your computer.
5. Extract the ZIP file.
6. Put (or *save* if you use an extraction wizard) the extracted folders in the `src` folder that we've just created inside the `papervision3d_source` folder.

At a certain moment, for instance when you need features that are incorporated in the most recent revision, you may decide you want to replace the code with the latest available version of the ZIP. Just look for the most recent, featured ZIP file on the list, repeat the download and extract process, and replace the folders in your `papervision3d_source` folder by your newly extracted folders. The source code will automatically be updated.

Next, we will configure the authoring tool of your choice so that we can actually use the code. Continue reading *Configuring your authoring tool for Papervision3D*.

Downloading the compiled source

If your authoring tool is Flex Builder, Flash Builder, or Flash CS4, both the non-compiled and the compiled source code will work for you. If you've decided to work with the compiled source code, you can download the SWC that contains this code from the Google Code page of Papervision3D. As the examples in this book are based on Papervision3D 2.1, revision 920, we will download this version to make sure that all the examples work. The next steps demonstrate how to get the SWC with revision 920.

1. Create a new folder somewhere on your computer. You can give it any name, but in this book we'll call it `papervision3d_source`.

2. Go to `http://code.google.com/p/papervision3d/downloads/list`.

3. Look for the SWC file, which has the following label:
   Papervision3D 2.1.920.swc (for use with "Papervision3D Essentials" book).

4. Download the SWC file, and save it in the `papervision3d_source` folder we've just created.

Every now and then you may want to download the latest version of the SWC to keep up with the changes that are being made to the project. Just look for the most recent, featured SWC file on the list, repeat the download process and replace your current SWC with the updated SWC.

Configuring your authoring tool for Papervision3D

Now that we have downloaded the source code, we will configure the authoring tool of our choice so that we can actually use Papervision3D. If your authoring tool is Flex Builder or Flash Builder, you can continue reading *Configuring Flex Builder and Flash Builder*.

Configuring Flash

We have downloaded the source code, but how can we make it work? Normally, if you download a software program, like we did with our SVN client, you would need to install it. But keep in mind that Papervision3D is not a software program—it's a library of folders and classes. What we need to do now is tell Flash where these folders are located so that we can access them when we work in the Flash IDE. In other words, within Flash we must set the path to the source code in our `papervision3d_source` folder. This is what we mean by **configuring** Flash.

Flash can handle the following two ways of setting such a path:

- You can set it separately for each FLA
- You can set it globally, which means that every FLA that you open or create automatically has access to the source

We will use the second approach in this book, so we'll only have to set the path once.

Both Flash CS3 and CS4 lets you set the path to the non-compiled source, but only Flash CS4 allows for setting the path to a SWC or SWC folder. If you decided to work with the SWC, you can continue reading *Set the path to the compiled source code in Flash (only CS4)*.

Set the path to the non-compiled source code in Flash (CS3 and CS4)

If you've downloaded the ZIP or used SVN, the following steps will set the path to the source code from within Flash:

1. Open Flash. You don't have to create a new FLA or open an existing one.
2. Go to **Flash | Preferences**. on MAC, or **Edit | Preferences** on Windows
3. Select **Actionscript** in the category list at the left. Click the **Actionscript 3.0 Settings** button.
4. The following step shows a slight difference between Flash CS4 and its predecessor CS3.
   - In Flash CS4: Click on the + icon next to **Source path**. Then click on the folder icon.

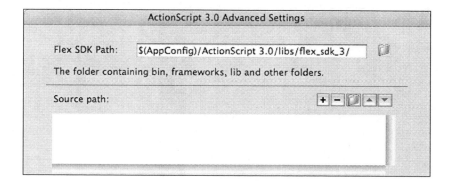

      °   In Flash CS3: Click on the + icon next to **Classpath**. Then click on the browse icon.

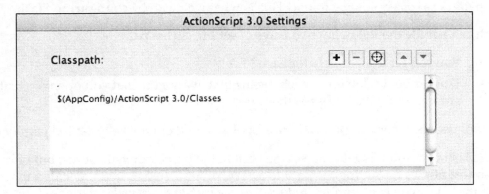

5. Browse to the folder where the source code is located — papervision3d_ source in our example.

6. Select **src** and click **Choose**. You will now see that the path has been added.

7. Click **OK** twice to close the dialog windows.

Now that the dialog windows are closed, it's a good idea to check if the process of downloading and setting paths went right. To do this, we will take a look at one of the examples that comes with this book. Continue reading *Running an example in Flash*.

Set the path to the compiled source code in Flash (Only CS4)

1. Open Flash. You don't have to create a new FLA or open an existing one.

2. Go to **Flash | Preferences** on MAC, or **Edit | Preferences** on Windows.

3. Select **Actionscript** in the category list at the left. Click the **Actionscript 3.0 Settings** button.

4. Click on the **+** icon next to **Library path**. Then click on the red SWC icon.

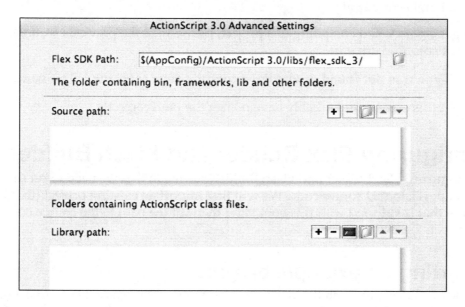

5. Browse to the folder where the SWC is located—`papervision3d_source` in our example.
6. Select the SWC and click **Choose**. You will now see that the path has been added.
7. Click **OK** twice to close the dialog windows.

Now that the dialog windows are closed and the path to the SWC is set, it may be a good idea to check if everything went right. To do this, we will take a look at one of the examples that comes with this book.

Running an example in Flash

Let's open the example that is shipped with this book using the Flash IDE. By doing this, we'll be able to find out if we installed and configured everything correctly. More than that, it gives us the chance to see some Papervision3D at work!

1. Open Flash.
2. Go to **File | Open**.
3. Browse to the `examples` folder, which can be found in the book downloads.
4. Browse to **CH01 | Flash | SetupTest**.
5. Open **SetupTest.fla** and publish it.

Do you see the earth turning and a 3D text? Congratulations, you've set up Papervision3D correctly!

If you get errors when compiling this project, please read the previous sections again. The most common error is:

Type was not found or was not a compile-time constant: [class name]

If you get this error, you probably have not set the path correctly.

Configuring Flex Builder and Flash Builder

By configuring Flex Builder and Flash Builder, we mean that we need to set the path to the Papervision3D source code. We will first import an existing project (that is, the example that is shipped with this book) and then set the path to the source code for this project.

Importing an example project

Both Flex Builder and Flash Builder allow you to import projects. Let's import one of the examples that come with this book.

1. Open the authoring tool of your choice.
2. Go to **File | Import | Other**.
3. Open the folder called `General` and select **Existing Projects into workspace**.
4. Click **Next**, and then select the radio-button **Select root directory** if it is not selected yet.
5. Click **Browse** and browse to the `examples` folder in the book download.
6. Go to **CH01 | FlexBuilder**.
7. By clicking **Choose** a list of projects will be displayed that are recognized as valid projects. Make sure that only the checkbox for **SetupTest** is selected.
8. Click **Finish**.
9. The project will now be imported. Flex Builder will display it in the **Flex Navigator** view, Flash Builder in the **Package Explorer** view. Open the project called **SetupTest** by double-clicking on it.

Take a look at the **Problems** view. Chances are that you will see some errors.

The project we imported uses the Papervision3D source code. The developer has set the path to the code from his authoring tool. But this path could be, and probably is, different on your computer, as it's most likely that we named our source folder differently and stored it somewhere else than the developer did. Therefore, let's fix that by changing the path.

Whether you import an existing project, or create a new one, you must always set the correct path to the external source code you would like to use. Keep in mind that in this example we are importing an existing project and that we will change the path that has previously been added. However, if you create a *new* project, no path has been added yet. Therefore, every time you create a new project, you must add the path to the source code that you want to access.

Setting the path to the SWC requires a different approach than setting it to the non-compiled source code. We'll first set the path to the non-compiled source. If you decided to use the SWC, you can continue reading *Setting the path to the SWC in Flex Builder and Flash Builder*.

Setting the path to the non-compiled source code in Flex and Flash Builder

If you've downloaded the ZIP or used SVN, the following steps will set the path to the source code from your project:

1. Right-click on the **SetupTest** project folder. You can find this in the **Flex Navigator** view in the Flex Builder, and in the **Project Explorer** view in the Flash Builder.

2. Select **Properties**.

3. Select **Actionscript Build Path** and click on **Source path** if it is not selected yet. You'll see a path that points to an additional source folder. To edit the path, double-click on it and browse to our `papervision3d_source` folder. Then select **src**.

4. Click **Choose** and OK.

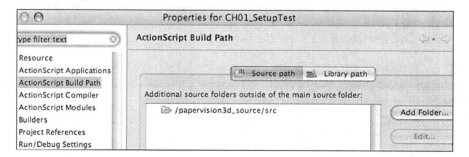

5. Click **OK** to close the **Properties** window.

The path that we've changed was set by the developer of the project, but would not have worked for us. We needed to set the path to the source folder on our computer.

Setting the path to the SWC in Flex and Flash Builder

If you've downloaded the SWC, the following steps will set the path to it from your project:

1. Right-click on the project folder in the **Flex Navigator** view (Flex Builder) or the **Package Explorer** view (Flash Builder).

2. Select **Properties**.

3. Select **Actionscript Build Path** and click on **Source path** if it is not selected yet. You'll see a path that points to an additional source folder. Highlight the folder by clicking on it and click the **Remove** button.

4. Select **Library path**.

5. Click on the **Add SWC Folder** button.

6. Browse to the `papervision3d_source` folder and select it. Click **Choose** and **OK**.

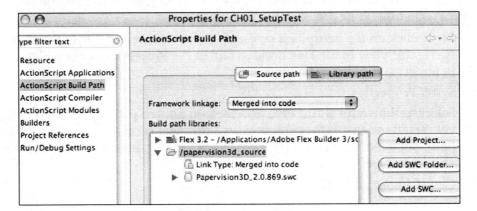

7. Click **OK** to close the Properties window.

The path we removed pointed to the Papervision3D source code that was stored on the developer's computer. We needed to remove this path because we have decided to use the SWC instead of the non-compiled source code.

Running the example in Flex Builder and Flash Builder

The errors in the **Problems** view should be gone now. But what just happened? First we imported an existing project that came with the examples. Then we edited the path so that it points to our Papervision3D source code. Now that we have configured this project correctly, we're ready to run the example. Select the project and publish it.

Your browser should open and show the compiled SWF. Do you see the earth turning accompanied by a 3D text? Congratulations, you've set up Papervision3D correctly!

If you get errors when compiling this project, please re-read the previous sections. The most common error is:

> **The definition of [class name] was not found.**

If you get this error, you probably have not set the path correctly.

Where to find the Papervision3D documentation

If you're familiar with the *ActionScript 3.0 Language Reference*, you will undoubtedly know that it's a good source for looking things up about ActionScript. It's an extensive and handy reference manual for the API's for Flash Player and Adobe Air.

Papervision3D also provides documentation. If you have downloaded the source code through SVN, you can find it inside the **papervision3d_source | docs** folder. Opening `index.html` gives you an overview of all the packages and classes.

In case you didn't choose to work with SVN, there is also an online version of the documentation. You can find it here: `http://docs.pv3d.org/`.

 The address of the online documentation may vary over time. If the address above is not valid, please visit the errata page that accompanies this book.

You can use documentation to look up how to use methods and properties, along with event handlers and listeners. It's a good idea to add either of the `index.html` pages as a bookmark in your browser. That way you always have easy access to the documentation. Keep in mind though that many open source projects are a constant work in progress. This may result in incomplete documentation and a lack of sample code.

Summary

Papervision3D is not a software program—it's basically a library of ActionScript classes. This open source library is available in two forms—compiled and non-compiled. The compiled code is downloadable as an SWC, which is compatible with Flex Builder, Flash Builder, and Flash CS4, but not with Flash CS3. The non-compiled code is downloadable through Subversion and as a ZIP file, and works for all four authoring tools.

We have discussed how to download and install SVN clients for both Windows and Mac OS X. With those clients we downloaded the non-compiled source code through SVN. We've also seen how to download the SWC and the ZIP. Then we configured the authoring tool of our choice by setting paths to Papervision3D. To test if our setup was done correctly, we ran some examples. Finally, we shed some light on where to find documentation.

In the next chapter, we're going to get our hands dirty by creating our first Papervision3D scene. Before we build this simple application, we will walk through some basics of 3D theory and object-oriented programming.

2

Building Your First Application

In this chapter, we will get our hands dirty by programming our first lines of code. Those who are new to object-oriented programming and classes can start with a short introduction about this subject. If you are already familiar with working with classes, you can skip these sections and learn what a 3D scene in Papervision3D is made of. Once this has been made clear, we can write our first basic application! Parts of this application will be wrapped up as the default class that we will use throughout the book.

This chapter covers the following:

- Introduction to classes and object-oriented programming
- Working with the document class/main application file
- Basics of a 3D composition in Papervision3D
- Building your first application
- Preparing for the book examples

Introduction to classes and object-oriented programming

In this book, we will make heavy use of Papervision3D classes. We will write our own classes that can be used in Flash, along with Flex Builder and Flash Builder. If you're a developer using the Flash IDE, it might be the first time you'll write your own classes. As classes and object-oriented programming are such an important part of getting along with this book, a short introduction will be given. If you work in Flex builder or Flash builder or if you are already familiar with classes, you can start reading the *Basics of a 3D scene in Papervision3D* section later in this chapter.

Don't worry about the difficulty level if you are new to classes—as book uses only the basics. Learning how to program in an OOP way using Papervision3D is a good way to become more familiar with classes and it might motivate you to learn more about this subject. You will not be the first who learned to program in an OOP way, as a side effect of learning an external library such as Papervision3D is.

So what are classes? In fact, they are nothing more than a set of functions (methods) and variables (properties) grouped together in a single file, which is known as the class definition. A class forms the blueprint for new objects that you create.

Sounds a bit vague? What if you were told that you've probably already used classes? Each object you create from the Flash API is based on classes. For example, `Sprites`, `MovieClips`, and `TextFields` are objects that you have probably used in your code before. In fact, these objects are classes. The blueprints for these objects and their classes are already incorporated in Flash. First, have a look at how you can use them to create a new `Sprite` object:

```
var mySprite:Sprite = new Sprite();
```

Looks familiar—right? By doing this, you create a new copy of the `Sprite` class as an object called `mySprite`. This is called instantiation of an object. There's no difference between instantiating built-in classes or instantiating custom written classes. Papervision3D is a set of custom classes. Chapter 1 illustrated how to instantiate a new instance of the Papervision3D-specific class called `DisplayObject3D`, after a successful installation:

```
var myObject3D:DisplayObject3D = new DisplayObject3D();
```

So, although you know how to use classes, creating your own classes might be new to you.

Creating a custom class

An ActionScript class is basically a text-based file with an `.as` extension stored somewhere on your computer, containing ActionScript code. This code works as the previously mentioned blueprint for an object. Let's see what that blueprint looks like:

```
package {
    public class ExampleClass
    {
            public var myName:String = "Paul";

            public function ExampleClass()
            {

            }
```

```
        public function returnMyName():String
        {
                return "My name is" + myName;
        }

    }
}
```

On the first line, you'll find the `package` statement, followed by an opening curly bracket and ended with a closing curly bracket at the bottom of the class. Packages are a way to group classes together and represent the folder in which you saved the file. Imagine you have created a folder called `myPackage` inside the same folder where you've saved an FLA or inside a defined source folder. In order to have access to the folder and its classes, you will need to define the package using the folder's name as shown next:

```
package myPackage {
    . . .
}
```

This works the same way for subfolders. Let's imagine a folder called `subPackage` has been added to the imaginary folder `myPackage`. The package definition for classes inside this subfolder should then look like this:

```
package myPackage.subPackage {
    . . .
}
```

If you don't create a special folder to group your classes, you can use the so-called default package instead of defining a name. All the examples in this book will use default packages. However, for real projects it's good practice to set up a structure in order to organize your files.

After the package definition, you'll find the class definition, which looks as follows.

```
public class ExampleClass
{
    . . .
}
```

The name of the class must be the same name as the class file. In this example, the file needs to be saved as `ExampleClass.as`.

 Besides the fact that working packages is a good way to organize your files, they can also be used to uniquely identify each class in a project.

At the top of the class definition you'll see the word `public`, which is a keyword defining that the class is accessible to all other code in the project. This keyword is called, an **access modifier**.

The defined name of the class will be used to intantiate new copies of the class. Instantiating this class could be done like this:

```
var classExample:ExampleClass = new ExampleClass();
```

Inside the class, a string variable is defined in pretty much the same way as you would when working with timeline scripting.

```
public var myName:String = "Paul";
```

The definition of a variable inside a class is called as a **class property**. You can add as many properties to a class as you want. Each definition starts off with an access modifier. In this case the access modifier is set to `public`, meaning that it is both readable and writeable by code located outside the class:

```
var classExample:ExampleClass = new ExampleClass();
classExample.myName = "Jeff";
```

As you can see, this creates an instance of `ExampleClass`. We also changed the `myName` property from `Paul` to `Jeff`. When a property is defined as public, this is allowed to happen. In case you want access to this property inside the class itself, you can mark the property as private:

```
private var myName:String = "Paul";
```

Executing the previous code to change `myName` from `Paul` to `Jeff` will result in a compile-time error.

In the next lines we see the creation of a new function called `ExampleClass` in the class. Functions that have the same name as the name of the class are known as **constructors**.

```
public function ExampleClass()
{

}
```

Constructors always have a public access modifier and are called automatically each time the class is instantiated. This means that the code inside this function will be executed automatically.

All other function definitions inside the class are called methods.

```
public function returnMyName():String
{
    return "My name is" + myName;
}
```

At the end of this method definition, you'll notice a colon followed by a data type. This defines the type of object the method returns. When you work with functions on the timeline in Flash, you can define this as well, but it's not required to do so. The method `returnMyName()` is defined to return a string. In case you do not want to return any data type, you can define this by using a `void` as the return type:

```
public function returnNothing():void
{
    //Do not return something
}
```

 We need to define return type only for methods and not for constructors.

Classes, as well as properties and methods, have access modifiers that define from where each of these objects can be accessed. So far we've seen that a **public** keyword allows code outside the class to access a property, or call a method inside the class. When you allow access from other code, you need to be aware that this code can mess up your class. You can prevent this by using the **private** keyword, which makes the property or method only accessible inside your class. Two other access modifiers that are often used are **internal** and **protected**. Classes inside the same package can access internal methods or properties and protected methods can only be used inside a related subclass. Subclasses are a part of inheritance, which will be explained in a bit.

As long as you have not planned to give access to scripts outside your class, it's a good practice to mark all properties and methods of a class as private by default. When defining a property or method, you should always ask yourself whether you want them to be accessed from outside your class.

Inheritance

Sometimes you want to create a new class that looks a lot like an existing one, except that you want to add a new functionality. You could copy the existing class, paste it into your new class, and add the functionality. However, that is not very efficient. This is where inheritance comes into play.

Inheritance is the technique of extending an existing class, called the **super class** or **base class**, with another class, called the **sub class**, which adopts the entire class definition from the super class. The new class has access to all non-private properties and methods that are defined inside the super class.

Imagine you are about to create a car and a motorbike by code. You could make two classes — one for the car and the other for the motorbike. However, you will soon notice that functionalities and properties of both classes will overlap. For example, they can both drive and steer, and have properties such as the amount of wheels and speed. In an abstract manner, these properties and functionalities overlap because the car and the motorbike are both vehicles. Creating a vehicle super class that is subclassed by a car class and a motorbike class prevents this overlap.

When needed, the subclass class can define how it differs or behaves differently from its parent class. For example, a car has four wheels and can drive in a reverse direction. A motorbike has two wheels and cannot drive in a reverse direction.

Take a look at how this can be achieved by two simple classes:

```
package {
    public class BasicClass
    {
            public function doSomething():void
            {
                    trace("I'm doing something");
            }
    }
}

package {
    public class SubClass extends BasicClass
    {
            public function saySomething():void
            {
                    trace("I'm saying something");
            }
    }
}
```

The first class will be the super class once it's extended and has only one method. Instantiating a `BasicClass` and calling a method is pretty straightforward.

```
var basicClass:BasicClass = new BasicClass();
basicClass.doSomething();
```

Nothing special so far. According to the class definition of `SubClass` we see that it extends `BasicClass`. By doing so, it is possible to use properties and methods from the `BasicClass`. Let's see what this looks like:

```
var subClass:SubClass = new SubClass();
subClass.doSomething();
subClass.saySomething();
```

This example calls the `doSomething` method on `SubClass`, which inherits this method from `BasicClass`.

Extending classes can be done not only with custom classes, but is also possible with built-in classes. Have a look at how you create an extended sprite:

```
package {
    import flash.display.Sprite;

    public class extendedSprite extends Sprite
    {

    }
}
```

Notice there's a new line right after the package definition:

```
import flash.display.Sprite;
```

To extend as well as instantiate classes that are not part of the current package, you need to define an import. Imports relate to packages and classes. In this case, the class `Sprite` was imported from package `flash.display`.

Extending is a good way to create new classes, based on other existing classes—isn't it? It keeps your code very clean and abstract. But what if you want to change an existing method in your super class? Changing the super class directly isn't always possible and is definitely not a good idea, as you want to leave the existing code intact to prevent breaking the class. When you're using a third-party library such as Papervision3D, it's not unthinkable that you'll update the classes in the future. When you apply changes directly to some of these classes, your code will break as soon as you update to a new version.

Luckily, object-oriented programming offers a solution. Have a look at how we can change the method doSomething() inside BasicClass, by overriding it in the SubClass:

```
package {
    public class SubClass extends BasicClass
    {
            override public function doSomething():void
            {
                    trace("Hi, you need to do something ");
            }

            public function saySomething():void
            {
                    trace("I'm saying something");
            }
    }
}
```

We've added the method doSomething() to the subclass. However you can't do this without explicitly saying that you want to override the doSomething() method from the super class. When you override a method, it will replace the original method. You can still call the overridden method in the super class from the overriding method in the sub class.

```
override public function doSomething():void
{
    trace("Hi, you need to do something ");
    super.doSomething();
}
```

When you now call the doSomething() method in the SubClass, it will trace:

**Hi, you need to do something
I'm doing something**

This is where the brief introduction to OOP ends. With some of the most relevant OOP basics explained, you should be able to get along with the rest of the book. If you want to know more, there are numerous books and online tutorials on the subject of OOP.

Working with the Document Class/Main Application File

The **Document Class** in the Flash IDE, or **Main Application File** in Flex Builder and Flash Builder, is a special class that contains a constructor, which will be called by the SWF file once it's loaded. You could say that the constructor inside your document class will be the entry point of your application. The document class requires that it is an extended `Sprite` or `MovieClip`, or any other class type that inherits from either of these objects.

> For the sake of simplicity, this book refers to the document class and not to the main application file. Although their names differ, their usage is exactly the same.
>
> Also note that a synonym for main application file is **Application Class**.

Flex Builder and Flash Builder have the same workflow to get the document class up and running. However, the Flash IDE takes another approach. Let's start by explaining how it is done in the Flash IDE.

Setting up the document class for Flash

In Flash, you can choose to define a document class as the entry point of your application. This class can extend the `MovieClip` that represents the timeline in Flash, and replaces the stage as the entry point of your application. Although you can use a combination of your stage and a document class as the entry point, it's not a very common thing to do.

Defining the document class is quite easy. Start Flash and follow the instructions.

1. Create a new ActionScript file and save it somewhere on your hard drive under the name `DocumentClassExample.as`.

2. Create a new Flash AS3 file and save it as `DocumentClassExample.fla` in the same location where you saved your `DocumentClassExample.as` file.

3. Open the **Properties** panel of your FLA file. At the bottom right you'll find an input field labeled as **Document class**. Just enter the class name that you want to use as our document class—DocumentClassExample in this case, just like in the following screenshot:

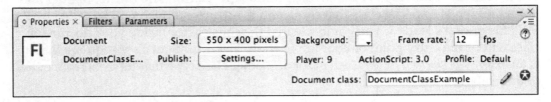

That's all you need to do to use a class as the entry point of your application. Easy, isn't it? Okay, it doesn't even look like 3D, but it's important basic information when you're new to working with classes in Flash.

Let's publish our movie now and see what happens. If you've followed the steps correctly, Flash will throw compiler error 5007.

5007: An ActionScript file must have at least one externally visible definition.

This is an expected error. We've defined the document class in the **Properties** panel, but we haven't written any class yet. We've only created an empty file that does not yet contain a class definition. For now, this file isn't understandable by Flash and that's why it threw this error. It's pretty reasonable that it warns us of this error. Let's write our first lines of code and define the class correctly. Open DocumentClassExample.as in Flash, add the following code, and save it.

```
package {
    import flash.display.Sprite;
    public class DocumentClassExample extends Sprite
    {
        public function DocumentClassExample()
        {
            trace("Hello world!");
        }
    }
}
```

Now you can publish your Flash file without getting any compiler errors. On line 3, you see that the class extends the sprite class, which is required as said at the beginning of this section. The constructor in this class contains only a trace and publishing this file should show the string in your output window.

Setting up the document class for Flex Builder and Flash Builder

Although it is possible, in this book we will not use Flex Builder or Flash Builder to create Papervision3D applications with the Flex Framework. Both authoring tools will be used only to manage our ActionScript projects.

Creating a document class in Flex Builder and Flash Builder is completely integrated in the way both programs works. If you don't know what a document class or main application file is, and if you've used Flex Builder or Flash Builder before, you've already created one without even knowing it. Let's see how we create a document class:

1. Start the wizard for creating a new **ActionScript project**.

2. Enter DocumentClassExample as your project name.

3. Click **Next** and look at the field called **Main application file**. By default, this value is the name of the project with the extension .as added to it. In our case that's DocumentClassExample.as.

   The following screenshot shows the second window from a **New ActionScript Project** wizard in Flex Builder. The name of the document class is automatically defined in the **Main application file** field.

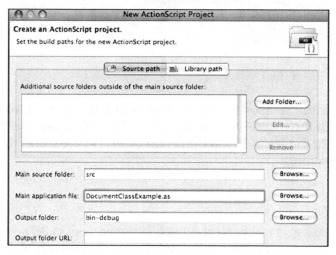

4. Click **Finish** and you've successfully set up your own document class. When you are working with multiple classes, you can always recognize your document class in the **Flex Navigator** (Flex Builder) or **Package Explorer** (Flash Builder) with the help of the 🔳 icon.

5. Let's finish this class and trace "Hello World" in the constructor.

There is no need to do more than this, as Flex Builder and Flash Builder always need to have a document class to be defined in order to run your code. Debug, run this code, and you'll see the trace.

Basics of a 3D scene in Papervision3D

Before we're ready to program some code for Papervision3D, we need to know a little bit more about 3D in Papervision3D. The following section is meant to give you a better understanding of the code that you will write later in this chapter. Each of these concepts relates directly to classes that are used by Papervision3D. Later in this chapter, these will be used to program your first application. All the object types that will be described are active elements in a 3D scene. Let's have a visualized look at all these objects:

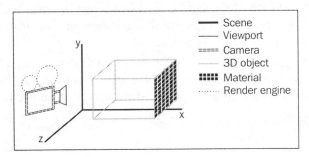

Scene

The **scene** is the entire composition of 3D objects in a 3D space. Think of it as your stage in Flash with three axes—x, y, and z. Each object that you want to be visible should be added to the scene. If you don't add objects to the scene, they will not appear on your screen.

Camera

You can think of this as a real **camera**, which is somewhere in 3D space recording activity inside the scene. The camera defines the point of view from which you are viewing the scene. Because a camera in 3D is not a visible object, it is not part of our scene and you don't need to add it. Like a real camera you can, for example, zoom and focus.

Cameras in 3D space can usually do more than real cameras. For example, in 3D you can, exclude objects to be rendered, when they are too close or too far away from the camera. The camera is able to ignore objects that are not in a certain, defined range. This is done for performance reasons. Objects that are too far away, or even behind the camera, don't need to be recorded, saving a lot of calculation for objects that are in a position where the camera simply can't see them.

Viewport

A **viewport** is a container sprite on your stage, and shows the output of what the camera sees. In the illustrative object overview, this has been compared with the lens of the camera. The lens is our window onto the 3D scene. We can make this window small and see just a small part of the scene, or make it big and see a lot. This works exactly as a real window in a wall—making it bigger will not affect how the world outside looks, but will have an effect on how much we can see from this world.

The following illustration contains the visualization of a relatively big viewport on the left, along with a relatively small and wide viewport on the right. The thick dark outlines represent the viewports. In the right image, you can clearly see how the window to the 3D world works and how changing its size will not stretch the view of the 3D object in the scene. It only affects how much we see of it.

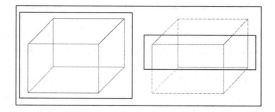

3D Objects

A shape in 3D space is called a 3D object, or **DisplayObject3D** in Papervision3D. You can think of 3D objects as more advanced display objects just like sprites and movie clips. The difference is that a `DisplayObject3D` has a third axis, so we can place it anywhere in 3D space and rotate over each of the three axes.

Material

A **material** is the texture that is printed on an object. When an object doesn't have a material applied, it will be invisible. There are a variety of materials available for you to use. For example, a very simple material is a color; a more advanced example of a material could be a live streaming video. In Chapter 4, you will learn how to use each material type.

Render engine

A **render engine** is like a rolling camera. As long as you trigger the render engine, it will output information of the scene recorded by the camera to the viewport. When you stop triggering the render engine, your viewport will not show any new image from the scene and shows the last rendered image. **Rendering** is actually the most intensive task for your computer, as it needs to recalculate each object that is placed inside your scene and output this to the viewport.

Left-handed Cartesian coordinate system

Flash, as well as Papervision3D, make use of the Cartesian coordinate system. In Flash, a regular visual object can be positioned on the stage by entering an x and y value. The object will be positioned according to these values and relative to the upper left corner of the stage. A higher x value moves the object to the right, whereas a higher y value moves it downward.

The coordinate system in Papervision3D works essentially the same, except for the following two differences.

- Flash uses Cartesian coordinates on two axes, whereas Papervision3D makes use of them on three axes
- The y-axis in Flash is inversed compared to the y-axis in Papervision3D

In Papervision3D, we want to position objects not only on the x and y axes, but also on an extra axis, in order to position objects in depth. This third axis is called the z-axis.

In Flash, objects are positioned relative to the upper left corner, which is the 0, 0 coordinate. This is called the center point, or the origin. Predictably, the position of the origin in 3D space is located at **0, 0, 0**. The three axes and the origin point are illustrated by the following image:

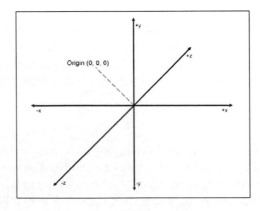

The plus and minus signs illustrate whether the coordinate values are increasing or decreasing in the direction away from the origin. Notice that the y-axis is inverted compared to 2D coordinates in Flash. When you want to position an object lower on your screen in Flash, you need to give it a higher y position. This is how 2D coordinates on a computer screen work. The above figure shows the y-axis as according to the coordinate system as it is used by Papervision3D.

Creating a basic class for Papervision3D

In the previous sections you've learned what a basic scene is made of, and how you can create your own classes. Now that we have gone through all this theory, it's now time that we get our hands dirty by writing some code.

Start your favorite authoring tool. The first application we'll build is a 3D scene containing a sphere that is rotating over its y-axis. A sphere is basically a "3D ball" and is built into Papervision3D as one of the default primitives.

The basic document class

First, have a look at the document class that defines the basic structure for the rotating sphere application.

```
package {
    import flash.display.Sprite;

    import org.papervision3d.cameras.Camera3D;
    import org.papervision3d.objects.primitives.Sphere;
    import org.papervision3d.render.BasicRenderEngine;
    import org.papervision3d.scenes.Scene3D;
    import org.papervision3d.view.Viewport3D;

    public class FirstApplication extends Sprite
    {
        private var scene:Scene3D;
        private var viewport:Viewport3D;
        private var camera:Camera3D;
        private var renderEngine:BasicRenderEngine;
        private var sphere:Sphere;

        public function FirstApplication()
        {
            scene = new Scene3D();
            camera = new Camera3D();

            sphere = new Sphere();
```

```
                     scene.addChild(sphere);

                     viewport = new Viewport3D();
                     addChild(viewport);

                     renderEngine = new BasicRenderEngine();
                     renderEngine.renderScene(scene,camera,viewport);
              }
       }
}
```

Let's have a look at this in detail. While we do that, you can create a new project in Flash, Flex Builder, or Flash Builder with a document class called FirstApplication. If you're using Flex Builder or Flash Builder, don't forget to configure the path to the Papervision3D source, just as we've learned in Chapter 1.

Previously in this chapter, we learned that we need to have a scene, a camera, a viewport, a 3D object with a material, and a render engine, in order to create a rendered output on the screen. Remember that the document class needs to extend Sprite. To make all these available inside the class, we need to import them first.

```
import flash.display.Sprite;

import org.papervision3d.cameras.Camera3D;
import org.papervision3d.objects.primitives.Sphere;
import org.papervision3d.render.BasicRenderEngine;
import org.papervision3d.scenes.Scene3D;
import org.papervision3d.view.Viewport3D;
```

Now that the imports are set, we define the properties of the class.

```
private var scene:Scene3D;
private var viewport:Viewport3D;
private var camera:Camera3D;
private var renderEngine:BasicRenderEngine;
private var sphere:Sphere;
```

We only define the properties and their class types here, without assigning any value. We'll do that inside the constructor. Let's first create the constructor.

```
public function FirstApplication()
{

}
```

We start by creating a scene inside the constructor. A scene is needed as the holder for our 3D objects. It's very easy to create one.

```
scene = new Scene3D();
```

All you have to do is create an instance of the Scene3D class, which doesn't take any parameters.

Next, we add a Camera3D, which is just as easy as the creation of a new Scene.

```
camera = new Camera3D();
```

A camera can take parameters when you create a new instance; however, the default values will do for now.

The scene and camera are useless as long as there are no 3D objects in the scene to film. For this example a sphere will be used, which is one of the built-in 3D objects.

```
sphere = new Sphere();
```

A camera, as well as a sphere, takes parameters when you instantiate it. However, when you do not pass any parameters, a default sphere will be created.

Now that we have created our sphere, we need to add it to the scene, otherwise it will not be seen by the camera. This works in exactly the same way as adding regular display objects to the display list in Flash, by using the addChild() method.

```
scene.addChild(sphere);
```

That looks familiar, right?

Now that we have a scene, a camera, and a sphere, we need to set up the window to the 3D scene, so we can see what is going on in there. We need to define our viewport and add it to the stage to make it visible.

```
viewport = new Viewport3D();
addChild(viewport);
```

While creating a new viewport, you can pass optional parameters to it, but the default parameters are again fine for now.

We are now just one step away from publishing our application. First we need to get our camera rolling. This is done by defining the render engine, which will render the current view of the camera to the viewport.

```
renderEngine = new BasicRenderEngine();
renderEngine.renderScene(scene,camera,viewport);
```

Now that the render engine is defined and an instruction to render the scene is added, we are ready to publish this project. This should result in the following image of triangles that together form something like a circle:

Case sensitivity

Pay attention to upper cases and lower cases in the examples. Not following these conventions might result in an error. A good example of this is the definition and instantiation of a sphere as we did in our `FirstApplication`.

```
var sphere:Sphere = new Sphere();
```

Here we see that we have defined a class property called sphere (lowercase) of a `Sphere` (uppercase) type, containing an instance of Sphere (uppercase). Giving a variable/property the same name as the defined object type will often cause problems.

The result of these few lines of code may not look very impressive yet, but in fact this is the beginning of something that will soon become exciting and could never be accomplished this easy by regular Flash use. When you have managed to compile this application that shows the triangles, you've made it through the hardest part of this example. Let's continue building your first application and see how we can add the illusion of 3D to our object, which still looks very 2D.

Finalizing your first application

The 2D look is caused by the fact that there's no perspective noticeable. Also, the scene is quite static. When we rotate the sphere over one of its axes, we will get a better 3D illusion. Because perspective changes, it adds the illusion of looking at a 3D sphere. But before we can implement rotation, we need to add a few extra lines of code. At this stage, we have executed only a single render, right after we've defined the render engine. However, this is not enough in a real 3D scene. Remember we talked about the need to have a rolling camera? Calling renderScene once will only render the output image once, similar as a camera that takes one picture. This isn't exactly rolling; we need to do this constantly. The most common way to do this is by adding an ENTER_FRAME event listener and by rendering the scene each time an ENTER_FRAME is dispatched.

We need to import the Event class, so we can listen for ENTER_FRAME events. This can be achieved by setting the following import at the top of your class:

```
import flash.events.Event;
```

Now that Event is available, we can add a listener. Place it right after the renderScene call, as shown in bold in the next snippet:

```
renderEngine.renderScene(scene, camera, viewport);
addEventListener(Event.ENTER_FRAME, render);
```

On each ENTER_FRAME event, a method called render will be triggered. This method needs to be implemented, together with a renderScene call inside of this method. Add the following code after the constructor method:

```
private function render(e:Event):void
{
    renderEngine.renderScene(scene, camera, viewport);
}
```

Each time the playhead enters a new frame, the scene will get rendered again. At this moment, that's just a waste of capacity. Why would you render the scene if nothing has been changed? So, let's start rotating the sphere around its y-axis. This can be achieved by constantly increasing the current rotation of the y-axis, right before the scene renders inside our render method.

```
private function render(e:Event):void
{
    sphere.localRotationY +=1;
    renderEngine.renderScene(scene, camera, viewport);
}
```

Every frame the current rotation of the object increases by one degree.

Publishing will lead to an animation as shown in the following sequence of screenshots:

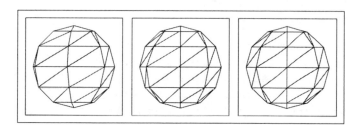

This immediately gives you the illusion of having a 3D object rotating! If you are working in Flash CS3, Flex Builder, or Flash Builder, the animation reveals an issue regarding the smoothness of the movement. This is because we haven't changed Flash's or Flex's default frame rate. This results in Flash CS3 playing at its default of 12 frames per second (fps), and Flex Builder and Flash Builder at 24 fps. By default, Flash CS4 does a better job, as it has a default fps of 30. Although the default frame rate of both Flex Builder and Flash Builder is 24, and Flash CS4's frame rate is 30, it can be a lot more. The higher you set this value, the smoother and faster everything will animate. Of course, getting smoother animations is not without extra costs. Higher frame rates consume more CPU power, maybe even more than is available on the user's computer. In that case the Flash player will try its utmost to draw as many new frames as it can, resulting in stalling animations. With our sphere this is far from an issue, but it can become one when render a more complex 3D scene.

For now, all we have to do is change the default FPS. There's no such thing as a best frame rate value. For all examples in this book, we'll use a value of 40. In Flash IDE you simply set a property of your FLA, but in Flex you can change this only by programming a line of code. This approach works for Flash as well. You can do this by setting the `frameRate` property of your stage:

```
stage.frameRate = 40;
```

Usually this value is set as one of the first instructions inside the constructor of a document class, but you can change it wherever and whenever you want in your application. To see a smoother animation, add the above line as the first command inside your constructor.

We have just finished our first application! Publish it and you'll see the same sphere rotating on its y-axis, but now it runs much smoother.

Let's recap and have a look at the updated class with the changes in bold:

```
package {
    import flash.display.Sprite;
    import flash.events.Event;

    import org.papervision3d.cameras.Camera3D;
    import org.papervision3d.objects.primitives.Sphere;
    import org.papervision3d.render.BasicRenderEngine;
    import org.papervision3d.scenes.Scene3D;
    import org.papervision3d.view.Viewport3D;

    public class FirstApplication extends Sprite
    {
```

```
        private var scene:Scene3D;
        private var viewport:Viewport3D;
        private var camera:Camera3D;
        private var renderEngine:BasicRenderEngine;
        private var sphere:Sphere;

        public function FirstApplication()
        {
                stage.frameRate = 40;
                scene = new Scene3D();
                camera = new Camera3D();

                sphere= new Sphere();
                scene.addChild(sphere);

                viewport = new Viewport3D();
                this.addChild(viewport);

                renderEngine = new BasicRenderEngine();
                renderEngine.renderScene(scene,camera,viewport);
                this.addEventListener(Event.ENTER_FRAME,render);
        }

        private function render(e:Event):void
        {
                sphere.localRotationY +=1;
                renderEngine.renderScene(scene,camera,viewport);
        }
    }
}
```

Smart programmers use less code

The FirstApplication example is a nice and minimal Papervision3D class. Each time we want to make a new Papervision3D application we could copy this class and add the specific logic for the new application to it. But isn't there a smarter way to do this? Each Papervision3D project contains minimal definitions of—a camera, a scene, a renderer, and a viewport. Defining these properties and importing the classes each time you start with a Papervision3D project sounds like a lot of work. Smart programmers ask themselves how they can do this in a more efficient way. Fortunately, Papervision3D includes a class called BasicView that contains the basic setup we need. As the BasicView class is, in the end, an extended Sprite, we can instantiate it and add it to the stage or extend our document class with it. In the book we'll use the last option.

So how does that work? Let's have a look at the improved version, with the same sphere rotating on its y-axis.

```
package {
    import flash.events.Event;

    import org.papervision3d.objects.primitives.Sphere;
    import org.papervision3d.view.BasicView;

    public class BasicViewExample extends BasicView
    {
        private var sphere:Sphere;
        public function BasicViewExample()
        {
            stage.frameRate = 40;

            sphere = new Sphere();
            scene.addChild(sphere);

            startRendering();
        }

        override protected function onRenderTick(e:Event=null):void
        {
            sphere.localRotationX +=1;
            super.onRenderTick();
        }
    }
}
```

Inside the constructor, we need to set only project specific values such as the frame rate and a sphere object. The sphere is added to the scene, without instantiating a Scene3D object. This was already done automatically inside the BasicView class. We then tell the BasicView class that it can start rendering by calling the startRendering() method which is part of the BasicView class. Once this method is called, it will add an ENTER_FRAME eventListener, re-rendering the scene each time the event is dispatched. This is already enough to see our sphere rendered on screen, but we need to increase the rotation-y value of the sphere which we do on each ENTER_FRAME. In most examples we will do something at each ENTER_FRAME. The easiest way to do this is to override the onRenderTick() method, which is part of the BasicView class, and will be called every frame. By overriding this method we can write our own code to be executed each time onRenderTick() gets called. As we want the original onRenderTick() to be executed as well, we'll call this method on the super class by calling super.onRenderTick();.

Due to some minor differences between the settings in the `BasicView` class and the settings we have used in `FirstApplication`, the size of the sphere will not be the same. Whereas the viewport in our example was predefined, `BasicView` automatically scales it to the size of the stage.

Using the `BasicView` class can save you a lot of code. When you compare this extended `BasicView` class to the `FirstApplication` class, you'll see that you've reduced the amount of lines from 43 to 26. So, this saved you 17 lines of code that you don't have to write over and over again. All examples in this book will make use of the `BasicView` class.

Preparing for the book examples

Now that we know how to set up a document class and extend it from the `BasicView` class, we will not go through these steps anymore in the examples that are coming up in the next chapters. Extending the `BasicView` class is a huge time saver, as you do not have to define the standard properties and methods over and over again. You can save even more time when working through this book because the examples always start based on the same extended `BasicView` class. So why not copy this class as a code snippet, which you can use each time you start working on a new example?

The class that you can use as the snippet is almost exactly the same as the class from our latest example. There are a few parts inside this class that make it too specific to use it as a snippet. For instance, we will not use the rotating sphere in every example. On the other hand, our class contains the changed frame rate and the overridden `onRenderTick()` method. Each example will use this setting and method.

It's up to you whether to create this template class as a project, or just as a single class file. Let's create this file, name it `BookExampleTemplate`, and add the following code:

```
package {
    import flash.events.Event;

    import org.papervision3d.view.BasicView;

    public class BookExampleTemplate extends BasicView
    {
        public function BookExampleTemplate()
        {
            stage.frameRate = 40;
            init();
            startRendering();
        }
```

```
        private function init():void
        {

        }

        override protected function onRenderTick(e:Event=null):void
        {
                super.onRenderTick();
        }
    }
}
```

As you can see this is exactly the same code as in the previous example, except that it's cleaned up by removing everything related to the sphere. The only thing you need to do next time when you create a new project is copy this code to your new document class, and replace the class definition and constructor method with the name of your new class.

Some examples in this book will make use of a non-default background color. Changing this in the Flash IDE is quite simple, as the background color is a property of the Flash document. If you work with Flex Builder or Flash Builder need to add a so-called **SWF metadata tag**, right after the imports inside the document class. This metadata tag can set several other document properties such as the width and height of the flash movie. The definition looks as follows:

```
[SWF(width="800", height="600", backgroundColor="#FF
FFFF")]
```

This sets the width and height of the SWF to 800 by 600 pixels and gives it a white background color.
In order to have consistent code examples for Flash, Flex Builder, and Flash Builder, this metadata tag will not be part of the examples as printed in this book.

If your authoring tool is Flex Builder or Flash Builder, you may want to add this line of code to your `BookExampleTemplate` class.

In some situations it is better to use the `super()` method, which calls the constructor of the inherited `BasicView` class. The constructor of `BasicView` takes several parameters. The first three affect the size of the viewport that is part of this class.

	Parameter	Data type	Default value	Description
1	viewportWidth	Number	640	Defines the width of the viewport.
2	viewportHeight	Number	480	Defines the height of the viewport.
3	scaleToStage	Boolean	true	When set to true, the BasicView class will automatically adjust its size to match the size of the stage. This can be useful to create a viewport at the full stage size.

To set the viewport size to a fixed value of 800 by 600 pixels, your BasicView super method call inside your constructor should look like this:

```
super(800,600,false);
```

The BasicView class takes some more parameters that will be explained later in this book, as soon as they are needed.

Working with the BookExampleTemplate class

If you want to follow along with the examples in this book by recreating them, then you can create a new project in the authoring tool of your choice, give it the name that is being proposed in the example, and paste the code of the BookExampleTemplate class into your document class.

Although keep in mind that you have to do two more changes. You'll have to change the class name that follows the class keyword. It still says BookExampleTemplate, so change it into the name of your document class. Likewise, the name of the constructor needs to be altered from BookExampleTemplate into the document class name. If you work in Flex Builder or Flash Builder, you should not forget to set the path for each example to the Papervision3D source code as described in Chapter 10.

Summary

The chapter started off with a short introduction to OOP and classes for those who are new to programming in an object-oriented way. We now know what classes are and how we can:

- Create a new class
- Set imports
- Define properties and methods
- Tell what access modifiers are
- Extend an existing class by using inheritance
- Override methods from a super class
- Create a new project with a document class/main application file

We also know what a Papervision3D application is made of and that it at least contains:

- A scene to hold 3D objects
- A camera that registrates the scene
- A viewport as the window to the world
- A render engine to render information to the viewport
- A 3D object as a visual object in 3D space
- A material to assign to the 3D object in order to make it visible

We've learned how to use these objects as the building blocks for a basic application by using a document class in Flash CS3, Flash CS4, Flex Builder, or Flash Builder. As an example, we've made a primitive sphere rotating around its y-axis.

An important thing you have learned is how we can program smarter by extending the `BasicView` class, which already contains the basic setup for a Papervision3D scene.

At the end of this chapter, we've created a template class that you can copy to your document class each time you create a new project. This class contains the basic setup that we'll use throughout the book.

In the next chapter, you will learn more about 3D objects including the built-in primitives such as planes, cubes, spheres, and cylinders.

3
Primitives

If you're familiar with 3D modeling software such as Maya, 3D Studio Max, or CINEMA 4D, you will undoubtedly know that programs like these usually have a set of built-in primitives. Primitives are basic geometric shapes such as the plane, sphere, and cube. In most 3D modeling programs you can easily add primitives to your scene by clicking and dragging, and if you like, you can modify them. In that respect primitives serve as the building blocks for advanced models. You could also create them yourself, but primitives included in 3D software programs definitely make life easier for the 3D modeler.

Papervision3D also has a set of primitive shapes. Although you cannot click and drag them to the stage, as Papervision3D is not a software program with a graphic user interface, they come in quite handy when you need basic shapes in your application.

Modifying primitives in Papervision3D is harder than in 3D modelling software, again because there is no user interface. However, working with more complex models is possible, as Papervision3D allows you to import models into your application that have been made in 3D modeling software. We'll take a look at exporting models from 3D software and importing them into Papervision3D in Chapter 8.

In this chapter, we will first take some time to deepen our understanding of vertices and triangles—the basic elements of every 3D object. Next, we will go through an example for each primitive, examining how to create one and how to add it to your scene. Then we will discuss how you can add objects as children of parent objects instead of adding them directly to the scene. Finally, we will build an example demonstrating how you can put to use the things we have discussed.

This chapter covers the following:

- A closer look at the geometry of 3D objects
- How Papervision3D transforms 3D information into a 2D screen
- Creating and adding primitives
- Nesting 3D objects

Before we create each of the seven primitives, we will take a closer look at what makes up a 3D object. We will also briefly discuss the sequence of processes that transform the data of a 3D object into a two-dimensional image, known as the rendering pipeline.

The basic elements of 3D objects

In our daily life it is not hard to imagine the third dimension, as we are part of it all the time. On a computer screen, 3D is different because a screen is 2D only. Let's get a little more familiar with the illusion of the third dimension on a two-dimensional screen.

Vertices

In 3D geometry, every object consists of a group of **vertices**, also known as **verts** (singular: **vertex**). A vertex is a point in 3D space. When you define the position of a sprite in Flash, you set it on two axes, the x- and y-axis. A vertex has a third coordinate, set on the z-axis. The order of the coordinates in 3D is always x, y, z.

Triangles

Vertices form **triangles**, also known as **faces**, or **triangle faces**, so every triangle is made of three vertices. Other 3D programs sometimes enable you to create faces that are made up of four vertices, also known as **quad faces**, but Papervision3D knows only triangle faces. The vertices define the shape of the triangle and because they have x, y, and z coordinates, it is possible to make the triangle face any direction along the three axes. When you draw multiple triangles and position them next to each other in 3D space, you can create all kinds of shapes. In Papervision3D such a shape is referred to as triangle mesh. By creating a mesh you create a 3D object.

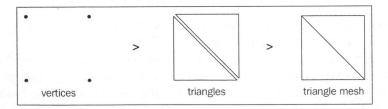

vertices   triangles   triangle mesh

The following drawing shows the same triangle mesh as in the previous figure, but we extended it by another pair of triangles with an angle of 90 degrees. Although all vertices and triangles are drawn on a 2D screen, it gives the illusion of a 3D object that has width, height, and depth.

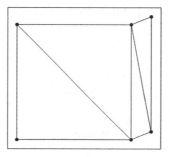

 If you are familiar with 3D modeling, you may wonder about the role of polygons in Papervision3D. In most 3D programs, a **polygon** is defined as an even surface, which has at least four corners and is made of two or more triangles. Papervision3D does not know polygons as such—for instance, it does not include a `Polygon` class. In fact, the only supported polygons in Papervision3D are triangles, or **triangular polygons**.

By setting the x, y, and z coordinates of vertices we can tell Papervision3D how to project them onto our 2D screen so that the illusion of depth is generated. In other words, Papervision3D knows how to represent three-dimensional shapes two-dimensionally.

In the Papervision3D library, the `Vertices3D` class takes care of creating the vertices for us and the `TriangleMesh3D` class handles the creation of 3D objects made of vertices and triangles. As we will see in a bit, this makes it very easy for us to create primitives.

While vertices define the shape of your object, triangles are the shapes onto which you put materials, varying from a simple color to bitmaps and even video. Papervision3D includes all kinds of classes to apply materials, resulting in interesting and realistic objects. As the subject of materials is beyond the scope of this chapter, we will only touch upon them and use two basic materials, wireframe material and color material. (See Chapter 4 for a thorough explanation of how to apply materials.)

The rendering pipeline

When you publish a project, Papervision3D handles several processes, resulting in the illusion of 3D that you see on your two-dimensional screen. The sequence of processes that transform 3D information into a 2D screen is called the **rendering pipeline**. The Papervision3D rendering pipeline looks like this:

When you built your first application in the previous chapter, you instantiated a sphere that appeared on the screen after publishing the file. Let's run through the pipeline with the sphere example in mind.

Initialization is the part where you set up your application by creating a viewport, a scene, a camera, a renderer, and one or more 3D objects. This is something that happens only once. In the example in Chapter 2, you created a sphere with default wireframe material in the init() method, which stands for **initialize**.

Projection converts 3D coordinates onto a 2D screen. As said in the previous section, a 3D object is made up of vertices, which have a third coordinate. Because the 2D screen has only an x and y-axis, you cannot simply map a 3D object on a 2D screen. Papervision3D takes the 3D coordinates of the vertices and projects them onto a 2D plane, calculating what the position of each vertex should be on the screen. Projection deals with only vertices, not with triangles or materials. In our sphere example, Papervison3D takes the 3D vertices of the sphere, and at each render calculates how they should be projected onto a 2D screen.

Rendering is the process of drawing the image that you see on the screen. It combines the 2D projection data with information about the material that is being used. The rendering process draws triangles with the lineTo() method from the Flash Graphics API. In order to add textures, the triangles are filled using another Flash method, beginBitmapFill(). The textures are usually BitmapData objects that are scaled and skewed when they are mapped onto the triangles.

The rendering part doesn't know about 3D coordinates. It is only interested in how they are projected in 2D. This is by far the most intensive task for the processor.

Creating and adding primitives

Papervision3D offers a set of seven primitives:

- **Plane**
- **Sphere**
- **Cylinder**
- **Cone**
- **Cube**
- **Arrow**
- **PaperPlane**

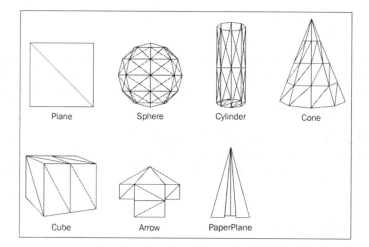

The arrow and the paper plane are shapes that are a little more specific than the other shapes that may have a broader use in real-world applications. The paper plane has been part of the Papervision3D library from the very start and has provided the developers with a simple object to carry out all kinds of testing. In that respect, there is an analogy between the paper plane and the famous "Utah teapot" that is included in many 3D software programs.

The Utah teapot is a 3D model that was created by Martin Newell back in 1975 after his wife Sandra suggested modeling their tea service. It is known to be quite useful for testing purposes. The original teapot model can be found in the Computer History Museum in Mountain View, CA.

The primitives that come with Papervision3D are easy to instantiate. For each primitive, we will go through an example that shows how to create one and how to add it to your scene.

In Chapter 2 we wrote a template class, so we don't have to rewrite the basic code that we will need over and over again. We have also seen how to start a new project based on this template, every time you want to follow along with an example in this book. Run through this process and call your first example `PlaneExample`. This should result in an FLA or, when you work in Flex Builder or Flash Builder, an ActionScript project with that name and an accompanying document class that carries the same name. Let's use this example project to create the first primitive that we will discuss—a plane.

Plane

The plane object is by far the simplest shape among the primitives. Actually it's a rectangle, and as long as you don't rotate it over the x- or y-axis, it looks like a 2D object. It's quite easy to add a plane. All you have to do is import the right class, create an instance, and add it to the scene.

In the previous section, we already created a project called `PlaneExample`. The following class looks exactly like the `PlaneExample` document class you have just created with only a few lines of code added. The extra lines are highlighted.

```
package {

    import flash.events.Event;

    import org.papervision3d.view.BasicView;
    import org.papervision3d.objects.primitives.Plane;

    public class PlaneExample extends BasicView
    {
        private var plane:Plane;

        public function PlaneExample()
        {
            stage.frameRate = 40;

            init();
            startRendering();
        }

        private function init():void
        {
```

```
            plane = new Plane(null,300,300,1,1);
            scene.addChild(plane);
    }

    override protected function onRenderTick
                            (e:Event=null):void
    {
            super.onRenderTick();
    }
  }
}
```

So what code did we add to create a plane? In order to use the `Plane` class, along with its properties and methods, we first had to import it. All the primitive classes are located at `org.papervision3d.objects.primitives`. Then we assigned our `Plane` object to an instance variable—`plane`. We used a class property, and not a local variable, to make sure we have access to the plane outside the constructor. This enables you to access the plane in other methods such as the render method. Next, we created our plane while passing some arguments to the `Plane` constructor and added it to the scene using the `addChild()` method. If you publish this example, you should see a simple plane made of two triangles.

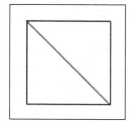

We passed five arguments to the `Plane` constructor. Let's see what they are:

	Parameter	Data type	Default value	Description
1	material	MaterialObject3D	null	Defines the material that you want to apply to the plane.
2	width	Number	0	Sets the desired width of the plane.
3	height	Number	0	Sets the desired height of the plane.
4	segmentsW	Number	0	Sets the number of segments horizontally.
5	segmentsH	Number	0	Sets the number of segments vertically.

In the example we passed `null` as a material, which results in applying the default `WireframeMaterial`. The fifth and sixth parameters define the number of segments. Take a look at the following illustration to see what segments are:

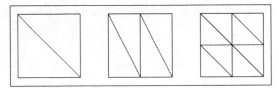

The plane on the left has one width and one height segment. The plane in the middle has two width segments and one height segment. And the plane on the right has two width and two height segments. As you can see, each width or height segment that you add results in two more triangles.

When you project an image on a plane, a common problem is that the image will distort when you rotate the plane. You can avoid this by increasing the number of segments. At the same time you should be cautious when adding segments. The more segments you add, the more processing power is required to render all the triangles. Adding too many triangles can result in an object that is hard to handle by the Flash player. You should generally try to keep the total number of triangles in a scene below 3000.

Although the default value for both segment parameters is 0, passing 0 or no value will result in a plane with one width and one height segment. Passing a width and height value of 0, or passing no values, results in a plane of 500 by 500 units.

Now that we have seen what arguments you can pass to the `Plane` constructor, let's take a look at some of the properties that you can set once you have created a plane. All primitives indirectly extend the `DisplayObject3D` class. In other words, primitives inherit all the properties and methods from `DisplayObject3D` unless they are private.

Let's play with some of the inherited properties to position the plane in our `PlaneExample` class, and set the x, y, and z in the `init()` method:

```
private function init():void
{
    plane = new Plane(null,300,300,1,1);
    scene.addChild(plane);
    plane.x = 200;
    plane.y = 200;
    plane.z = 300;
}
```

In Chapter 2, we discussed the difference between the coordinate systems in Papervision3D and Flash. In Papervision3D, increasing the y coordinate moves the plane up and increasing z moves it away from us. Increasing x will do the same as in Flash—moving the plane to the right.

> Equivalent to Flash movie clips, every primitive has a registration point. In movie clips the registration point is by default set at (0,0). In 3D objects this point is set at (0,0,0), which is located at the center or origin of the object. Whereas in movie clips you can change the registration point, you cannot simply change the origin of a Papervision3D object.

In the method that renders our scene, we add another property, `localRotationY`, and we increment its value every frame by 1.

```
override protected function onRenderTick(e:Event-null):void
{
    plane.localRotationY++;
    super.onRenderTick();
}
```

This will cause the plane to rotate around its own y-axis.

As you can see some of the properties are similar to the properties of the ActionScript `DisplayObject` class, like x and y. But Papervision3D's `DisplayObject3D` has a set of extra properties (and methods) that enable its instances to move and rotate in 3D space such as z and `localRotationY`.

> There are several ways of rotating objects in Papervision3D. The `localRotationX`, `localRotationY`, and `localRotationZ` properties set the rotation of the object around its own x-, y-, and z-axis respectively. The value is set in degrees, so `plane.localRotationY = 45` sets the plane's rotation around the y-axis to 45 degrees.

If you publish the project it should show you a rotating plane. However, only one side of the plane has a wireframe material applied to it. This is the default material when you do not apply a material to a primitive or when Papervision3D does it for you when you pass `null` as the material argument. One way of displaying material on two sides is accessing the plane's `material` property, which in turn has a `doubleSided` property that we set to `true`.

```
plane.material.doubleSided = true;
```

Adding this line of code to the init() method after you have created the plane will result in a plane that has a material applied to both sides.

 PlaneExample

---

A closer look at DisplayObject3D

The Papervision3D documentation describes DisplayObject3D as follows:

The DisplayObject3D class represents instances of 3D objects that are contained in the scene

That sounds like a pretty relevant class when you figure that a 3D scene would not be worth much worth without 3D objects.

You could say the relevance of DisplayObject3D lies in the fact that so many subclasses extend it. Not only do primitives inherit from DisplayObject3D, but also the Camera class and the DAE class for instance, a class that can be used to load external models into Papervision3D. DisplayObject3D has a number of crucial properties and methods that can be used by 3D objects. These properties and methods will be discussed throughout the book, starting in this chapter.

With the increasing popularity of the mailing list, the Papervision3D community soon adapted **do3D**, which is an abbreviation of **display object 3d**. It not only refers to *an instance of DisplayObject3D* but also to *an instance of a class that extends DisplayObject3D*. Therefore, an instantiated Plane object cannot only be described as *an instance of the Plane class* but also as a do3D.

Sphere

We have already created a sphere in the previous chapter. In order to keep our examples consistent, we will copy the code of the BasicViewExample class and paste it into the document class of a new project called SphereExample. If you do so and rename both the class definition and the constructor to SphereExample, then this is what your document class should look like:

```
package {

    import flash.events.Event;
    import org.papervision3d.objects.primitives.Sphere;
    import org.papervision3d.view.BasicView;

    public class SphereExample extends BasicView
    {
```

```
        private var sphere:Sphere;

        public function SphereExample ()
        {
                init();
                startRendering();
        }

        private function init():void
        {
                sphere = new Sphere();
                scene.addChild(sphere);
        }

        override protected function onRenderTick(e:Event=null):void
        {
                sphere.localRotationY--;
                super.onRenderTick();
        }
    }
}
```

The sphere that we have instantiated has only a material applied to its outside. Keep in mind that not passing any material is the same as passing `null` — both will default to wireframe material. Let's elaborate on this code by passing some arguments to the `Sphere` constructor. In the `init()` method, change this line:

```
sphere = new Sphere();
```

to the following line:

```
sphere = new Sphere(null,300,16,12);
```

If you want to know what arguments you can pass to the `Sphere` constructor (or to the constructor of any other object), you could look it up in the documentation. Look for the `Sphere` class and then for the *Constructor detail* paragraph. It will show you the following lines:

```
public function Sphere(material:MaterialObject3D = null, radius:Number
                         = 100, segmentsW:int = 8, segmentsH:int = 6)
```

This is the first part of the constructor in the `Sphere` class. It shows us what the available parameters are when you instantiate the class. They are also listed and described in the following table:

	Parameter	Data type	Default value	Description
1	material	MaterialObject3D	null	Defines the material that you want to apply to the sphere
2	radius	Number	100	Sets the radius of the sphere, meaning the distance between the center and the vertices
3	segmentsW	Number	8	Sets the number of segments horizontally
4	segmentsH	Number	6	Sets the number of segments vertically

Take some time to experiment with these values. One thing you might notice is that raising the number of segments makes the movement of the sphere less fluid. The reason for this is that the more segments you add, the more vertices and triangles will be created, and the harder the Flash player has to work to render your object.

{Ex.} SphereExample {Ex.}

Cylinder

Creating a cylinder and adding it to the scene is quite similar to what we did in our plane and sphere examples. If you want to follow along hands-on, we will call this example and our project and document class `CylinderExample`. The import line for the `Cylinder` class looks like this:

```
import org.papervision3d.objects.primitives.Cylinder;
```

We instantiate the primitive and assign it to a local variable in the `init()` method. After we have done that, we add the cylinder to the scene.

```
private function init():void
{
    var cylinder:Cylinder = new Cylinder(null,80,400,8,
                            2,-1,false,true);
    scene.addChild(cylinder);
}
```

If you publish the file you should see the shape of a cylinder.

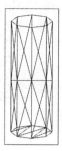

 Keep in mind that when you instantiate an object within a method using a local variable, you don't have access to the object outside that method. If you would like to add some movement to the object in the onRenderTick() method such as a rotation, you would have to use a class property as we have done when we created the plane and the sphere.

We can pass eight arguments to the Cylinder constructor.

	Parameter	Data type	Default value	Description
1	material	MaterialObject3D	null	Sets the material that you want to apply to the cylinder
2	radius	Number	100	Sets the radius of the cylinder
3	height	Number	100	Sets the height of the cylinder
4	segmentsW	Number	8	Sets the number of segments horizontally
5	segmentsH	Number	6	Sets the number of segments vertically
6	topRadius	Number	-1	Sets the radius of the top face. This parameter allows you to create cylinders with a diverging or converging top. The default value of -1 results in a top radius equal to the radius that is passed as the second parameter
7	topFace	Boolean	true	Defines whether the top face should be created
8	bottomFace	Boolean	true	Defines whether the bottom face should be created

Setting both `topFace` and `bottomFace` to `false` will create a cylinder that has neither a top nor a bottom, resulting in the shape of a tube, as shown in the next screenshot:

 CylinderExample

Cone

As you've probably noticed, the keyword is uniformity when it comes to instantiating primitives. The same goes for the cone. We will assume a new project as a starting point, but this time we will call it `ConeExample`. First, we import the `Cone` class.

```
import org.papervision3d.objects.primitives.Cone;
```

Then we instantiate the cone in the `init()` method, passing null as the material and four other arguments, and add it to the scene.

```
private function init():void
{
    var cone:Cone = new Cone(null,150,400,8,4);
    scene.addChild(cone);
}
```

The following parameters are available in the `Cone` constructor:

	Parameter	Data type	Default value	Description
1	material	MaterialObject3D	null	Defines the material that you want to apply to the cone.
2	radius	Number	100	Sets the radius of the cone.
3	height	Number	100	Sets the height of the cone.
4	segmentsW	Number	8	Sets the number of segments horizontally.
5	segmentsH	Number	6	Sets the number of segments vertically.

A cone always has a converged top, so you set only the radius for the bottom of the cone.

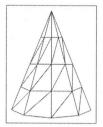

 ConeExample

Cube

In the previous sections we have instantiated a plane, a sphere, a cylinder, and a cone. In all four examples we passed null as a material, resulting in primitives that had the default wireframe material applied to them. Although instantiating a cube is quite similar to instantiating the previously discussed primitives, applying materials differs from what we have seen so far. The first parameter of the `Cube` constructor is not a material, but a **materials list**. As a cube has six sides, this allows you to apply a different material to each side, by adding it to the list. To create a materials list we need to import the `MaterialsList` class. We also import the `Cube` class, and this time we will use a color as our material, so we need to import `ColorMaterial`.

```
import org.papervision3d.materials.utils.MaterialsList;
import org.papervision3d.materials.ColorMaterial;
import org.papervision3d.objects.primitives.Cube;
```

Add this line to create a class property:

```
private var cube:Cube;
```

In the `init()` method, we first create three color materials passing a hexadecimal color value to the `ColorMaterial` constructor:

```
private function init():void
{
    var red:ColorMaterial = new ColorMaterial(0xFF0000);
    var blue:ColorMaterial = new ColorMaterial(0x0000FF);
    var green:ColorMaterial = new ColorMaterial(0x00FF00);
```

Then we instantiate a materials list.

```
    var materialsList:MaterialsList = new MaterialsList();
```

Now we can add the materials to the list using the `addMaterial()` method. We apply each color material to two opposite faces of the cube.

```
materialsList.addMaterial(red,"front");
materialsList.addMaterial(red,"back");
materialsList.addMaterial(blue,"left");
materialsList.addMaterial(blue,"right");
materialsList.addMaterial(green,"top");
materialsList.addMaterial(green,"bottom");
```

Notice that a second argument is being passed in this method such as `"front"` and `"back"`. This argument is a string and represents the face of the cube. Earlier in this chapter we referred to faces as another word for triangles. However, when we speak of the faces of a cube, we refer to the six sides, not to triangles.

> If you want to apply the same material to all six faces you can pass the `"all"` string to the `addMaterial()` method:
> ```
> materialsList.addMaterial( green,"all");
> ```

Finally we create the cube, pass the materials list and three more arguments, and add it to the scene.

```
cube = new Cube(materialsList,300,300,300);
scene.addChild(cube);
}
```

`Cube` takes quite a few parameters, so let's sum them up:

	Parameter	Data type	Default value	Description
1	materials	MaterialList		A list that contains the material properties of the object.
2	width	Number	500	Sets the width.
3	depth	Number	500	Sets the depth.
4	height	Number	500	Sets the height.
5	segmentsS	int	1	The number of width segments.
6	segmentsT	int	1	The number of height segments.
7	segmentsH	int	1	The number of depth segments.
8	insideFaces	int	0	Defines the sides that are visible from the inside of the cube.
9	excludeFaces	int	0	Defines the sides that will not be created.

The fifth, sixth, and seventh argument define the number of segments, and deserve a closer look. The three cubes in the following illustration show how each parameter has subdivided sides with one segment into sides having two segments:

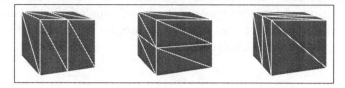

When the cubes above were instantiated, the fifth, sixth, and seventh parameter were given the following values:

- The cube at the left: 2, 1, and 1, creating two width segments in the x direction
- The cube in the middle: 1, 2, and 1, creating two height segments in the y direction
- The cube at the right: 1, 1, and 2, creating two depth segments in the z direction

Let's take a moment to examine the eighth and ninth parameter, which we did not pass as arguments in our example.

The `insideFaces` parameter defines the sides that are visible from the inside of the cube. Suppose your camera is placed inside the cube and you only want to show the backside. To achieve this you would pass `Cube.BACK`. You can also add or subtract sides when passing the argument, for instance `Cube.ALL-Cube.LEFT`. This would show all sides except the left side.

The `excludeFaces` parameter defines the sides that will not be created. Here too you can add or subtract. Passing `Cube.FRONT+Cube.BACK` results in a cube without the front- and backside.

> Note that in the list of parameters the default value of both `insideFaces` and `excludeFaces` is 0, which is the equivalent of `Cube.NONE`.

As we created a class property for our cube, we are able to access it in the render method. Let's rotate the cube around its three axes, so we can see all sides:

```
override protected function onRenderTick(e:Event=null):void
{
    cube.localRotationX++;
    cube.localRotationY++;
    cube.localRotationZ++;
    super.onRenderTick();
}
```

{Ex.} CubeExample {Ex.}

PaperPlane

In the introduction of this chapter we saw that the paper plane was built at the start of the Papervision3D project for testing purposes. What makes the paper plane such a suitable testing object is its specific shape—the fact that you can always see in which direction it is pointing and what its approximate rotation is. This can be quite handy when you are building an application in which 3D objects are moving and rotating.

Suppose you have a sphere in your scene with a wireframe material and suppose you want the sphere to rotate 270 degrees. When the rotation would be completed it would be hard to tell if the front of the sphere is facing the direction that you expected it to face. Replacing the sphere temporarily with a paper plane probably would give you a much better idea of what's happening to the object, as you can constantly see the position and rotation of the paper plane.

You will have to import the PaperPlane class in order to use it.

```
import org.papervision3d.objects.primitives.PaperPlane;
```

The constructor of the PaperPlane class takes two parameters—material and scale. In the following lines we instantiate a paper plane with its size scaled up by a factor of three, and add it to the scene:

```
var paperPlane:PaperPlane = new PaperPlane(null,3);
scene.addChild(paperPlane);
```

The paper plane constructor has neither width, depth, and height parameters available, nor are their default values listed in the documentation. But what if you need to know these values, for instance because you want to scale the object to a size that fits your needs? There are more situations in which you don't know or may not have fast access to the size of 3D objects, for instance because you have set it randomly.

Getting the size of a 3D object

The `Vertices3D boundingBox()` method calculates a 3D bounding box and enables us to get the width, depth, and height of any 3D object that inherits from `Vertices3D`, which actually goes for all the built-in Papervision3D objects that you can display on the screen. A bounding box is the smallest enclosing box that an object fits into. The illustration below shows a paper plane with a visual representation of its bounding box:

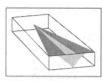

 You get the size of the bounding box of an object as follows:

```
trace(paperPlane.boundingBox().size);
```

The `size` property returns three numbers that represent the difference between the maximum and the minimum vertex of the object over each axis. The trace call above will output this:

x:100 y:33.33z:200

The output shows the size in the x, y, and z direction. The paper plane apparently has a default width of 100, a default height of 33.33, and a default depth of 200. You can also get the size per dimension. The next trace call outputs only the width:

```
trace(paperPlane.boundingBox().size.x);
```

Therefore, if you want a paper plane to have a width of 200 units, you should scale it by a factor 2. As the paper plane inherits from `DisplayObject3D`, you can also use `scaleX` and `scaleY`, to scale in the x and y direction independently.

The next figure shows a paper plane with a local rotation around its own x-axis of 90 degrees:

{Ex.} PaperPlaneExample {Ex.}

Arrow

Although not unthinkable, the arrow is probably not a primitive that you would use a lot in real-world projects. But just like the paper plane, the arrow too can be of good service as a testing object, as it also gives you a clear view on its orientation. By now you probably can guess how to import the class, but here it is:

```
import org.papervision3d.objects.primitives.Arrow;
```

The only parameter inside the `Arrow` constructor is the one for material, so creating a new arrow looks like this when we do not pass a material:

```
var arrow:Arrow = new Arrow();
scene.addChild(arrow);
```

As seen before, not passing any material defaults to wireframe material. Similar to `PaperPlane`, the `Arrow` constructor does not have size parameters available. By default, the arrow has a width of 400, a height of 100, and a depth of 600. If you would like to change the size of the arrow, use the `scale` property that it inherits from `DisplayObject3D`:

```
arrow.scale = 0.5;
```

The following figure shows an instance of `Arrow` with a local rotation around its own x-axis of 45 degrees:

 ArrowExample

Nesting

Nesting is the technique of adding one or multiple objects—the child or children—to a parent object. A benefit of nesting is that you can create a hierarchal structure in which children show behavior relative to their parent. For instance, you can group one set of objects by nesting them in one parent and group another set of objects by nesting them in another parent. This gives you a lot of control over both groups of objects.

In the previous examples, every time we created a primitive we added it directly to the scene using the `addChild()` method. But not only `Scene3D` has this method, so does `DisplayObject3D`. In the documentation we can look up the path of inheritance for both classes:

- `DisplayObject3D` inherits from `DisplayObjectContainer3D`
- `Scene3D` inherits from `SceneObject3D`, which inherits from `DisplayObjectContainer3D`

Both `Scene3D` and `DisplayObject3D` inherit the `addChild()` method from `DisplayObjectContainer3D`. This means that we can also use the `addChild()` method on primitives as they inherit their properties and methods from `DisplayObject3D`.

Let's create a project and call it `NestingExample` in which one sphere will be added to another. After we have imported `Sphere`, we assign an object of the class to a class property.

```
private var parentSphere:Sphere;
```

In the `init()` method we first create the parent sphere and add it to the scene.

```
private function init():void
{
    parentSphere = new Sphere(null,200,16,12);
    scene.addChild(parentSphere);
```

Then we create the child sphere using a local variable and we set the x coordinate to `400`.

```
    var childSphere:Sphere = new Sphere(null,100,12,8);
    childSphere.x = 400;
```

Now we add the child sphere, not directly to the scene, but to the parent sphere.

```
    parentSphere.addChild(childSphere);
}
```

The child sphere has an x value of `400`. We didn't set the coordinates of `parentSphere`, so it is positioned at the origin of the scene with x, y, and z being `0`. Let's see what adding `childSphere` to `parentSphere` does to the way we perceive the coordinate system as we know it.

World space versus local space

The moment we add childSphere to parentSphere, the coordinates of childSphere are relative to its new parent. They are not relative to the global scene coordinate system, but to a local coordinate system. We call the global coordinate system (the coordinate system relative to our scene) **world space** and a local coordinate system **local space**. Therefore, every time you add one instance of DisplayObject3D to another, it has its own local space.

Compare this with 2D Flash, where you also can add objects to other objects. For instance, you can nest a movie clip within another movie clip. Suppose you add one movie clip, the child, to another movie clip, the parent. The x and y coordinates of the child are now relative to the position of the parent. Moving and rotating the parent will move and rotate the child. Likewise, scaling the parent will scale the child proportionally.

Let's continue with our NestingExample class and rotate parentSphere around its y-axis by incrementing the y rotation in the onRenderTick() method:

```
override protected function onRenderTick(e:Event=null):void
{
    parentSphere.localRotationY++;
    super.onRenderTick();
}
```

When you publish this example you should see the parent sphere rotate around its y-axis just as expected. The child sphere moves too, although we didn't tell it to move. It moves in world space, not in local space. It is moving along with its parent because its coordinate system is relative to parentSphere. If you would trace the x coordinate of childSphere in the render method, it would remain 400 because the child sphere is not moving in local space. This is an important principle to keep in mind when you work with nesting.

If you would like to know the x coordinate of the child sphere relative to the scene coordinate system (world space), you can use the sceneX property. Tracing childSphere.sceneX in the render method would output values from 400 to -400 and back. DisplayObject3D also has a sceneY and a sceneZ property.

The following sequence of screenshots shows the parent sphere rotating. Notice that the x value of the child sphere stays 400, whereas the sceneX value changes.

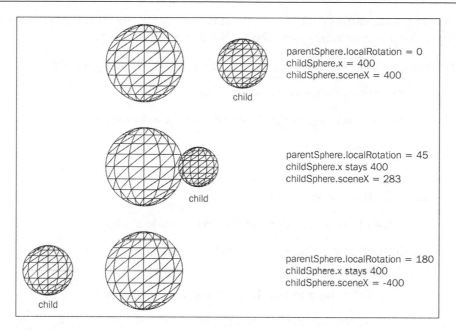

parentSphere.localRotation = 0
childSphere.x = 400
childSphere.sceneX = 400

child

parentSphere.localRotation = 45
childSphere.x stays 400
childSphere.sceneX = 283

child

parentSphere.localRotation = 180
childSphere.x stays 400
childSphere.sceneX = -400

child

Nesting 3D objects inside other 3D objects clearly has an important benefit. You can add multiple objects to one parent object and then tell the parent object to do something, for instance move from one point to another. Because the coordinates of each child object are relative to the parent object, they will move along relatively to this parent. Therefore, instead of telling each child object separately to go from one point to another, you can simply tell the parent object to move and all its children will follow.

{Ex.} NestingExample {Ex.}

Creating a pivot point with DisplayObject3D

A common nesting technique is to create an instance of `DisplayObject3D` and use it as a holder to which you add other objects such as primitives. This technique is similar to the one described in the previous section. However, this time you do not use a primitive as the parent, but an instance of `DisplayObject3D`. If you create a do3D and add it to the scene, you will not see it on screen because it is not made up of vertices and triangles. However, similar to primitives it does have the `addchild()` method meaning that you can add other objects to it. It also has all the properties and methods that enable you to move and rotate it. The do3D will serve as a pivot point for its children just like the parent sphere did for the child sphere in the previous example. To have access to the `DisplayObject3D` class you need to import it.

```
import org.papervision3d.objects.DisplayObject3D;
```

The following code shows part of a class called `PivotDO3DExample`. Notice the similarity with the previously described `Nestingexample` class.

This time we assign an instance of `DisplayObject3D` to a class property.

```
private var pivotDO3D:DisplayObject3D;
```

In the `init()` method we create the do3D and add it to the scene.

```
private function init():void
{
    pivotDO3D = new DisplayObject3D();
    scene.addChild(pivotDO3D);
```

Next, we create the child sphere and set its x coordinate at `400`.

```
    var childSphere:Sphere = new Sphere(null,100,12,8);
    childSphere.x = 400;
```

Then we add the child sphere to the do3D that serves as the parent:

```
    pivotDO3D.addChild(childSphere);
}
```

In the render method we rotate the parent around its own y-axis.

```
override protected function onRenderTick(e:Event=null):void
{
    pivotDO3D.localRotationY++;
    super.onRenderTick();
}
```

If you compare this code with the `NestingExample` class you can see that we only replaced `parentSphere` from our previous example by `pivotDO3D`, which is an instance of `DisplayObject3D`. Adding the child sphere to `pivotDO3D` makes the coordinate system of the sphere relative to it. If you publish this file you should see the sphere turning circles around an imaginary point, `pivotDO3D`, just as the child sphere was moving along with the parent sphere in the `NestingExample` project.

{Ex.} PivotDO3DExample {Ex.}

Accessing vertices

Let's go back for a moment to the basic elements of a 3D object—vertices. The vertices of every `do3D` are stored in an array. You can access them through the `geometry` property.

```
do3D.geometry.vertices
```

Suppose you would like to know the x and y coordinates of all the vertices of the plane that we built in `PlaneExample`. Because the vertices are stored in an array, you can find out how many there are by using the `length` property.

```
var numberOfVertices = plane.geometry.vertices.length;
```

Then you can iterate through the array using a `for` loop.

```
for(var i:uint = 0; i < numberOfVertices; i++)
{
    trace("x: " + plane.geometry.vertices[i].x,
        "y: " + plane.geometry.vertices[i].y,
        "z: " + plane.geometry.vertices[i].z)
}
```

This will output:

```
x: -150 y: -150 z: 0
x: -150 y: 150 z: 0
x: 150 y: -150 z: 0
x: 150 y: 150 z: 0
```

As you can see, only the x, y, and z positions of four points are given. Maybe you would have expected the positions of six points because every triangle has three vertices and we have two triangles. However, as we don't need two vertices on the same position, they are shared by the triangles. You can undoubtedly imagine that for a complex object with hundreds or thousands of triangles, getting rid of double vertices can really make a difference when the object is being rendered. It saves the Flash player calculations and memory, which results in a higher performance of your movie.

The x, y, and z coordinates are read-write properties. We have just read them, writing them is just as easy. This line of code sets the value of the x property of the first vertex in the array to -300:

```
plane.geometry.vertices[0].x = -300;
```

This will result in an altered shape. The first vertex in the array is apparently the vertex at the bottom left of the left triangle.

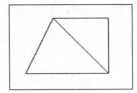

Let's see what happens when instead of the x property we set the z property for that vertex:

```
plane.geometry.vertices[0].z = 100;
```

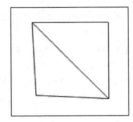

This immediately gives us a 3D illusion on our 2D screen. The bottom left vertex has moved further away from us. Of course these are just simple alterations, but they show that you can customize objects to your own needs.

 The geometry property also lets you access the triangles of an object:

```
do3D.geometry.faces
```

Example—building a sphere of spheres

To give an example of what's possible when you know the coordinates of the vertices of a primitive, we will do the following:

- Create a sphere
- Find out what the coordinates of the vertices are
- Place a smaller sphere on the position of each vertex of the big one

Let's call this example VerticesExample. First we need to import DisplayObject3D to create a pivot point.

```
import org.papervision3d.objects.DisplayObject3D;
```

Next, we assign a `DisplayObject3D` instance to a class property. This instance will serve as a pivot point or holder for the small spheres.

```
private var pivotDO3D:DisplayObject3D;
```

In the `init()` method we instantiate the `DisplayObject3D` object. We also create the big sphere.

```
private function init():void
{
    pivotDO3D = new DisplayObject3D();
    scene.addChild(pivotDO3D);
    var bigSphere:Sphere = new Sphere(null,500);
```

We don't need to add the big sphere to the scene, nor do we have to add a material to it because we don't want to see it. But even if we don't add the sphere, we still can obtain and use information about it, in our case the coordinates of its vertices. Once we know the values of the x, y, and z properties of each vertex, we can place other objects exactly on these coordinates.

Still in the `init()` method, we add a `for` loop and iterate through the array that holds all the vertices of the big sphere.

```
var numberOfVerts:uint = bigSphere.geometry.vertices.length;
for(var i:uint = 0; i < numberOfVerts; i++)
{
```

In the `for` loop we instantiate a small sphere in each iteration, passing `null` as the material and using the `Math.random()` method to give the sphere a random radius. We keep the number of segments low, which will give the small primitives a diamond-like shape.

```
var smallSphere:Sphere = new Sphere(null,Math.random() * 30,2,2);
```

Now we are ready to position the small sphere on the coordinates of the vertex of the big sphere using the `geometry.vertices` property.

```
smallSphere.x = bigSphere.geometry.vertices[i].x;
smallSphere.y = bigSphere.geometry.vertices[i].y;
smallSphere.z = bigSphere.geometry.vertices[i].z;
```

Finally, we add the small sphere to `pivotDO3D`—the instance of `DisplayObject3D` that does not have a visual representation, but will serve as a container and pivot point.

```
pivotDO3D.addChild(smallSphere);
    }
}
```

To finish off this example, we add the following line in the `onRenderTick()` method:

```
override protected function onRenderTick(e:Event=null):void
{
    pivotDO3D.localRotationY--;
    super.onRenderTick();
}
```

What you should see if you publish the example is a number of small spheres that form the shape of an imaginary bigger sphere that is rotating around its y-axis.

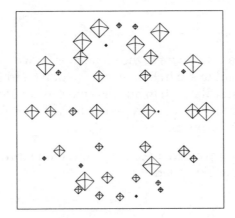

We didn't add the small spheres directly to the scene because that would make it tedious to control all of them at the same time. Adding them to a parent do3D makes it a lot easier to add animation to all the children, resulting in the rotation of our imaginary sphere.

{Ex.} VerticesExample {Ex.}

Summary

Primitives are basic geometric shapes such as the cone, cube, and sphere. The Papervision3D library contains a set of primitives meaning you won't have to build them yourself. For each primitive, we worked through an example that demonstrated how to instantiate it and how we can add it to our scene. We also discussed the parameters that are available such as the number of segments and the material you want to apply.

Every 3D object is made of vertices, which are coordinates in 3D space. Vertices are projected onto the 2D screen and form triangles. Every triangle is made of three vertices, and multiple triangles form a 3D object or a triangle mesh.

The sequence of processes that takes place when you publish a project is called the rendering pipeline. The Papervision3D rendering pipeline looks as follows:

- **Initialization** is the part where you set up your application by creating a viewport, a scene, a camera, a renderer, and one or more 3D objects and their materials.

- **Projection** converts 3D coordinates onto a 2D screen. Projection only deals with vertices, not with triangles or materials.

- **Rendering** is the process of drawing the image that you see on the screen, combining the 2D projection data with information about the material that is being used. It only deals with triangles, not with vertices. This is the most intensive task for the processor.

You can add a 3D object directly to the scene, but you can also add it to another 3D object, a technique known as nesting. A common nesting trick is using an instance of a `DisplayObject3D` that serves as a holder for other objects. Adding a 3D object to the scene or to another do3D is done by using the `addChild()` method.

Primitives inherit properties and methods from `DisplayObject3D`. The properties that we have discussed in this chapter are:

- `x`: The x coordinate of the object relative to the origin of its parent
- `y`: The y coordinate of the object relative to the origin of its parent
- `z`: The z coordinate of the object relative to the origin of its parent
- `localRotationX`: The rotation of the object around its own x-axis
- `localRotationY`: The rotation of the object around its own y-axis
- `localRotationZ`: The rotation of the object around its own z-axis
- `geometry`: Accesses the geometry (vertices and triangles) of the object
- `sceneX`: The x coordinate of the object relative to the scene coordinate system
- `sceneY`: The y coordinate of the object relative to the scene coordinate system
- `sceneZ`: The z coordinate of the object relative to the scene coordinate system
- `scale`: The 3D scale as applied from the origin of the object

In this chapter, we used two materials—wireframe and color material. But Papervision3D has much more to offer. In the next chapter, we will make our objects look more interesting by applying all sorts of other materials.

4
Materials

In this chapter, we will have a close look at materials and how we can map them onto 3D objects. There are a variety of material types that can be used, from simple images to movie clips with mouse interaction and streaming video. Each type takes another approach and has its pros and cons. Having a look at all of the available materials will make it easier for you to find the right one for the job.

This chapter covers the following:

- Introduction to materials
- Basic materials such as a wireframe and a color
- Strategies for loading a bitmap as material
- Strategies for using a movie clip as material
- Streaming video as a material
- Combining materials
- Object and material interactivity
- Tips and tricks for using materials
- Example—creating a carousel

Introduction to materials

A **material** is like a texture on an object. Without a material, objects are invisible. By choosing the right material you can make a simple object look detailed and interesting.

The difference between a texture and a material is that a texture is the source image that is being used by the material. The material can then be used to define properties that affect how the texture is mapped on an object. You can think of it as an extended texture.

Before we discuss each type, we will examine how materials work. Materials in Papervision3D have their issues. Knowing how they work helps you solve these issues.

In the previous chapter, you learned that 3D objects are made of triangles. These triangles are used as the skin of a 3D object. Every single triangle relates to a part of the material. The triangle information will be used to transform the flat material to something that seems to be placed in perspective. The more triangles an object has, the more seamless materials appear on your screen. However, more triangles also result in more transform calculations, and is therefore heavier on the processor.

Basic properties

All materials inherit from a special base material class called `MaterialObject3D`. This class contains properties, which are valid for all materials, although some of them only make sense for specific material types. For example, properties that control a material's tiling allow an image to be repeated several times in a horizontal and vertical direction, but this technique would not make sense for a basic color material. Before we discuss each material type, we will take a look at three properties that are useful to all materials:

- Double-sided and one-side mapping
- Opposite mapping
- Smoothing

When you set a material's `doubleSided` property to `true`, you make the triangles of an object visible on both sides, allowing you for instance to see the front and the back of a plane, or the inside and outside of a cube. Setting the property looks as follows:

```
material.doubleSided = true;
```

The same results can be achieved by setting the `oneSide` property of a material to `false`.

```
material.oneSide = false;
```

Either can be used; choosing one of the two options is just a matter of taste.

By default, all materials are visible only on the defined front side of an object. But what if you would like it to be mapped to the other side of the object exclusively? For instance, what if you want only the inside of a cube textured instead of the default outside? Performance-wise it wouldn't be a good idea to set the material to double sided. For those situations, the `opposite` property of a material can be set to `true`.

```
material.opposite = true;
```

Due to the transformation and scaling of materials for a 3D perspective, materials can become **pixelated**. Changing the **smoothing** property of a material can solve this.

```
material.smooth = true;
```

Unfortunately, smoothing costs you performance, so think twice before enabling it. We will have a closer look at smoothing in the section about the `BitmapMaterial` class, and in Chapter 13, where we'll talk about performance optimization techniques.

Basic materials

There are two types of basic materials. These are:

- **Wireframe materials**
- **Color materials**

We consider them as basic materials because their practical use is limited. Other materials offer more functionalities and are often more useful while working on real-world projects. These will be discussed after we have seen how to apply a wireframe and color as material.

Wireframe material

All examples we've seen so far used **wireframe material**. Papervision3D sets this as the default material type for most objects. It draws lines between all the vertices that form the triangles of a 3D object. This comes in handy for debugging purposes because it visualizes how the triangles are drawn at runtime. Although it might sound like a lightweight material, it is actually quite heavy to render. It makes use of Flash's line drawing, which is a relatively slow operation.

By default, a wireframe material is generated when working with primitives. However, we can create a wireframe material by hand as well. Let's create a new project called `WireframeMaterialExample` and define the material manually.

Before we can use the wireframe material, we need to import the class that creates it. Like most materials, it is located in the `org.papervision3d.materials` package. Add the following new imports at the top of your class, right after the other imports:

```
import org.papervision3d.materials.WireframeMaterial;
import org.papervision3d.objects.primitives.Cone;
```

Depending on your project, it may or may not be a problem to define a material inline as a local variable, instead of making it a class property. When a material is defined inline, you'll assign it to an object and never use it again. If you want to access the material, you can do this by using the `material` property of the object and cast it to the material type. For example:

```
var material:WireframeMaterial = do3D.material as WireframeMaterial;
```

Instantiation of `WireFrameMaterial` takes three parameters as shown in the next table:

	Parameter	Data type	Default value	Description
1	color	Number	0xFF00FF	A color defined by a 24-bit number, which can be in the hexadecimal format, used as the line color of the wires.
2	alpha	Number	1	An alpha value between 0 and 1, used as line transparency.
3	thickness	Number	0	A number between 0 and 255 that defines the line thickness of the wires in points. The default value of 0 indicates hairline thickness.

Flash uses both **24-bit colors** and **32-bit colors**. A 24-bit color value is what we know as RGB colors, containing 256 possible red values, 256 green values, and 256 blue values. A 32-bit color contains alpha information as well, which adds alpha values to the RGB notation and is called RGBA. This adds 256 possible alpha values to the color notation. An alpha value of **0** stands for **completely transparent** and a value of **256** stands for no transparency.

Both 24-bit and 32-bit colors can be represented in the hexadecimal format. A 24-bit hexadecimal color looks like `0x00FF00`, which indicates 00 red colors, FF green colors, and 00 blue colors.

A 32-bit color notation looks pretty similar, but has alpha values added at the end. Again, this looks like `0x00FF00FF`, which represents a 00 red color, FF green color, 00 blue color and a FF alpha value. A value of FF means no transparency and a value of 00 means completely transparent.

Most of the time you work with 24-bit colors and supply an alpha value as a separate parameter to add transparency. However, in some occasions you need to set 32-bit colors instead. In case of a wireframe material, you will use a 24-bit color value and a separate alpha value.

When you do not set any parameter, a wireframe material will use its default values. But let's have a look at how we can create a cone with a 50% transparent black wireframe that has a thickness of 2:

```
private function init():void
{
    var material:WireframeMaterial = new WireframeMaterial(0x000000,0.
5,2);
    var cone:Cone = new Cone(material,500,500);
    scene.addChild(cone);
}
```

{Ex.} WireframeMaterialExample {Ex.}

Now that we know how to create wireframe materials, it's time to have a look at how to apply a color as material.

Color material

The second basic material is **color material**. As the name suggests, it is a color as a material. You create it just as easy as wireframe material. In the previous chapter about primitives, you've already learned how to apply this material type to a cube.

`ColorMaterial` can be instantiated with the following parameters:

	Parameter	Data type	Default value	Description
1	color	Number	0xFF00FF	A 24-bit color in hexadecimal format as the fill color of the material.
2	alpha	Number	1	A value between 0 and 1, used as the transparency of the color fill.
3	interactive	Boolean	false	Sets the interactive property of a material.

Except for the `interactive` parameter, this pretty much looks the same as the parameters for instantiating `WireframeMaterial`. When you do not pass any parameter, `ColorMaterial` will be instantiated with its default parameters, resulting in a magenta color as material, without interactivity.

The `interactive` property defines whether a material should be interactive. This property is implemented by the `MaterialObject3D` class and makes interaction with a material possible. For now, we're not going to use that, so you can leave this value as it is.

Have a look at how we can create the same cone, but now with a 50% transparent green color material.

```
private function init():void
{
    var material:ColorMaterial = new ColorMaterial(0x00FF00,0.5);
    var cone:Cone = new Cone(material,500,500);
    scene.addChild(cone);
}
```

Do not forget to import the `ColorMaterial` class from the `org.papervision3d.materials` package, before running this code.

{Ex.} ColorMaterialExample {Ex.}

As you can see the use of color material and wireframe material is very similar.

Three ways of using bitmaps as a material

Although, defining wireframes and colors as materials is easy, the results aren't very spectacular. For many applications you will want to assign bitmap materials to add detail and interest to your objects. With clever use of images, even simple 3D objects can look far more realistic.

Creating bitmap textures can be done with imaging programs such as Photoshop or Paintshop Pro. It is strongly recommended to edit the bitmaps before using them in Papervision3D, as this can add much more detail and realism to the rendered objects.

A trick to give objects an extra dimension without loss of performance is called **baking textures**. This can be done in most 3D programs and is a smart way to add, for example, lighting and shadows or reflection to your objects, without the need of using the limited functionalities for doing this real-time with Papervision3D. It simply saves the lighting and shadows, or reflection, in a regular image. This will not lead to a lower performance, and your objects will look more realistic. In Chapter 7, real-time shading with the presence of light objects will be discussed. By having lights in your scenes, you can affect how your textured objects look in real-time.

There are several approaches for creating good textures; however, this is not in the scope of this book. There are many books and online tutorials available if you want to know more about texture creation.

Using a bitmap as material is just as simple as defining color or wireframe materials. Depending on your needs, you can use a regular bitmap object, an external bitmap, or a library asset as material.

BitmapMaterial

As you probably have guessed already, the BitmapMaterial class creates a material that is made of a bitmap. This can be a drawing you made by code, an external image, or an image asset from your library. For the, external images and asset images, there are special material types available that handle the loading for you. These classes all inherit from BitmapMaterial and will be discussed in a bit.

As an example, we will draw a circle by code and use it to instantiate BitmapMaterial. We'll also have a look at how we can load and use external images manually.

Instantiating BitmapMaterial takes two parameters as shown next:

	Parameter	Data type	Default value	Description
1	asset	BitmapData	null	The object that holds BitmapData.
2	precise	Boolean	false	When precision is set to true, this dynamically creates extra triangles to draw the material in a more precise way.

The following two examples will show how to work with BitmapMaterial.

Using a bitmap shape as material that is generated by code

For the first example called BitmapMaterialShapeExample, we're going to create a circle with Flash's graphics API and convert it to a BitmapData type. A plane will be added as our 3D object using the generated bitmap as material. To do this, we need to import the Shape, BitmapData, BitmapMaterial, and Plane classes.

```
import flash.display.BitmapData;
import flash.display.Shape;

import org.papervision3d.materials.BitmapMaterial;
import org.papervision3d.objects.primitives.Plane;
```

In the `init()` method we define a new shape and draw a circle on it, exactly as we would normally do when drawing a circle by code. We create a red circle at x and y `100`, with a radius of `200`:

```
private function init():void
{
    var circle:Shape = new Shape();
    circle.graphics.beginFill(0xFF0000);
    circle.graphics.drawCircle(100,100,100);
```

Instantiation of a `BitmapMaterial` class takes only a `BitmapData` instance as parameter, so the created shape needs to be converted. Don't confuse this with converting it to a `Bitmap`, as for this purpose you need a `BitmapData` object. Let's see how we instantiate the `BitmapData` class. The first two parameters are defining the width and height, followed by a boolean value for transparency. The last parameter is a 32-bit integer as the base fill color. In order to see the circle as a transparent shape, we need to define a hexadecimal fill color of 0x0. This way we won't see any fill around the drawn shape. After the `BitmapData` class is instantiated, we can draw the circle on the `BitmapData` canvas.

```
    var bmp:BitmapData = new BitmapData(200,200,true,0x0);
    bmp.draw(circle);
```

Now that we have successfully created a `BitmapData` object, we can continue by creating the material.

```
    var material:BitmapMaterial = new BitmapMaterial(bmp);
```

The material is now ready to be assigned to a plane.

```
    var plane:Plane = new Plane(material);
    scene.addChild(plane);
}
```

Publish your work and you'll see a circle as the material of a plane. When you look closely, you'll notice that the circle has very rough edges.

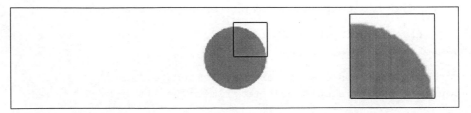

This is where smoothing comes in. Add `material.smooth = true` after the material is defined and before the creation of the plane. This will smooth the edges of the circle, but keep in mind that this costs performance. Therefore, you should carefully consider whether or not you set this to `true`.

{Ex.} BitmapMaterialShapeExample {Ex.}

Manually loading and assigning an external bitmap as material

Before we learn how to load an external bitmap as a texture using a specific Papervision3D class, let's look at how you can do this by hand. There are some situations where you do not want this to be done automatically. Have a look at the following code:

```
package {
    import flash.display.Bitmap;
    import flash.display.Loader;
    import flash.events.Event;
    import flash.net.URLRequest;

    import org.papervision3d.materials.BitmapMaterial;
    import org.papervision3d.objects.primitives.Plane;
    import org.papervision3d.view.BasicView;

    public class BitmapMaterialImageExample extends BasicView
    {
        public function BitmapMaterialImageExample()
        {
            stage.frameRate = 40;

            init();
            startRendering();
        }

        private function init():void
        {
//Start loading the image and define an on complete event listener
            var imgLoader:Loader = new Loader();
            imgLoader.contentLoaderInfo.addEventListener
                                (Event.COMPLETE, loadComplete);
            imgLoader.load(new URLRequest("assets/mill.jpg"));
        }

        private function loadComplete(e:Event):void
        {
            //Loading complete. Cast target content as a Bitmap
```

```
            //and use its bitmapData for creating a BitmapMaterial
            var bitmap:Bitmap = e.target.content as Bitmap;
            var material:BitmapMaterial = new
                                BitmapMaterial(bitmap.bitmapData);

            var plane:Plane = new Plane(material);
            scene.addChild(plane);
        }

        override protected function onRenderTick(e:Event=null):void
        {
            super.onRenderTick();
        }
    }
}
```

Please note that this code is loading an image from the assets folder. You can find this image in the code download, but you could use any image you like.

The code results in an image on your screen, which is nice. However, as of now, we could still do this without Papervision3D. So, why don't you try to set a rotation value for the image?

Note that creating a rotating plane leads to problems in the current example. The above class has no property that holds a reference to the plane, so we can't access the plane in the render method and increase its rotation values. Also note that the example starts rendering before the plane has been instantiated. It may be a good exercise to get this working. The example in the next section will show how to start rendering after a material is loaded and a plane has been instantiated.

If you haven't launched your authoring tool yet, this is the time you should do it. Change the above example and rotate the plane on one of its axes. Make sure you create a plane with enough segments and set your material to double sided, and you will see something like this:

Play around with this material a bit. For example, try if you can draw a circle as material for a rotating plane.

BitmapFileMaterial

So far we've seen how we can create a `BitmapMaterial` and apply it to a plane. We've also loaded an image and created a new `BitmapMaterial` from this image. This works fine, but there is a smarter way to load external images as a material. The `BitmapFileMaterial` class inherits from `BitmapMaterial` and takes care of all the hassle regarding loading external images, such as setting up listeners.

Creating a `BitmapFileMaterial` instance is very easy. It takes two parameters as shown in the next table:

	Parameter	Data type	Default value	Description
1	url	String	" "	A URL that refers to the image that needs to be loaded as the texture for this material.
2	precise	Boolean	false	Defines whether or not to use precision of the material.

You must at least pass the URL parameter. We don't pass the second parameter, as the default value `false` is fine for now. As long as the image is not loaded, the texture will have a black color. Have a look at how we can load the image that we used in the previous example.

We'll call this example `BitmapFileMaterialExample`, which is, like all examples, based on our template class. First, we configure the right imports on top of the class. Additionally, we need to have the `BitmapFileMaterial` and `Plane` class available in the code:

```
import org.papervision3d.materials.BitmapFileMaterial;
import org.papervision3d.objects.primitives.Plane;
```

Inside the `init()` method we instantiate `BitmapFileMaterial`, which takes a string as the URL for the image that you want to load. Do not forget that you need to have a file located on the given URL, relatively to the published SWF.

```
private function init():void
{
    var material:BitmapFileMaterial = new BitmapFileMaterial
                                ("assets/mill.jpg");
```

The created material will be assigned to a new plane, which we'll give a size of 500 by 375, and which consists of 2 horizontal and vertical segments.

```
var plane:Plane = new Plane(material,500,375,2,2);
scene.addChild(plane);
}
```

{Ex.} BitmapFileMaterialExample {Ex.}

That's all the code in order to use the `BitmapFileMaterial` class. It's so easy and hassle free as compared to doing this manually!

Set width and height when using a plane in combination with a BitmapFileMaterial

When using a plane object in combination with a file material, you should always set the width and height parameters. When plane objects are instantiated with a bitmap material type, Papervision3D looks at the size of the material and takes this as the size for the plane. Papervision3D doesn't know the size of the bitmap that's still loading; therefore, it sets the size of the plane to 0 by 0 resulting in a plane that you can never see.

When you publish the code above and look very carefully at the plane, you'll notice that it is black for a fraction of a second before the loaded bitmap is shown. This is because the material is black while it is loaded. A way to prevent this behavior is by not rendering the scene as long as the texture is being loaded.

But how do we know when the image is loaded? We do not have access to the loader that loads the image inside the `BitmapFileMaterial` class. A way to achieve this is by adding an `EventListener` to the `BitmapFileMaterial` instance and listen for `FileLoadEvent.LOAD_COMPLETE` events. `FileLoadEvent` is a custom Papervision3D event class, used by several other Papervision3D classes. There are four events that are relevant listening for in combination with a `BitmapFileMaterial` instance:

- `FileLoadEvent.LOAD_COMPLETE`: Dispatched as soon as the external bitmap is loaded

- `FileLoadEvent.LOAD_PROGRESS`: Dispatched on progress during loading of the bitmap

- `FileLoadEvent.LOAD_ERROR`: Dispatched when the image could not be found

- `FileLoadEvent.SECURITY_LOAD_ERROR`: Dispatched when there's a security error

In order to use `FileLoadEvent`, you first need to import it from the `org.papervision3d.events` package.

```
import org.papervision3d.events.FileLoadEvent;
```

We can now add an `EventListener` directly after instantiating `BitmapFileMaterial` and listen for a LOAD_COMPLETE event.

```
material.addEventListener(FileLoadEvent.LOAD_COMPLETE,loadComplete);
```

This defines `loadComplete()` as the listener method. Let's create this method and trace, which file we've loaded. This information might be useful when working with multiple instances of `BitmapFileMaterials` that are loading images and sharing a single `loadComplete()` method:

```
private function loadComplete(e:FileLoadEvent):void
{
    trace("Completed loading file: " + e.file);
    startRendering();
}
```

Inside this method we called `startRendering()` so that Papervision3D will start rendering as soon as the load is complete. This means you need to remove this method call from the constructor.

When you publish this code, you should see the following output:

```
Completed loading file: assets/mill.jpg
```

And you got rid of the black flickering texture!

{Ex.} BitmapFileMaterialEventListenerExample {Ex.}

BitmapAssetMaterial

The `BitmapAssetMaterial` class also inherits `BitmapMaterial` and is another handy class for defining a bitmap as your material. The `BitmapAssetMaterial` uses a graphical library asset and takes its `BitmapData` as the texture. Because Flex Builder and Flash Builder do not have a library like Flash has, this class and the following example are compatible only with the Flash IDE.

The class takes two parameters on instantiation, which looks pretty similar to how we instantiated a `BitmapMaterial` and `BitmapFileMaterial` before:

	Parameter	Data type	Default value	Description
1	linkageID	String	—	A reference to the linkage ID of an asset in the Flash library
2	precise	Boolean	false	Defines whether or not to use precision of the material.

Let's have a look at how we define the library asset in Flash, so we can use it in combination with a `BitmapAssetMaterial` instance:

1. Import a new image to your library (not to your stage!).
2. Right-click on the image inside the library and choose **Properties**.
3. A new window called **Bitmap Properties** shows up.
4. Open the **Advanced** panel if not opened already.
5. Check the **Export for ActionScript** checkbox.
6. Check the **Export in first Frame** checkbox in Flash CS3 or **Export in frame 1** when using Flash CS4, if not checked already.
7. **Class** and **Base class** are auto-filled after checking the checkboxes. Change the class name if you like, but leave the base class as it is. Remember this class name because we will pass it as the first parameter when instantiating `BitmapAssetMaterial`.
8. Click **OK** to finish.

The following screenshot shows the **Linkage** properties in Flash CS3, used for this example:

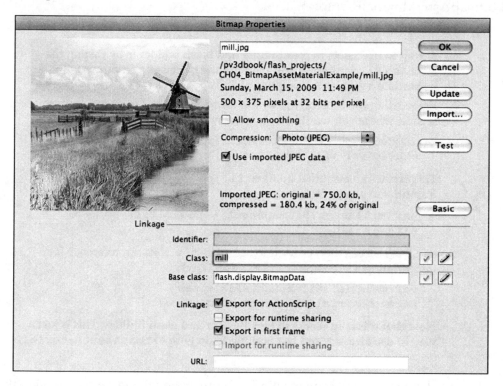

Now that we've set up a library asset, we can write our class. As always this starts off with importing the classes we're going to use.

```
import org.papervision3d.materials.BitmapAssetMaterial;
import org.papervision3d.objects.primitives.Plane;
```

Next, we can instantiate a new `BitmapAssetMaterial` instance and pass the asset's class name as a string.

```
private function init():void
{
    var material:BitmapAssetMaterial = new BitmapAssetMaterial("mill")
;
```

Once that's done, we define and add a plane like we've done a couple of times before now.

```
    var plane:Plane = new Plane(material,500,375,2,2);
    scene.addChild(plane);
}
```

That's it. You're all set to publish your project now.

 BitmapAssetMaterialExample

A way to use assets in Flex Builder and Flash Builder is by casting the asset as a `BitmapAsset` and then use the `bitmapData` property to instantiate a regular `BitmapMaterial`.

Embedding can be achieved by the following embed meta tag, in the same section where you would create a class property:

```
[Embed (source="assets/mill.jpg")]
public var mill:Class;
```

This creates an asset that holds `mill.jpg` as a class that can be instantiated as a `BitmapAsset`.

```
var millAsset:BitmapAsset = new mill() as
BitmapAsset;
```

`millAsset` can then be used to access its `bitmapData` reference for instantiating a `BitmapMaterial` as follows:

```
var material:BitmapMaterial = new
BitmapMaterial(millAsset.bitmapData);
```

Note that this only works in Flex Builder and Flash Builder. This is just a way to use an asset, and has nothing to do with `BitmapAssetMaterial`.

Now that we have seen how bitmaps work as your material, we can move on to the next category of materials — movie clips.

Two ways of using a movie clip as material

Being able to use a bitmap as a material is already pretty handy for a lot of situations. These materials are similar to the types available in 3D modeling software. But we're not working in a 3D modeling program, we're working in Flash. The main reason why the Flash player has become so popular is because of its ability to produce stunning, lightweight animations. From the beginning this has been something Flash has excelled at. More recently, the Flash platform has proved itself as being a good tool for building **Rich Internet Applications** (**RIAs**). Wouldn't it be nice if we could use those Flash strengths while building Papervision3D scenes, or if we could apply animations as our materials, or use RIA elements as materials?

Everything that you can make with a `MovieClip` can be used as a material using the `MovieMaterial` type. Essentially this works in much the same way as `BitmapMaterial`, although there are only two types of movie materials:

- `MovieMaterial`
- `MovieAssetMaterial`

Although you might expect something similar as `BitmapFileMaterial`, there is no such thing as a `MovieFileMaterial`. Let's have a look at how the two movie materials work.

MovieMaterial

A movie clip-based material works with every type of object that inherits from a `DisplayObject`. This is usually a sprite or a movie clip. The `MovieMaterial` class works with any display object that is accessible by code. Instantiation of a `MovieMaterial` takes a few new parameters. Let's have a look at each in the following table:

	Parameter	Data type	Default value	Description
1	movieAsset	DisplayObject	null	A reference to the display object you want to use as source for this material.
2	transparent	Boolean	false	Defines whether or not to create a material that supports transparency.
3	animated	Boolean	false	If set to `true`, every frame a new snapshot of the referenced `movieAsset` will be drawn and used as the new image for this material. This is a CPU consuming property.
4	precise	Boolean	false	Defines precision of the material.
5	rect	Rectangle	null	An optional rectangle object used to define the boundary for a material. This can be useful when you have defined a movie whose size changes during the animation. Without the boundary definition, the boundary of the current frame from the `movieAsset` will be used.

In order to explain how this material works, we'll create a new sprite, draw a rectangle shape, and add a text to it. We'll create a movie material from the sprite and apply it to a rotating plane. As the sprite is a display object, we can add it to the stage as well.

To do this we need to import several classes.

```
import flash.display.Sprite;
import flash.text.TextField;
import flash.text.TextFieldAutoSize;
import flash.text.TextFormat;

import org.papervision3d.materials.MovieMaterial;
import org.papervision3d.objects.primitives.Plane;
```

Because we want to rotate the plane, we need to make it a class property, so we will have access to it inside the onRenderTick() method.

```
private var plane:Plane;
```

In the init() method, we'll start by creating a new sprite and draw a gray rectangle on it.

```
private function init():void
{
    var materialSprite:Sprite = new Sprite();
    materialSprite.graphics.beginFill(0x333333);
    materialSprite.graphics.drawRect(0,0,200,200);
```

The next thing we need to do is define a text field. This is just regular ActionScript and takes a few lines of code.

```
var textfield:TextField = new TextField();
textfield.text = "Hello 3D world!";
textfield.autoSize = TextFieldAutoSize.LEFT;
textfield.setTextFormat(new TextFormat("Arial",25));
```

To place the text exactly in the middle, we can subtract the text field width from the materialSprite width and divide the rest value by 2. The same can be done for vertical alignment using height values.

```
textfield.x = (materialSprite.width - textfield.width) / 2;
textfield.y = (materialSprite.height - textfield.height) / 2;
```

Then, add the text field to the material sprite and add the material sprite to the stage, so we can see what we've created.

```
materialSprite.addChild(textfield);
addChild(materialSprite);
```

Now that we've created a sprite, we can define a new `MovieMaterial` instance, set it to smooth and double sided, and assign it to a plane that we create. This works pretty much the same as the other materials we've created so far. To instantiate, only the first parameter is required. All other parameters have default values that are fine for now.

```
var material:MovieMaterial = new MovieMaterial(materialSprite);
material.smooth = true;
material.doubleSided = true;

plane = new Plane(material);
scene.addChild(plane);
}
```

As a final step, we rotate the plane in the `onRenderTick()` method, which is a good way to see that it is really 3D.

```
plane.localRotationY++;
```

{Ex.} MovieMaterialExample {Ex.}

At the beginning of this section we saw that the `MovieMaterial` class has some properties that we have not seen before. These properties require animations and will be demonstrated in the next section.

MovieAssetMaterial

The `MovieAssetMaterial` class is the equivalent of the `BitmapAssetMaterial` and uses movie clip assets from the library as the source of a material. Just like `BitmapAssetMaterial`, this type works only in the Flash IDE and not in Flex Builder and Flash Builder.

With a movie clip asset as material, you have the same methods and properties available as a regular movie clip as material, as it inherits from the `MovieMaterial` class. The class makes it easy to use movie clip assets from your library as the material. At instantiation, you can pass the following parameters:

	Parameter	Data type	Default value	Description
1	linkageID	String	" "	The string of the linkage ID from the asset in the library that you want to apply as the material.
2	transparent	Boolean	false	Defines whether or not to create a material that supports transparency.
3	animated	Boolean	false	If set to true, every frame a new snapshot of the movie clip will be drawn and used as the material.
4	createUnique	Boolean	false	Defines if you want to create a new instance of the defined asset, or if you want to reuse a previously instantiated instance.
5	precise	Boolean	false	Stands for precision of the material.

Assigning a movie clip as a material gives you the ability to animate your material. This can be done by code in combination with a regular `MovieMaterial` class, or you can do this on the timeline in combination with the `MovieAssetMaterial` class. So, let's start by creating an animation in Flash. Create a new **MovieClip** symbol and add some animation to it. To understand how movie assets work as materials, a simple tween will do. The example included in the book download has a background shape, two animating texts, and a thick line from the left to the right. The line will illustrate some problems that you can run into when working with the `MovieAssetMaterial` class and materials in general.

After you've created your animation, you need to define the linkage properties of the symbol. This works just like setting up the linkage for a bitmap asset as material, except that this base class is a `MovieClip`.

1. Right-click on the symbol in the library that you want to use as your material and click on **properties**.

2. A new window called **Symbol Properties** shows up.

3. Open the **Advanced** panel if not opened already.

4. Select **Export for ActionScript**.

5. Check **Export in first frame** in Flash CS3, or **Export in frame 1** in Flash CS4.

6. Define a class name, which will be passed as the linkage ID when we instantiate a `MovieAssetMaterial`. In the example we'll name it **material.**

7. Leave the base class set to `flash.display.MovieClip`.

8. Click **OK** to finish.

With the asset defined, you're ready to instantiate `MovieAssetMaterial` and assign it to a primitive. For now we'll use the rotating plane again because it's a good object to point out some problems and solutions.

The only new class used in this example is `MovieAssetMaterial`. This class needs to be imported along with all the other classes that we need for this example.

```
import flash.events.Event;

import org.papervision3d.materials.MovieAssetMaterial;
import org.papervision3d.objects.primitives.Plane;
import org.papervision3d.view.BasicView;
```

As said before, we'll rotate the plane, meaning it needs to be a class property.

```
private var plane:Plane;
```

In the `init()` method, we instantiate `MovieAssetMaterial`. The first parameter is a string "material", which is the name of the class we defined for our library item in Flash. The second parameter is for transparency, which is set to `false`. Because the movie we'll use as a material contains an animation, we set the animated value to `true` in the third and last parameter that we pass. When the animated value is set to `true`, a new bitmap from the movie will be redrawn on each render.

```
private function init():void
{
    var material:MovieAssetMaterial = new MovieAssetMaterial("material
",false,true);
    material.doubleSided = true;

    plane = new Plane(material,500,500);
    scene.addChild(plane);
}
```

Publish this and you'll immediately notice some problems. The problems discussed below are based on the animation described earlier in this section. This animation can be found in the examples folder under MovieAssetMaterialExample. If you've made your own animation, these problems may or may not occur. Let's address those and solve them.

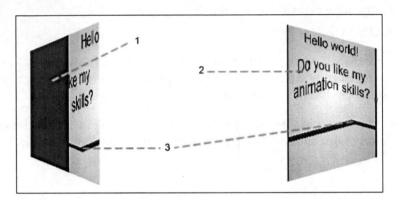

The following table lists the problems along with their probable causes:

Problem	Cause
Floating texture	Caused by the movie that changes size during animation
Flickering and pixelated text	Caused by skewed bitmaps
Texture distortion	Caused by using a low number of segments

The texture floating from left to right is caused by the changing size of the movie clip during the animation. The black background color you'll see is caused by the transparent property, which is set to false. This floating can be prevented in an easy way. All you have to do is define a rectangle object as the area of your texture. In the section about the MovieMaterial class, you saw that a rectangle was the fifth parameter of the MovieMaterial class constructor. The MovieAssetMaterial class works in a slightly different manner. Instead of passing the rectangle as a parameter, we need to access it as a property of the class. This is also possible with the MovieMaterial class. In this example, the texture has the same rectangle parameters as the gradient shape that is used as the background of the asset. It has a width and height of 200 and starts at the 0 coordinate for both x and y. To create a rectangle object, we first need to import flash.geom.Rectangle. We can then add the following line after instantiating the material:

```
material.rect = new Rectangle(0,0,200,200);
```

Publish again, and you won't see the floating texture. This problem is fixed!

The second problem is flickering and the text is pixelated. We saw pixilation before when we used a bitmap as material. This was solved by turning on smoothing. Here the solution is the same. Pixelation changes depending on the way an image is skewed, which can especially be noticed without smoothing turned on. When these changes take place in an animation, you'll notice this as a flickering image. So, let's turn on smoothing:

```
material.smooth = true;
```

After publishing this, you'll see (generally spoken) a good improvement. When you're a pixel perfect person, you'll notice some issues when there's a lot of perspective. This is an issue that is especially noticeable with animated 3D objects and text as part of the material. The following image clearly illustrates this problem:

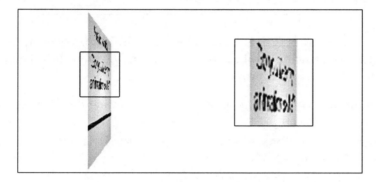

Due to the heavy distortion you can't read the text on the plane. Animating this leads to small flickering artifacts, which is an issue that is inherent to working with Papervision3D.

The third and final issue regards texture distortion on the material. Previously we have learned that 3D objects are made of vertices and triangles. Triangles are used as the skin of an object and its texture gets distorted in a certain perspective. The more triangles used, the smaller the distortion changes are per triangle, resulting in an image that seems to be in perspective.

Papervision3D distorts materials in 2D to add a perspective illusion. You can see this like skewing and distorting images so that it will look as if they are placed in 3D perspective. The way Papervision3D maps textures on 3D objects is called **affine texture mapping**.

We haven't provided height and width segments for the plane, meaning that it will consist of just one height segment and one width segment. With text and a line in the material, you can clearly see that the object consists of only two distorted triangles. In the following image, you'll see these triangles, illustrated by a dashed line:

Setting the `precision` property to `true` solves this problem. We've already seen this parameter in the constructor of all the bitmap and movie materials. There are two ways to enable the `precision` property:

- At instantiation of `MovieAssetMaterial` by setting the fifth parameter to `true`.

  ```
  var material:MovieAssetMaterial = new MovieAssetMaterial("material
  ",false,true,false,true);
  ```

- By setting the `precise` property to `true`.

  ```
  material.precise = true;
  ```

With `precision` set to `true`, Papervision3D will dynamically subdivide each triangle for you, creating more new triangles and giving a more precise result. This will immediately be noticeable. However, this introduces a new problem , which is caused by our animation. On each angle change relative to the camera, Papervision3D creates new triangles for you, which can differ from the previous ones. This will result in a shaking and flickering text. We have the following two ways to stabilize this behavior:

- Adding more triangles
- Defining the precision mode

The plane we've instantiated made up of only one height and width segment. We could give the plane more segments at instantiation, resulting in more triangles, as a stable basis from which triangles can be subdivided. In combination with `precision` set to `true`, flickering will be unnoticeable.

The other way to get rid of the shaking text is by defining the precision mode, which by default is set to `PrecisionMode.NORMAL`. Setting `PrecisionMode.STABLE` instead solves our issue as well. To define the precision mode, we need to import the `PrecisionMode` class, which is part of the material utilities:

```
import org.papervision3d.materials.utils.PrecisionMode;
```

And to use it we can set the following material property:

```
material.precisionMode = PrecisionMode.STABLE;
```

This solution reduces the problem to an acceptable level. However, remember that the more segments and triangles you create, the heavier your scene will become to render. With just one rotating plane you won't notice these differences, but in real-world applications chances are that you'll experience performance issues. Also keep in mind that you should always try to play around with the class properties to get the best results for your situation.

[Ex.] MovieAssetMaterialExample [Ex.]

VideoStreamMaterial

Although you can apply video as a material manually when using `MovieMaterial`, the `VideoStreamMaterial` class does this automatically for you.

The class is called `VideoStreamMaterial` and extends `MovieMaterial`. Its constructor takes four parameters:

	Parameter	Data type	Default value	Description
1	video	Video	—	A `video` instance used as the source to take snapshots from.
2	stream	NetStream	—	A `NetStream` instance used to control the video.
3	precise	Boolean	false	Stands for precision of the material.
4	transparent	Boolean	false	Defines whether or not to create a material that supports transparency.

This class allows you to show streaming or progressive videos. You can also use your webcam output as the input for this class. Let's create an example based on video coming from your webcam. This example uses quite a few different classes.

```
import flash.events.Event;
import flash.media.Camera;
import flash.media.Video;
import flash.net.NetConnection;
import flash.net.NetStream;

import org.papervision3d.materials.VideoStreamMaterial;
import org.papervision3d.objects.primitives.Plane;
import org.papervision3d.view.BasicView;
```

The first parameter for instantiating the `VideoStreamMaterial` class is a video object. We need to define a video object and attach a camera to it. This is done exactly the same as you would normally attach a camera to a video object.

```
private function init():void
{
    var video:Video = new Video();
    video.attachCamera(Camera.getCamera());
```

If you use a camera as video input, and you don't broadcast the camera output to a streaming server, neither a `NetStream` object nor a `NetConnection` object are needed. However, these classes are essential when you want to play streaming or progressive video. As for this example, we create a new `NetConnection` object which connects with nothing (`null`) and we create a new `NetStream` object. We connect with nothing, as the `NetStream` class requires a connected net connection in order to instantiate. Connecting it with null is a little trick to flag a net connection as connected. When you want to connect to a streaming server, you need to make a real connection.

```
    var conn:NetConnection = new NetConnection();
    conn.connect(null);
    var stream:NetStream = new NetStream(conn);
```

The next thing we need to do is creating a new material from the input video and stream. As a video is like an animation and changes constantly, we need to set the `animated` property to `true`.

```
    var material:VideoStreamMaterial = new VideoStreamMaterial
                                (video, stream);
    material.animated = true;
```

Our final step is to create a plane. In this case, give it a size of 640 by 480, so it will appear on screen with the correct aspect ratio.

```
var plane:Plane = new Plane(material,640,480,3,3);
scene.addChild(plane);
}
```

After publishing this code, Flash will first ask you to grant access to your camera. Once access is granted, you should see the video input on the created plane object.

 VideoStreamMaterialExample

Security sandbox violation issues

There are two situations in which the Flash player throws a security sandbox violation:

- Progressive streaming from another domain
- Streaming through a non-Flash Media 3 server

Playing a progressive video file coming from another domain than the one from which the SWF file is located will throw a security violation error. This is a known issue in Flash and can't be solved, unless you copy the FLV files to the same domain.

Streaming a video by using a streaming server instead of a progressive download also leads to security sandbox violation problems. In the past, there has been a workaround hack to get this to work, which is implemented in the `VideoStreamMaterial` class. Don't get confused when looking at the comments inside the class or reading mailing list messages about this issue. The only way to fix it is by using Flash Media Server 3 and setting `client.videoSampleAccess` to `publicdomain` on the server.

Combining materials

In some cases you might want to combine multiple materials and use them together as one single material. For example, during development it can be pretty useful to combine a wireframe material with another material type. This can be achieved with the `CompositeMaterial` class.

Usage of this material type differs from what we've seen before with other material types, as it doesn't take any parameters on instantiation. Instead, you add materials to the CompositeMaterial class, similar to adding materials to a materials list, which we did in the previous chapter. Having a look at how this works makes it clearer:

```
import flash.events.Event;

import org.papervision3d.materials.BitmapFileMaterial;
import org.papervision3d.materials.WireframeMaterial;
import org.papervision3d.materials.special.CompositeMaterial;
import org.papervision3d.objects.primitives.Plane;
import org.papervision3d.view.BasicView;
```

In the init() method we create two materials, which will be combined by the composite material. In this example a bitmap file material will be combined with a wireframe material.

```
private function init():void
{
    var bmpMaterial:BitmapFileMaterial = new BitmapFileMaterial
                                            ("assets/mill.jpg");
    var wireMaterial:WireframeMaterial = new WireframeMaterial();
```

Next, we define a composite material. After it is instantiated, we add the bitmap file material and wireframe material to the composite material by calling its addMaterial() method.

```
    var material:CompositeMaterial = new CompositeMaterial();
    material.addMaterial(bmpMaterial);
    material.addMaterial(wireMaterial);
```

Adding the material to a 3D object is just as usual:

```
    var plane:Plane = new Plane(material,500,375,3,3);
    scene.addChild(plane);
}
```

After publishing you'll see the combined material, containing a bitmap and a wireframe:

{Ex.} CompositeMaterialExample {Ex.}

Note that some of the material properties you set on the sub-materials are ignored when using them as elements of the composite material. For example, when we change the double-sided property of the bitmap material in this example and set it to `true`, it won't result in any visual changes. Instead these values need to be defined on the composite material itself. On the other hand, when you want to apply material smoothing, you can try setting the `smooth` property of the composite material to true; however, this won't change anything. In this particular case, you should set the `smooth` property on the bitmap file material to `true`. In most cases, you'll be fine by setting the properties on the materials that are part of the composite material.

Interactivity

You can have the following two types of mouse interaction with your 3D scene:

- On a material
- On a 3D object

To make both types work, you need to define your viewport as well as your material as interactive. First look at how to set viewport interactivity to `true`, which will cause the viewport to listen for mouse events. By default, the interactivity value is set to `false`. There are several ways to set it to `true`, each of them require just a single line of code.

The first way is to change the `interactive` property of the viewport and set it to `true`.

```
viewport.interactive = true;
```

You can add this line anywhere in your code, as long as you have access to the viewport instance.

If you extend the `BasicView` class, like we do in all our examples, you can also use the fourth parameter in the `super()` method call, which stands for `interactive`:

```
super(640,480,false,true);
```

Make sure you add the `super()` call before calling `startRendering()`.

When you're not working with an extended `BasicView` class, you can also define interactivity as the fourth parameter during instantiation of the `Viewport3D` class.

```
var viewport:Viewport3D = new Viewport3D(640,480,false,true);
```

For interactivity with materials, as well as interactivity with objects, you need to set interactivity of the used material to `true`.

```
material.interactive = true;
```

The interactive property is part of the MaterialObject3D class. As all material types inherit from this class, they all have the interactive property available.

Notice that you need to set both viewport and material interactivity to true. A common mistake is that only one of these values is set to true, resulting in no interactivity at all.

Material interactivity

By **material interactivity** we mean making all mouse events that you have with regular movie clips available in combination with a material. This technique is mainly used to make parts of a material clickable. Defining listeners that are waiting for mouse interactivity can be done in exactly the same way as you would normally do with a movie clip or sprite. This works out of the box, as long as viewport interactivity and material interactivity are set to true.

When working with a movie clip asset as material, you can even use timeline scripting to define the listeners. In the examples download you'll find two working examples based on movie clip assets. These have mouse interactivity and a button to stop and play the animation in the movie asset material.

Using ButtonMode

A common issue is that by default you don't see a hand cursor when hovering an interactive part of your material. In order to make this work, a little trick should be used that sets up a MOUSE_OVER event listener and a MOUSE_OUT event listener on the buttons. Each time a MOUSE_OVER event is dispatched, you can set the buttonMode parameter of the viewport to true. On each MOUSE_OUT you can set it to false again. This will result in the same behavior as you would have with a sprite or movie clip that has buttonMode set to true:

```
private function mouseOver(e:MouseEvent):void
{
    viewport.buttonMode = true;
}

private function mouseOut(e:MouseEvent):void
{
    viewport.buttonMode = false;
}
```

As you need to have access to the viewport, this works only when you are not working with movie clip assets that make use of timeline scripting, and when the event listeners are locally defined on the timeline. A way to solve this is to make the asset aware of the viewport by setting a reference to the viewport after the asset has been instantiated by the `MovieAssetMaterial` class. `localViewportReference.buttonMode` can then be set to `true` on mouse rollovers that are locally defined in the asset.

Defining the event listeners

If you're working with the `MovieAssetMaterial` class and want to set up listeners, you need to have access to the movie that it automatically instantiates. All inherited `MovieMaterial` class types have the special property called `movie`. This class property holds an instance of the display object used as your material. Assuming that you have a button called **btn** defined inside your movie clip asset, you can access it as follows and set up the event listeners:

```
MovieClip(material.movie).getChildByName("btn").addEventListener(
MouseEvent.CLICK,click);
MovieClip(material.movie).getChildByName("btn").addEventListener(
MouseEvent.MOUSE_OVER,mouseOver);
MovieClip(material.movie).getChildByName("btn").addEventListener(
MouseEvent.MOUSE_OUT,mouseOut);
```

Because `material.movie` holds a display object as a reference, we need to cast it to `MovieClip`, in order to use `getChildByName()` and get a reference to the button defined in the asset.

An example of the `MovieAssetMaterial` class can be found in the book downloads.

{Ex.} MaterialInteractivity {Ex.}

Material interactivity is very useful when you want parts of the material to be clickable. If you want the entire object to be clickable, you could use a movie material, add a transparent button to the top layer, and listen for `MouseEvent.CLICK` events. This would work, but then you're limited to movie materials exclusively. This is where object interactivity comes in.

Object interactivity

Beside material interactivity, we have object interactivity, which is used specifically when you want the entire 3D object to be interactive. This allows you to add event listeners to 3D objects and wait for them to get fired. These events can be found inside the `InteractiveScene3DEvent` class, which is located in Papervision3D's event package `org.papervision3d.events`.

Setting this up is essentially the same as setting up interactivity for materials. Both your viewport interactivity and the material interactivity property must be set to `true`.

```
private function init():void
{
    viewport.interactive = true;

    var material:ColorMaterial = new ColorMaterial();
    material.doubleSided = true;
    material.interactive = true;

    var plane:Plane = new Plane(material);
```

This is just setting viewport interactivity to `true`, instantiate a double-sided interactive color material, and apply it to the plane that we create.

Once the plane has been instantiated, we can add an event listener for interactive scene 3D events, and add the plane to the scene.

```
    plane.addEventListener(InteractiveScene3DEvent.
                            OBJECT_CLICK,click);
    scene.addChild(plane);

}
```

Each time the user clicks the plane, it will result in a `click` method call with an `InteractiveScene3DEvent` as parameter. This event contains interesting information such as which face of the 3D object was clicked and which 3D display object was clicked. Knowing which 3D object was clicked can be very useful when you have defined multiple listeners for multiple objects. This way you easily have control over the object that was clicked. For now, we use the information to rotate the plane over its y-axis.

```
private function click(e:InteractiveScene3DEvent):void
{
    e.displayObject3D.localRotationY +=12;
}
```

{Ex.} ObjectInteractivity {Ex.}

The following self-explanatory events can be dispatched by a do3D:

- `InteractiveScene3DEvent.OBJECT_ADDED`
- `InteractiveScene3DEvent.OBJECT_CLICK`
- `InteractiveScene3DEvent.OBJECT_DOUBLE_CLICK`
- `InteractiveScene3DEvent.OBJECT_MOVE`

- `InteractiveScene3DEvent.OBJECT_OUT`
- `InteractiveScene3DEvent.OBJECT_OVER`
- `InteractiveScene3DEvent.OBJECT_PRESS`
- `InteractiveScene3DEvent.OBJECT_RELEASE`
- `InteractiveScene3DEvent.OBJECT_RELEASE_OUTSIDE`

As you can see, most of the events relate to mouse events.

Tips and tricks

We have already seen some tips and tricks regarding materials between the lines. But there are a few others left that are worth mentioning.

Tiling

When developing for the web, file size is always something to keep in mind. Using a lot of textures with Papervision3D can soon result in a big download. Any savings that keep the file size as low as possible should be taken into consideration—especially when you're working on larger projects.

A smart technique often used in 3D is texture tiling. It repeats the texture in a horizontal and vertical direction, creating a new, larger texture out of this.

The code described below demonstrates how this works. For this example, we use a bitmap file material having a size of 128 by 128 pixels and we create a plane of 1024 by 512 units. The loaded image will be tiled 8 times horizontally and 4 times vertically.

First we can just instantiate `BitmapFileMaterial` as you would do this normally.

```
private function init():void
{
    var material:BitmapFileMaterial = new BitmapFileMaterial("assets/
tile.jpg");
```

To define the tiling parameters, the image needs to be loaded first. A new tiled image can't be created as long as there's no image. Therefore, we have to define an event listener that will be triggered as soon as the loading is completed.

```
material.addEventListener(FileLoadEvent.LOAD_COMPLETE,
                                loadComplete);
```

Now we can create the plane and add it to the scene as usual.

```
var plane:Plane = new Plane(material,1024,512);
scene.addChild(plane);
}
```

Once the image has been loaded, the `loadComplete()` method will be triggered. Inside this method, we have to change a few material settings. To gain easy access to the material object, we cast the event target to a `BitmapFileMaterial` type.

```
private function loadComplete(e:FileLoadEvent):void
{
    var material:BitmapFileMaterial = BitmapFileMaterial(e.target);
```

To apply tiling we change three material properties. The first one sets tiling to `true`. The second and third properties set the number of tiles horizontally (`maxU`) and vertically (`maxV`).

```
material.tiled = true;
material.maxU = 8;
material.maxV = 4;
}
```

After publishing this code, you'll see that the plane now is made of 8 x 4 copies of the original image.

{Ex.} MaterialTiling {Ex.}

The `maxU` and `maxV` properties come from **UV mapping**. UV mapping is a way to map a transformed 2D image on a 3D object. Instead of using x, y, and z coordinates, it uses U and V coordinates. U and V stand for the x and y-axis in 2D; however, the letters U and V have been used in order to avoid confusion by x and y in 3D.

More information about UV mapping can be found on Wikipedia at
`http://en.wikipedia.org/wiki/UV_mapping`

With tiling it is important to have an image that is made to be tiled and can be copied seamlessly in a horizontal and vertical direction. Creating textures is a skill in its own right and hence not in the scope of this book.

Flipping your material

Sometimes you need to flip a material because you find out that it is mirrored on the 3D surface. This happens when you set `material.doublesided` or `material.opposite` to `true` and have a camera looking at the back-face of an object. A good example is when you have a camera looking at the inside of a cube.

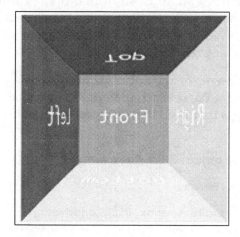

Papervision3D does not include a property on the material object, which defines that the image should be mirrored. Fortunately, flipping is nothing more than setting a negative scale value. For movie materials this can be done in a very straightforward way, which has nothing to do with Papervision3D.

Just create two sprites—one sprite to use as the movie material, along with the other that will be flipped and will hold display objects.

```
var materialSprite:Sprite = new Sprite();
var flippedSprite:Sprite = new Sprite();
```

Setting a negative `scaleX` value flips display objects horizontally.

```
flippedSprite.scaleX = -1;
```

Add some graphics to the flipped sprite.

```
flippedSprite.addChild(graphic1);
flippedSprite.addChild(graphic2);
```

Because Papervision3D maps materials on the surfaces of a 3D object, you can't affect the size of a material. It will always be mapped onto the object, no matter what the aspect ratio of a material is. This also limits the use of scaling and negative scaling materials. In order to make negative scaling possible, we nest movie clips. Therefore, you need to add the `flippedSprite` as a child to the `materialSprite`.

```
materialSprite.addChild(flippedSprite);
```

The final step—creating a movie material based on the `materialSprite`—is left out for the sake of brevity. It should now be clear how this works.

Flipping a bitmap material is a bit different from flipping sprites and movie clips. To achieve this in an easier way, the Papervision3D team developed a class called `BitmapMaterialTools`, which can be found inside the materials utilities package `org.papervision3d.materials.utils`.

To demonstrate we create a new cube out of six images, using the `BitmapFileMaterial` class. We set each material to be visible on the opposite side, resulting in flipped images that need to be flipped back, so that they will have their initial look again.

The following imports are required for this example:

```
import flash.events.Event;

import org.papervision3d.events.FileLoadEvent;
import org.papervision3d.materials.BitmapFileMaterial;
import org.papervision3d.materials.utils.BitmapMaterialTools;
import org.papervision3d.materials.utils.MaterialsList;
import org.papervision3d.objects.primitives.Cube;
import org.papervision3d.view.BasicView;
```

In the `init()` method, we start by defining the six bitmap file materials.

```
private function init():void
{
    var frontMat:BitmapFileMaterial = new BitmapFileMaterial
                                ("assets/front.jpg");
    var backMat:BitmapFileMaterial = new BitmapFileMaterial
                                ("assets/back.jpg");
    var leftMat:BitmapFileMaterial = new BitmapFileMaterial
                                ("assets/left.jpg");
    var rightMat:BitmapFileMaterial = new BitmapFileMaterial
                                ("assets/right.jpg");
    var topMat:BitmapFileMaterial = new BitmapFileMaterial
                                ("assets/top.jpg");
    var bottomMat:BitmapFileMaterial = new BitmapFileMaterial
                                ("assets/bottom.jpg");
```

Because we can only flip a material that is loaded, we define a load complete event listener for each material.

```
frontMat.addEventListener(FileLoadEvent.LOAD_COMPLETE,
    loadComplete);
backMat.addEventListener(FileLoadEvent.LOAD_COMPLETE,
    loadComplete);
leftMat.addEventListener(FileLoadEvent.LOAD_COMPLETE,
    loadComplete);
rightMat.addEventListener(FileLoadEvent.LOAD_COMPLETE,
    loadComplete);
topMat.addEventListener(FileLoadEvent.LOAD_COMPLETE,
    loadComplete);
bottomMat.addEventListener(FileLoadEvent.LOAD_COMPLETE,
    loadComplete);
```

As we've learned in Chapter 3, cubes require a `MaterialsList` object. Let's create one and add each material to it.

```
var materialsList:MaterialsList = new MaterialsList();
materialsList.addMaterial(frontMat,"front");
materialsList.addMaterial(backMat,"back");
materialsList.addMaterial(leftMat,"left");
materialsList.addMaterial(rightMat,"right");
materialsList.addMaterial(topMat,"top");
materialsList.addMaterial(bottomMat,"bottom");
```

The final step in the `init()` method is creating and adding the cube to the scene.

```
var cube:Cube = new Cube(materialsList,800,800,800,5,5,5);
scene.addChild(cube);
}
```

Each time one of the six materials has been loaded, the `loadComplete()` method will be called. The dispatched `FileLoadEvent` contains a reference to the target object which can be casted to a `BitmapFileMaterial` type.

```
private function loadComplete(e:FileLoadEvent):void
{
    var material:BitmapFileMaterial = BitmapFileMaterial(e.target);
```

We could set each `material.opposite` to `true` immediately after instantiation, but we can save ourselves some work by doing this once the material is loaded. This way we need to type it just once, instead of six times.

```
material.opposite = true;
```

Setting the `opposite` property of a material to `true` will make the inside faces of the cube visible.

In the final line of code, the bitmap material tools come in handy. This utilities class has a static method that converts the input bitmap data into a flipped version. You have the choice to flip the bitmap on the x-axis or the y-axis by using `BitmapMaterialTools.mirrorBitmapX()` or `BitmapMaterialTools.mirrorBitmapY()`. In this case we need to flip the material around the x-axis.

```
        BitmapMaterialTools.mirrorBitmapX(material.bitmap);
    }
```

After publishing this code, you'll see the inside of a cube with the images on the sides flipped so that their text is no longer mirrored.

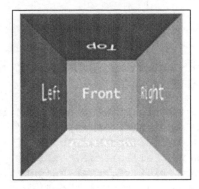

{Ex.} MaterialFlipping {Ex.}

Power of two textures

When you work with textures that have dimensions of a power of two, this will enable **mipmapping** (also spelled as **MIP Mapping** or **MIP-Mapping**) in the Flash player. This is a mathematical operation that is done natively by the Flash player, creating multiple versions of the bitmap. Once the bitmap is used and is scaled up or down, the Flash player gets the two closest bitmaps from memory, and interpolates between these to get a smoothed image at every size. Rendering smoothed mipmapped images is extremely fast. It is so fast that setting smoothing on your materials has a negligible effect on performance.

So, in order to profit from mipmapping you should use power of two bitmaps. This way you can set smoothing on your materials for free! Valid power of two dimensions in Flash are 2, 4, 8, 16, 32, 64, 128, 256, 512, 1024, and 2048. The dimensions of the images do not have to have a 1:1 aspect ratio; you can combine the power of two values to create a 1024 x 256 pixels image for example.

When it is not possible to use power of two dimensions, we can use of the automatic mipmapping feature that is implemented in Papervision3D. It is a static property that can be set on the BitmapMaterial class.

```
BitmapMaterial.AUTO_MIP_MAPPING = true;
```

When you set this static property to true, all newly-created bitmap materials will be corrected by Papervision3D so that they support mipmapping.

Example—creating a carousel

We've learned about quite a few material types in this chapter. Let's wrap up this knowledge and make an interactive carousel of planes that randomly use a color-based material, a bitmap file material, or a movie material. Each time the user hovers a plane with a color-based material, the material will change to a new random-colored material. The bitmap file material will randomly load one of the available images. And the movie material contains a button, which will flip the image on click.

The code for creating a carousel is based on the sphere of spheres example in Chapter 3. Although this time we will base it on a cylinder, and the 3D objects are planes.

This example uses quite a few different object types, which means that we have to import a list of 18 different classes at the top of our class:

```
import flash.display.DisplayObject;
import flash.display.Loader;
import flash.display.Sprite;
import flash.display.StageAlign;
import flash.display.StageScaleMode;
import flash.events.Event;
import flash.events.MouseEvent;
import flash.net.URLRequest;

import org.papervision3d.core.proto.MaterialObject3D;
import org.papervision3d.events.InteractiveScene3DEvent;
import org.papervision3d.materials.BitmapFileMaterial;
import org.papervision3d.materials.ColorMaterial;
import org.papervision3d.materials.MovieMaterial;
import org.papervision3d.objects.DisplayObject3D;
import org.papervision3d.objects.primitives.Cylinder;
import org.papervision3d.objects.primitives.Plane;
import org.papervision3d.view.BasicView;
```

Just like the sphere in spheres example, this project will create a pivot do3D as a class property, which will be used in the `onRenderTick()` method to rotate the carousel around.

```
private var pivotDO3D:DisplayObject3D;

private function init():void
{
    pivotDO3D = new DisplayObject3D();
    scene.addChild(pivotDO3D);
```

The carousel is based on the vertices of a cylinder. The cylinder has a radius of 250 and a height of 180, containing 15 width segments and 2 height segments. Because two height segments will use three vertical vertices, this will result in a carousel made of 3 rows.

```
var cylinder:Cylinder = new Cylinder(null,250,180,15,2);
```

Next, we loop through the vertices of the cylinder and place a plane on each coordinate.

```
var numberOfVerts:uint = cylinder.geometry.vertices.length
for (var i:uint = 0; i < numberOfVerts; i++)
{
```

In order to apply a random material to each plane, we add a method called `getRandomMaterial()`, which returns a `MaterialObject3D` instance containing the random material type. This method will be showed in a bit.

```
var plane:Plane = new Plane(getRandomMaterial(),75,75);
```

Then we position the plane on the coordinates of the vertex.

```
plane.x = cylinder.geometry.vertices[i].x;
plane.y = cylinder.geometry.vertices[i].y;
plane.z = cylinder.geometry.vertices[i].z;
```

All planes in the carousel should be rotated, as if they're facing the center of the carousel. Without the rotation, all objects would face the same direction, which wouldn't give us the effect we're looking for. The following formula calculates the rotation angle in radians, based on `plane.x` and `plane.z`, and then converts this into degrees.

```
plane.localRotationY = -Math.atan2(plane.x,plane.z) * 180 /
                        Math.PI;
```

To detect a rollover event, we need to define an event listener. The `objectRollOver()` method will be explained in a bit.

```
plane.addEventListener(InteractiveScene3DEvent.OBJECT_OVER,
                       objectRollOver);
```

Add the plane to the pivotDO3D object.

```
pivotDO3D.addChild(plane);
}
```

As we want interactivity for both objects and materials, we need to set `viewport` interactivity to `true`.

```
viewport.interactive = true;
```

To get a nice view of the carousel, we need to change the camera position and zoom a little bit.

```
camera.z = 200;
camera.zoom = 80;
}
```

The following method returns one of the three chosen material objects, based on a random number. New methods will be used to generate the random material type.

```
private function getRandomMaterial():MaterialObject3D
{
    var random:Number = Math.round(Math.random() * 2);
    if(random == 0)
    {
        return createMovieMaterial();
    }
    else if(random == 1)
    {
        return createBitmapMaterial();
    }
    else
    {
        return createColorMaterial();
    }
}
```

One of the random materials is of the `MovieMaterial` type, which is created by calling the following method. It contains a nested sprite, which we use to flip the material. The user can flip the material by clicking the flip arrow that is loaded inside this class.

```
private function createMovieMaterial():MovieMaterial
{
    var materialSprite:Sprite = new Sprite();
    var flippedSprite:Sprite = new Sprite();
    flippedSprite.graphics.beginFill(0x3366FF);
    flippedSprite.graphics.drawRect(0,0,512,512);
```

The loaded image serves as the button. Create a loader, position it, and add it to the `flippedSprite`.

```
    var imgLoader:Loader = new Loader();
    imgLoader.load(new URLRequest("assets/flip.png"));
    imgLoader.x = 300;
    imgLoader.y = 350;
    flippedSprite.addChild(imgLoader);
```

On click we flip the material and on rollover we set `viewport.buttonMode` to `true`, so that the button on the sprite gives us the idea that it is clickable. We do this by adding regular event listeners.

```
    imgLoader.addEventListener(MouseEvent.CLICK,flipClick);
    imgLoader.addEventListener(MouseEvent.MOUSE_OVER,spriteRollOver);
    imgLoader.addEventListener(MouseEvent.MOUSE_OUT,spriteRollOut);
```

The flipped sprite needs to be part of the material sprite. Next, a `MovieMaterial` instance can be created and returned. Note that the `animated` property is set to `true` in the constructor, which is to keep this class simple for now. We will automatically see an updated material once the image has been loaded. This saves us from setting up listeners, waiting for the loader to complete, and updating the `MovieMaterial` instance.

```
    materialSprite.addChild(flippedSprite);

    var material:MovieMaterial = new MovieMaterial(materialSprite,
                                  false,true);
    material.interactive = true;

    return material;
}
```

A random bitmap is our second random material type. This method loads one of the 10 available random images, numbered from `image_0.jpg` to `image_9.jpg`.

```
private function createBitmapMaterial():BitmapMaterial
{
    var random:Number = Math.round(Math.random() * 9);
    var material:BitmapFileMaterial = new BitmapFileMaterial("assets/
image_" + random + ".jpg");
    return material;
}
```

The last random material is a random interactive color as material, which is returned by this method.

```
private function createColorMaterial():ColorMaterial
{
    return new ColorMaterial(0xFFFFFF * Math.random(),1,true);
}
```

Each time the user hovers over one of the planes in the carousel, the following method will be triggered. For now, we want to react on this only when the plane has a material of the `ColorMaterial` type. If that's the case, a new random `ColorMaterial` will replace the current material.

```
private function objectRollOver(e:InteractiveScene3DEvent):void
{
    if(e.displayObject3D.material is ColorMaterial)
    {
        e.displayObject3D.material = createColorMaterial();
    }
}
```

The next two methods are to simulate button behavior, by changing the mouse pointer to a hand cursor when it's over the flip button that is part of the movie material. Don't confuse this with object rollovers—these are only for the flip button.

```
private function spriteRollOver(e:MouseEvent):void
{
    viewport.buttonMode = true;
}

private function spriteRollOut(e:MouseEvent):void
{
    viewport.buttonMode = false;
}
```

When the user clicks the flip button, this method is triggered and changes the scaleX value to flip the material.

```
private function flipClick(e:MouseEvent):void
{
    var flippedSprite:DisplayObject = Loader(e.target).content.parent;
    if(flippedSprite.scaleX == -1)
    {
            flippedSprite.scaleX = 1;
    }
    else
    {
            flippedSprite.scaleX = -1;
    }
}
```

Each onRenderTick() looks at the mouse position on the stage and translate this to a localRotationY value giving you control over the rotation of the carousel by moving your mouse to the left or to the right.

```
override protected function onRenderTick(e:Event=null):void
{
    pivotDO3D.localRotationY +=(stage.mouseX -
                                 stage.stageWidth / 2) / 200;
    super.onRenderTick();
}
```

{Ex.} Carousel {Ex.}

Publishing this example will result in an interactive carousel, containing several techniques that we've discussed in this chapter.

Summary

Materials are the skin on your 3D objects. Wireframe materials and color-based materials are the most basic materials. More advanced materials are bitmaps and movie clips. Both have inherited classes available that make it easier for you to create new instances of them.

In this chapter we looked at the following material classes in detail:

- `WireframeMaterial`
- `ColorMaterial`
- `BitmapMaterial`
- `BitmapFileMaterial`
- `BitmapAssetMaterial`
- `MovieMaterial`
- `MovieAssetMaterial`
- `VideoStreamMaterial`
- `CompositeMaterial`

We have seen several general and material-specific techniques. We have learned how to:

- Smooth materials with `material.smooth = true`.
- Make double-sided materials by using `material.doubleSided = true`.
- Animate materials and set `material.animated` to `true`.
- Prevent distortion in materials using `material.precise = true`.
- Make interactive materials and objects. Both require `viewport.interactive` and `material.interactive` set to `true`.
- Flip materials by using a `DisplayObject`'s `scaleX` property, or using the `BitmapMaterialTools` utilities class, in order to mirror bitmap data with the static method call `BitmapMaterialTools.mirrorBitmapX( material.bitmap)`.
- Tile materials by using `material.tiled = true`, along with `material.maxU` and `material.maxV`.

At the end of the chapter, we combined a lot of what we've learned into the creation of a carousel. The class introduced a few camera settings in order to get a good view of the carousel. In the next chapter, we'll discuss the various types of cameras available in Papervision3D and how we can use them.

5
Cameras

In the previous chapters, we have only touched upon the use of cameras. In this chapter, we will see what cameras in 3D are and what they can do. Obviously, there is nothing like a real, physical camera in Papervision3D and it doesn't even have a visual representation on the 2D screen. The camera merely represents a virtual point from which we view the scene and the objects present in it.

The chapter will cover the following:

- The camera as a `DisplayObject3D`
- Camera settings
- Camera types
- Setting a camera target

First, let's briefly examine how the camera and its classes are implemented in the Papervision3D library.

Cameras inherit from DisplayObject3D

Not only primitives inherit their properties and methods from `DisplayObject3D`, but also the `CameraObject3D` class, which is the super class of `Camera3D`. To sum up, `Camera3D` inherits from `CameraObject3D`, which inherits from `DisplayObject3D`.

So what does this mean? Because each camera inherits the x, y, and z properties from `DisplayObject3D`, we can move it around over the axes of the scene coordinate system (world space). Furthermore, you can rotate the camera in the same way as you would rotate any other instance of `DisplayObject3D`. Although the camera doesn't have a visual representation on the screen, we have a lot of tools to manipulate it. The camera even has some properties and methods that no other do3D has.

Basic camera settings

Basic settings that specifically apply to cameras are:

- **Zoom**
- **Focus**
- **Field of view**, also known as **fov** or **FoV**
- **Near** and **far**

To get familiar with these settings, we will briefly examine some basics of 3D computer graphics. We will then look at a demo to get a better understanding of how the settings relate to each other.

The following illustration shows the camera and what it sees. Also notice the pyramid shape, cut off by a **far plane** and a **near plane**. The space inside the truncated pyramid is the **viewing volume** or **frustum**. The near and far planes are imaginary planes that define the frustum.

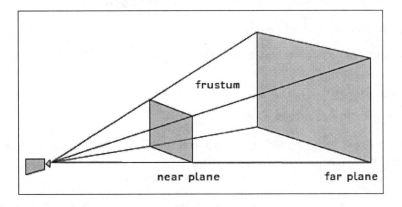

Now, let's take a look at how the frustum relates to the viewport sprite in which everything inside the frustum is eventually drawn. Different 3D programs have different ways of setting the viewport. In Papervision3D the viewport is set at the near plane. Therefore, although the viewport is a 2D sprite and the near plane is an imaginary plane perpendicular to the camera, the two are virtually related. Now, let's imagine we add a cube to our scene. In the following illustration you can see the cube inside the frustum, containing 3D information such as the number and position of vertices and the material assigned to it. Papervision3D projects the vertices on the 2D viewport and renders the cube so that we see it on our screen.

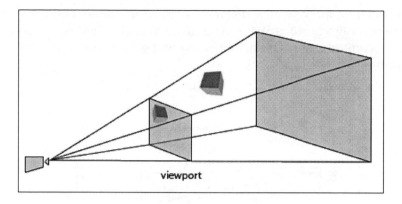

The frustum is the 3D area visible on the screen, so objects outside the frustum will not appear on the screen. It would be a waste of capacity if Papervision3D would render objects that are outside the frustum. The process of identifying what is inside the frustum and not rendering what is outside is known as **culling**, and is crucial in optimizing 3D applications. It saves a lot of processing if Papervision3D does not render all the vertices that we cannot see anyway. Culling will be discussed in more detail at the end of this chapter.

Focus and field of view

Focus is a positive number that represents the distance between the camera and the near plane (and thus our viewport). It is the shortest distance possible between the observer and a visible object.

Field of view is the camera's vertical angle of view in degrees. The following illustration shows that there is a relationship between focus, field of view, and the height of the viewport:

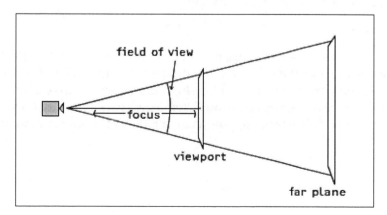

A higher focus value increases the distance between the camera and the near plane. Close and distant objects will appear to be closer to each other, regardless of the distance between them. Also, the field of view will get smaller as can be seen in the next illustration:

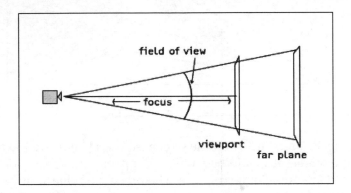

Lowering the focus increases the field of view. This is like using a wider lens resulting in an exaggerated view, where close objects appear to be larger and distant objects appear to be smaller. Setting the focus very low leads to distortion of perspective where parallel lines seem to converge. In photography you can take extremely wide images using a **fisheye** lens, which is popular for its distorted perspective.

Setting the focus is done as follows:

```
camera.focus = 12;
```

Due to the way different camera types are initialized, the default value of `camera.focus` may vary. It defaults to approximately 8.66 in all types that we will discuss in a bit, except in the debug camera where it defaults to 10.

Use the `fov` property to set the field of view.

```
camera.fov = 90;
```

The constructor of the `Camera3D` class has an `fov` parameter that defaults to 60. But as we have seen, one of the factors that define the field of view is the height of the viewport. However, the width and height of the viewport are set by you, the developer, and may vary per application. Therefore, chances are that if you do not set a value for `fov` and then trace it, you will get a different output than the default value of 60.

Zoom

Zoom is a familiar concept to most of us. When you zoom in with a photo or video camera, the image that you see in the viewer scales up. The whole scene magnifies without moving the camera towards the scene. Distances between close and distant objects seem to decrease leading to a more compressed view. The same happens when you increase the zoom value of a camera in Papervision3D.

Have a look at the following illustration. Zooming the camera magnifies objects that are seen in the region represented by the small white rectangle. You can see that if we keep the focus the same, we need to make the field of view smaller in order to make the objects that we see appear bigger.

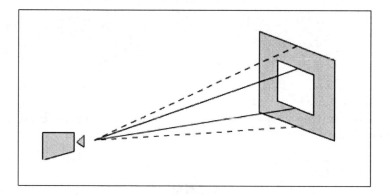

The default value of zoom is set to 40, but you can adjust it to your liking. In the carousel that we built in the previous chapter, we changed the zoom of the camera to get a better view at the carousel.

```
camera.zoom = 80;
```

Zoom, focus, and field of view relate to each other

As we have seen, zoom, focus, and field of view are clearly related to each other. Changing one of these leads to different results.

- If you decrease either zoom or focus, the field of view will increase
- If you increase either zoom or focus, the field of view will decrease
- Increasing or decreasing the field of view will decrease or increase the focus respectively, but will not change the zoom

But what does all this mean to our perception of the scene? To get a better grasp on what happens visually, open CH05_CameraSettingsDemo.swf. You will see a number of red planes—four at the left and four at the right. There's also one blue plane set far away on the z-axis. Playing around with the sliders can be helpful in understanding the relationship between zoom, focus, and field of view. You can also adjust the z coordinate of the camera. If you move the zoom, focus, or field of view slider, you can see how the other values are being updated as described in the previously shown bullet list.

Let's set zoom to 12, focus to 6, and the z position to -160. This will give you a heavily distorted perspective with a very deep view.

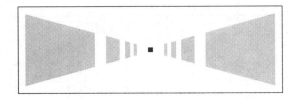

On the other hand, setting zoom to 60, focus to 55, and camera to -2500 results in a very compressed view.

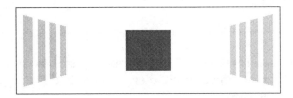

Near and far

The truncated pyramid that defines the frustum is cut off by the near and the far plane. The distance from the camera to both planes is defined by the properties near and far. As focus also defines the distance between the camera and the near plane, near and focus are equivalent. Setting the near property does exactly the same as focus.

```
camera.near = 30;
```

The far property is the distance between the camera and the far plane. Setting it goes like this:

```
camera.far = 15000;
```

Suppose you are building a game with many objects in a very wide and deep space. Objects can be close to the camera, but they also can be so far away that you cannot or hardly see them on the screen. But objects will be drawn anyway, no matter how far they are. Because there are so many triangles to be drawn, the rendering process can be very hard on a user's computer. Bringing the far plane closer to the camera would result in fewer objects inside the frustum and less triangles to render.

Take this into consideration when you build a game or any other 3D application. Some games even give the player the option to set the distance of the far plane. If a user has a computer that is not so fast and chooses to bring the far plane closer to the camera, the result would be a better CPU performance and a more enjoyable game.

 To prevent objects from being rendered when they are beyond the far plane, you need to set `camera.useCulling` to `true`. We will discuss the `useCulling` property later in the *Culling* section in this chapter.

Another property that you can use when working with the camera is **target**. Let's see what that is by examining what kind of cameras Papervision3D provides.

Camera types

Papervision3D includes four types of cameras:

- Target camera
- Free camera
- Debug camera
- Spring camera

The target camera and the free camera are the most common types and will be discussed first. The debug camera is handy for testing purposes as it has some basic built-in navigation, and continuously displays information about its settings. A special type is the spring camera that provides an easy way to follow a moving 3D object, something that can be useful in game applications.

You set the camera type of your choice by passing it as an argument to the constructor of the `BasicView` class. Because we extend `BasicView`, we can use the `super()` call in our constructor to do so.

```
super(stage.stageWidth,stage.stageHeight,true,false,
      CameraType.TARGET);
```

In Chapter 2 we have seen what the first three arguments do. And in the previous chapter we added a fourth one to set the interactivity of the viewport. Now we have added a fifth argument, which sets the type of camera you would like to use. This argument is a static variable of the string type, defined in the `CameraType` class.

- `CameraType.TARGET`
- `CameraType.FREE`
- `CameraType.DEBUG`
- `CameraType.SPRING`

Keep in mind that you will have to import the `CameraType` class when you want to pass one of the above types.

```
import org.papervision3d.cameras.CameraType;
```

If you do not pass an argument, the type defaults to the target camera. Therefore, if we take a look again at the `super()` call, we actually could have left out the third, fourth, and fifth argument, as they are all default values.

Let's take a closer look and see what the differences are between the available camera types.

The target camera

The **target camera** is a type of camera that always looks at a target. The data type of the `target` property is `DisplayObject3D`, so the target can, for instance, be a blank do3D or a primitive. You define the target as follows:

```
camera.target = myTarget;
```

If you pass `CameraType.TARGET` as your camera type and do not set a target, Papervision3D will create one for you. By using `DisplayObject3D.ZERO`, it will create an empty do3D positioned at the center of the global coordinate system. In effect, the camera will always look at the origin point of your scene.

 `DisplayObject3D.ZERO` returns an empty `DisplayObject3D` object positioned at the center of the 3D coordinate system (0,0,0).

The free camera

The free camera behaves exactly the same as the target camera except that it has no target. The free camera is always looking straight ahead in the direction of its local z-axis. If you pass `CameraType.FREE` as the type argument, the target will return null.

Demonstrating the difference between the free camera and the target camera

To become more familiar with the differences between the target camera and the free camera, open `CameraTypesDemo.swf`. You will see a plane with a wireframe material applied to it. You will also see a red x-axis, a green y-axis, and a blue z-axis. The axes are a visual representation of the global 3D coordinate system and give you a better sense of where your camera and your 3D objects are at any moment. The plane is positioned at the center of the coordinate system. The camera is lifted a little so that we are able to see the z-axis. The y position of the camera is `80`.

Notice the mouse interaction in the demo. When you move your mouse to the left, the camera will move to the left; and when you move your mouse to the right, the camera will move to the right.

By clicking the **Target** button we change the camera to the target type, and the plane is set as the camera's target.

```
camera.target = plane;
```

No matter what the camera's x position is, it is always looking at the plane. Depending on its x position it is actually rotating towards the plane. Once you have set a target for a camera, the camera will always be rotated facing the target. As a consequence, the camera will ignore any attempts to change that rotation. To keep things simple, we are moving the camera in this demo only over the x-axis. But moving the camera position over the y and z-axis would also cause the camera to rotate towards the plane.

Select the free camera by clicking the other button and you will see a clear difference. When the camera moves, it just keeps looking in the direction of the z-axis of its local coordinate system. Although it sees the plane, the camera does not rotate towards it.

The following illustrations demonstrate the difference between the two types. The illustration at the left depicts a target camera that follows an object, which has been set as the camera's target and moves from left to right. In the illustration at the right you see a free camera that does not follow the moving object.

Switching between the free camera and the target camera

Switching from target camera to free camera and back is easy. The only difference between the two is that the target camera has a target, whereas the free camera doesn't. Therefore, to switch to a free camera, set the target to `null`:

```
camera.target = null;
```

If you want to switch from a free camera to a target camera, just set the do3D that you would like the camera to look at as the target.

This is just a simple example to demonstrate the difference between the two types. However, working with cameras can be quite confusing. Especially while using the free camera it's easy to lose your sense of orientation.

Let's move on to the next camera, the debug camera.

The debug camera

You can imagine that with all the available settings it is quite easy to get lost in 3D space when you are building an application. To keep track of where your camera is and what its settings are while you are testing, the debug camera has been developed. It has some basic built-in navigation using keys and mouse interaction implemented, and it displays some stats that continuously tell you what is going on.

Let's build a simple application that uses this camera. We will generate a galaxy of random colored planes and add a sphere to it. The sphere will have a bitmap of the earth wrapped around it. If you have tried the `SetUpTest` project in Chapter 1, you've already seen the earth turning. Now let's see how to create it in a couple of minutes and examine the galaxy with our debug camera.

Taking the `BookExampleTemplate` from Chapter 2 as our starting point, we will first do some imports that should speak for themselves by now:

```
import org.papervision3d.cameras.CameraType;
import org.papervision3d.events.FileLoadEvent;
import org.papervision3d.materials.BitmapFileMaterial;
import org.papervision3d.materials.ColorMaterial;
import org.papervision3d.objects.primitives.Plane;
import org.papervision3d.objects.primitives.Sphere;
```

Right under the class definition we assign an instance of `Sphere` to a variable `earthSphere`.

```
private var earthSphere:Sphere;
```

You can set the debug camera type similar to how you set a target or a free camera, by passing a string in the `super()` call as shown next:

```
super(stage.stageWidth,stage.stageHeight,true,false,CameraType.DEBUG);
```

In our `init()` method we create the material for the sphere, add a listener to check if the material is loaded, and set the `precise` property to `true`. This assumes that you have an `assets` folder in your `src` folder with a bitmap `earth.jpg` in it. You can find this bitmap in the code download:

```
var material:BitmapFileMaterial = new BitmapFileMaterial
                                ("assets/earth.jpg");
material.addEventListener(FileLoadEvent.LOAD_COMPLETE,
                            loadComplete);
material.precise = true;
```

In Chapter 4, we saw that we do not need the event listener to apply the material to the sphere. We are using it so that we will not start rendering the scene before the material has loaded. We can instantiate the sphere and apply the material to the sphere right away.

```
earthSphere = new Sphere(material,200,24,16);
scene.addChild(earthSphere);
```

Next, still in the `init()` method, we create 150 planes and give them a random color, position, and rotation.

```
for(var i:uint = 0; i <  150; i++)
{
    var plane:Plane = new Plane(new ColorMaterial(Math.random()
                            * 0xFFFFFF),50,50,1,1);
    plane.material.doubleSided = true;
    scene.addChild(plane);
    plane.x = Math.random()*20000 - 10000;
    plane.y = Math.random()*1500 - 750;
    plane.z = Math.random()*20000 -10000;
    plane.localRotationY = Math.random() * 180 - 90;
}
```

`Math.random() * 20000 – 10000` will return a random number between -10,000 and 10,000, providing a good way to divide the planes randomly over the scene in the direction of the x and z-axis. The same goes for randomizing the y position, but here we apply a shorter range resulting in a galaxy that looks a bit "flat".

Now that we have built our galaxy, let's set some camera settings:

```
camera.z = -2000;
camera.focus = 20;
camera.far = 20000;
```

We increased the focus in order to prevent too much perspective distortion when the earth will be at the side of our scene. The particular value of 20 is a matter of taste and you can change it to see the difference it makes in depth of view and perspective distortion. Finally, we set the far plane at 20000. This will allow us to see our objects even when the camera is quite far away from the galaxy.

We have added an event listener to check if the material is loaded. This is the accompanying listener method that contains the render call:

```
private function loadComplete(e:FileLoadEvent):void
{
    startRendering();
}
```

Don't forget to remove the startRendering() call from the constructor!

By adding a local rotation to the sphere, we will make the earth turn slowly. Add the following line in the onRenderTick() method before the super.onRenderTick() call:

```
earthSphere.localRotationY += 0.2;
```

Publish the file and you should see a galaxy of planes with the earth in the middle. Also notice the information being displayed at the top left of the screen.

It shows the camera's values for the following properties:

- Coordinates
- Rotation
- Field of view
- Near and far

Use your *W*, *A*, *S*, and *D* keys or the arrow keys to move the camera. Notice that you can manipulate the rotation of the camera over the x and y-axis by dragging your mouse. You can use the *Q* and *E* keys to rotate over the z-axis.

As you navigate through the scene and rotate the camera every now and then, you will probably notice how easy it is to lose your orientation, especially when you're not an experienced gamer or game developer. Although the information that the debug camera gives does not provide an ultimate fix, it can give a better understanding of what is going on. This makes the debug camera a useful tool when you are developing and debugging your 3D application.

You could even do some exercising to get familiar with moving through 3D space. Move around for a while and then try to get back somewhere close to the position where you started, $(0,0,-2000)$ in our example. Also, try to restore the initial rotation, which was 0 for all three axes. It's not very easy and it may take some time, but it can be done with the help of the information the debug camera supplies.

The information display not only shows coordinates and rotation, but also gives you the field of view, along with the distance from the camera to the near plane and the far plane. We have set the far plane at 20,000 units from the camera. This enables us to see all the planes and the earth sphere even if we move the camera quite far away from the galaxy. When you move back the camera to a z value of less than -20,000, the earth sphere will disappear. It is now behind the far plane and not being rendered anymore.

For example, changing `far` to 8000 will bring the far plane closer to the camera. This results in a less deep frustum, and now when you move the camera backward, planes will start disappearing right away. Moving the camera forward brings them back inside the frustum and they are rendered again.

{Ex.} DebugCameraExample {Ex.}

The spring camera

The spring camera type is a camera that follows a 3D object. Think of cars and spaceships that are tailed by a third person or chase camera as seen in many 3D games. You can also use it as a first person camera. The camera does not just follow the object, it adds a nice spring effect when the object accelerates and makes turns. The camera makes use of physics, creating an imaginary spring between the camera and the object. When the object moves, the imaginary spring with the camera attached to it will be extended and will then be pulled back, resulting in a natural and smooth movement.

Let's build an example that is based on the previous one. We will add a flying object to the scene and we will tell the spring camera to chase it. There is one thing we will have to do before we can use the camera. Although it takes care of tailing our object, we first need to make the object move. We have seen that the debug camera has some built-in camera navigation using keyboard keys and the mouse. We need to build some navigation like that ourselves to make the object fly. More advanced navigation techniques will be discussed in Chapter 6, but for now, let's take the opportunity to get familiar with basic navigation.

We will call this project `SpringCameraExample`. As this example is based on the example of the debug camera, you can copy and paste the complete code of `DebugCameraExample` in the document class of your new project. Just don't forget to change the class definition and the constructor name into `SpringCameraExample`. Also, copy the `assets` folder from the previous project and paste it into the `src` folder of the current one as it contains the bitmap for the earth sphere.

Before we create the camera, we will first build a simple object and add navigation so that we can fly it around. We will be using paper plane as our flying object.

Import the `PaperPlane` class and add the following line to assign the object to an instance variable:

```
private var paperPlane:PaperPlane;
```

To apply a composite of two materials to the paper plane, we need to import both `WireframeMaterial` and `CompositeMaterial`:

```
import org.papervision3d.materials.WireframeMaterial;
import org.papervision3d.materials.special.CompositeMaterial;
```

In the `init()` method, right after the code that creates the galaxy planes but before the camera settings, add the following:

```
var planeMaterial:CompositeMaterial = new CompositeMaterial();
planeMaterial.addMaterial(new ColorMaterial(0xFFFFFF));
planeMaterial.addMaterial(new WireframeMaterial(0x484848));
planeMaterial.doubleSided = true;
```

The composite material is made of a color and a wireframe material and will be applied to the paper plane that we instantiate and position.

```
paperPlane = new PaperPlane(planeMaterial);
scene.addChild(paperPlane);
paperPlane.y = 250;
paperPlane.z= -1000;
```

We are done creating the paper plane, let's take a look at how we can build basic keyboard navigation.

Adding basic navigation

The kind of navigation we are about to create is quite common in 2D Flash, so the code may look familiar. Because we will use the keys of our keyboard to navigate the paper plane, we need the following two imports:

```
import flash.events.KeyboardEvent;
import flash.ui.Keyboard;
```

To keep track of what key is pressed, we create some class properties.

```
private var keyRight:Boolean;
private var keyLeft:Boolean;
private var keyForward:Boolean;
private var keyBackward:Boolean;
```

At the top of the `init()`, method we add two event listeners that listen to the stage:

```
stage.addEventListener(KeyboardEvent.KEY_DOWN,keyDownHandler);
stage.addEventListener(KeyboardEvent.KEY_UP,keyUpHandler);
```

As you can see, the event listeners expect two methods—`keyUpHandler()` and `KeyDownHandler()`. The `keyDownHandler()` method looks like this:

```
private function keyDownHandler(e:KeyboardEvent):void
{
    switch( e.keyCode )
    {
            case "W".charCodeAt():
            case Keyboard.UP:
                keyForward = true;
                break;

            case "S".charCodeAt():
            case Keyboard.DOWN:
                keyBackward = true;
                break;

            case "A".charCodeAt():
            case Keyboard.LEFT:
                keyLeft = true;
                break;

            case "D".charCodeAt():
```

```
        case Keyboard.RIGHT:
                keyRight = true;
                break;
    }
}
```

The method checks which key has been pressed and sets the accompanying boolean to `true`. The `keyUpHandler()` looks very similar, and sets the booleans to `false` again.

```
private function keyUpHandler(e:KeyboardEvent):void
{
    switch(e.keyCode)
    {
        case "W".charCodeAt():
        case Keyboard.UP:
                keyForward = false;
                break;

        case "S".charCodeAt():
        case Keyboard.DOWN:
                keyBackward = false;
                break;

        case "A".charCodeAt():
        case Keyboard.LEFT:
                keyLeft = false;
                break;

        case "D".charCodeAt():
        case Keyboard.RIGHT:
                keyRight = false;
                break;
    }
}
```

This code will not do much yet, except that it listens for keys being pressed. But as we continuously need to check if a key is pressed and then tell the plane to respond, we need another method and call it from inside the `onRenderTick()` method.

The method to check the state of the booleans on every frame looks like the following:

```
private function moveObject():void
{
    if(keyForward)
    {
            paperPlane.moveForward(30);
    }
```

```
        else if(keyBackward)
        {
                paperPlane.moveBackward(30);
        }

        if(keyRight)
        {
                paperPlane.localRotationY -=2;
        }
        else if(keyLeft)
        {
                paperPlane.localRotationY +=2;
        }
}
```

It holds two `if-else` statements. The first takes care of the paper plane moving forward and backward, while the second handles its steering. Notice that we have used two new methods. They are part of the `DisplayObject3D` class and pretty self explanatory:

- `moveForward()`: Moves the object forward in the direction of its own z-axis

- `moveBackward()`: Moves the object backward in the direction of its own z-axis

`DisplayObject3D` includes four similar methods that we did not use in this example but are worth mentioning here:

- `moveLeft()`: Moves the object to the left in the direction of its own x-axis
- `moveRight()`: Moves the object to the right in the direction of its own x-axis
- `moveUp()`: Moves the object upward in the direction of its own y-axis
- `moveDown()`: Moves the object downward in the direction of its own y-axis

All six methods require a numeric argument, which defines how many units the object should be moved per frame.

Once you have added the `moveObject()` method right after the key handlers, you need to call it every frame to cause the paper plane to move. Add the following line inside the render method, but make sure you add it before the `super.onRenderTick()` call, otherwise you will constantly see the position of the paper plane one frame late:

```
moveObject();
```

If you publish the file now, you should see the newly-added paper plane. However, our navigation will not work yet because the camera is still set to the debug type. The debug camera listens to the same keyboard keys and "overrules" our listeners. We will not yet set the type to spring because we first want to see the navigation of the plane without a camera following it. Therefore, let's set the camera type to `CameraType.TARGET` for the time being, allowing us to test the navigation code we have written. Change the `super()` call into the following:

```
super(stage.stageWidth,stage.stageHeight,true,false,
    CameraType.TARGET);
```

Now publish the file again and use your keyboard to move the paper plane. The example shows how to move and rotate a 3D object, but instead you could also apply the code to the camera, resulting in behavior similar to what we have seen when using the debug camera class. You would simply have to replace `paperPlane` in the `moveObject()` method by `camera`. Notice that, to see the camera rotate, you would have to set its target to `null`.

Putting the spring camera to work

Now that we have built some basic navigation to fly the paper plane, let's put the spring camera to work and see what it does. Instantiating the spring camera requires a slightly different approach than the other types. The camera that we normally have in our document class is instantiated in `BasicView` as a `CameraObject3D` object. The `SpringCamera3D` class has some unique properties that are not inherited from `CameraObject3D`. Because our regular camera is a `CameraObject3D` object, we will not be able to access the properties of the `SpringCamera3D` class. One way to handle this is to typecast the camera as a `SpringCamera3D`.

To accomplish this, we need to import the `SpringCamera3D` class. Importing the `Number3D` class enables us to work with some of the properties of `SpringCamera`.

```
import org.papervision3d.cameras.SpringCamera3D;
import org.papervision3d.core.math.Number3D;
```

 The `Number3D` class stands for a value in a three-dimensional coordinate system. Take a look at the following line of code where `number3D` represents a 3D value with an x, y, and a z coordinate:

```
var number3D:Number3D = new Number3D(0,50,20);
```

Now set the type to spring by changing the `super()` call again:

```
super(stage.stageWidth,stage.stageHeight,true,false,
    CameraType.SPRING);
```

In the `init()` method, right before the camera settings, we assign a `SpringCamera3D` object to a local variable and typecast the camera as `SpringCamera3D`.

```
var camera:SpringCamera3D = SpringCamera3D(camera);
```

After this line, add the following:

```
camera.mass = 20;
camera.damping = 4;
camera.stiffness = 1;
camera.positionOffset = new Number3D(0,150,-500);
camera.lookOffset = new Number3D(0,0,100);
```

Here we have set the properties we wanted to change, and that we have access to, as we typecasted the camera as a `SpringCamera3D`. Before we discuss what they do, let's set the target for the spring camera. At the end of the `init()` method, right after the camera settings, add the following line:

```
camera.target = paperPlane;
```

Publish the file again. This time the camera is brought into position right away, ready to tail the paper plane. If you move the paper plane around, the camera follows as if a spring is connecting camera and paper plane, resulting in smooth moves and turns. We have set a list of spring camera properties, so let's see what they do.

Property	Data type	Default value	Description
mass	Number	40	The mass or weight of the camera. It defines how hard it is to pull. A higher mass makes the camera harder to move.
damping	Number	4	Controls the internal friction or how much the spring resists the elastic effect. Raising the value will decrease the elastic effect, resulting in smoother movement. Keep the value somewhere between 1 and 20.
stiffness	Number	1	The stiffness of the spring or how hard the spring is to extend. The higher the value, the more fixed the camera seems to be, as if the spring has a fixed length. Keep the number somewhere between 1 and 20.

Property	Data type	Default value	Description
positionOffset	Number3D	Number3D(0,5, -50)	The position of the camera in relation to the target's local space.
lookOffset	Number3D	Number3D(0,2,10)	Sets the point for the camera to look at, again defined in the local space of the target. An offset of Number3D(0,100,0) causes the camera to look 100 units higher than the position of the target.

The last two properties contribute a lot to the camera's viewing perspective, and hence to the 3D experience of the user. Let's look a little closer at the position offset, which should be considered as the position to which the camera always wants to return, as it changes all the time while in motion to cause the desired spring effect. An offset of Number3D(0,50,200) sets the camera 50 units higher than the target and 200 units behind it. If you would set this property in our example to a value of Number3D(0,0,-300), the camera would be right behind the paper plane. Because that is not such an interesting view, we lifted the camera by 150 units. In some 3D games the user can switch between a third person view, where the camera is behind the head of the avatar; and a first person view, where the camera's position and behavior seem to replace the "eyes" of the avatar. This is also something that could be achieved by changing the position offset.

{Ex.} SpringCameraExample {Ex.}

Setting a target with the lookAt() method

The lookAt() method enables you to make a camera look at a target. In this respect it behaves similarly to the previously discussed target property. However, besides target being a property and lookAt() being a method, there is a difference in how to use them. The target property needs to be set only once, for instance in the init() method, whereas lookAt() requires that you put it in the render method in order to keep being executed after the first frame is rendered. Therefore, to make the camera look at an object assigned to a variable plane, the following line should be added to the onRenderTick() method:

```
camera.lookAt(plane);
```

The camera will continuously rotate in such a way that its own z-axis is pointing at the origin of the target, as shown in the following illustration:

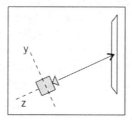

The `lookAt()` method is inherited from the `DispayObject3D` class. This means you can tell any do3D to look at any other do3D. So, you can't only tell a camera to look at a 3D object, but also make a 3D object look at a camera or at another 3D object.

Use this to make the plane in the previous line of code look at the camera:

```
plane.lookAt(camera);
```

Notice that in the following illustration the plane's own z-axis is pointed at the camera:

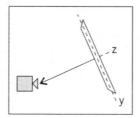

Finally, we can also tell one 3D object to look at another. Although this does not directly involve the camera or its settings, we might as well run through an example now that we are discussing `lookAt()`.

```
plane.lookAt(sphere);
```

The next illustration shows what this would look like. Again, the plane's own z-axis is pointing at the origin of target—the sphere in this case.

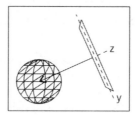

To demonstrate the difference between the camera looking at an object and vice versa, open `LookAtDemo.swf`. The demo has the same mouse interaction implemented as the camera type demo we have seen earlier, where moving the mouse to the left moved the camera to the left and moving the mouse to the right moved the camera to the right. If you make the plane look at the camera, notice that you will not see the blue line anymore that represents the plane's own z-axis demonstrating that this axis is indeed pointing right at the camera. The axes are drawn with the `Line3D` class (which we will discuss in Chapter 12) and a line that is exactly directed at the camera is simply not visible. On the other hand, if the plane is the target of the camera, you will still be able to see the line that represents the local z-axis of the plane. Also notice that when you switch the relationship between the camera and the plane, the rotation of the object that is looking changes over the x-axis.

Culling

The following illustration shows a camera and the frustum with the near plane and the far plane. The light grey objects are outside the frustum, the black objects are inside the frustum, and the dark grey objects are partially inside the frustum.

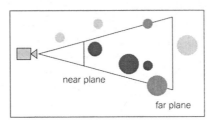

Rendering objects that are outside the frustum would be a waste of performance. Even triangles that are not on the screen because objects are partially outside the frustum should better not be rendered.

Culling is the process of identifying what is totally or partially inside the frustum and getting rid of what is not inside (in the illustration, the light grey objects and parts of the dark grey objects). Papervision3D includes culling and does not render objects and triangles that are outside the frustum, which increases performance. Before we examine how we can tell Papervision3D to apply culling, let's see which types of culling are generally used in 3D computer graphics.

Culling origins from the Latin word **colligere**, which means to collect. In a broader sense, the term is used for dividing a collection of objects into two groups, ignoring or throwing away one group and using the other. The set of objects being rejected is called the **cull**.

Types of culling in 3D computer graphics

3D computer graphics usually implement different types of culling. Let's walk through them and see whether they are implemented in Papervision3D:

- **Frustum culling**: This is what we have just seen—everything outside the frustum is culled. Papervision3D includes this type of culling.

- **Back-face culling**: The triangles that face away from the camera are culled. This is also included in Papervision3D.

- **Contribution culling**: An object is too small or far away to contribute to the image and can be culled. This type is not included as such, but you can tell Papervision3D to cull objects that are beyond the far plane.

- **Occlusion culling**: An object that is entirely behind another object is culled. This type of culling, also known as **hidden surface removal**, is not included in Papervision3D.

The first two types in the above list are included in Papervision3D. On one hand where back-face culling is done automatically, frustum culling can be turned on and off. We will take a closer look at frustum culling in the next section, but let's first address back-face culling briefly.

Suppose you add a sphere to your scene. Rendering the triangles at the back of the sphere, relative to the camera's point of view, would cause the engine to make superfluous calculations. Papervision3D supports back-face culling, so triangles not facing the camera are automatically culled, unless they have a double sided material applied to them. You can imagine that this saves a lot on performance.

Two levels of culling in Papervision3D

Papervision3D can handle culling on two levels:

- **Object-based**: The object is culled when it is entirely outside the frustum.

- **Triangle-based**: A triangle is culled when partly or entirely outside the viewport. Triangles are also culled when they intersect with the near plane.

Object-based culling is similar to frustum culling, which in Papevision3D is also known as **camera based** culling. Culling triangles that are partly or entirely outside the viewport is a technique specific to Papervision3D and does not fit into one of the four types listed in the previous section.

Applying frustum culling

You apply frustum culling by setting the camera's `useCulling` property to `true`:

```
camera.useCulling = true;
```

With the above setting objects outside the viewing frustum will not be rendered. This type of culling is object based and not triangle based, meaning that the entire object is culled when it is entirely outside the frustum.

 Earlier in this chapter we have discussed four types of cameras. They all inherit the `useCulling` property from `CameraObject3D`. This property defaults to false for all types, except for the debug camera, in which it defaults to true.

You can check if a do3D is being culled by using the `culled` property. The next trace call outputs `true` when the do3D is culled.

```
trace(do3D.culled);
```

Applying culling on viewport level

When you apply frustum culling, an object has to be entirely outside the frustum to be culled. However, if an object is partially outside the frustum, triangles of the object that are outside the frustum are not culled when setting the `useCulling` property. With the help of the `autoCulling` property of `Viewport3D`, Papervision3D culls these triangles.

```
viewport.autoCulling = true;
```

The property is set to `true` by default, so you do not have to add the previous line to make it work. When `autoCulling` is set to `true`, the viewport creates a rectangle with its own size and every triangle outside the rectangle (and thus outside the viewport) will not be rendered. Note that frustum culling is object based, whereas viewport culling is triangle based.

Seeing culling at work

To see culling at work, open `CullingDemo.swf`. It shows a sphere made of 760 triangles. You can move around the camera by using the keyboard arrows or by clicking and dragging the mouse.

At the left top of the screen, you see some statistics displayed about the movie.

A Papervision3D class called `StatsView` generates the statistics, which are displayed in the demo. Chapter 13 discusses how to use this class and explains the statistics that it shows.

The first statistic on the second line tells us that 760 triangles are rendered, which is the expected number as we have added a sphere made up of this number of triangles.

Now take a look at the fourth line. **COb** stands for the number of culled objects and **CTr** for the number of culled triangles. The statistics show that no triangles are being culled. Also the number of culled objects is **0**.

First, let's see what happens if we move the camera forward, until the sphere disappears partially because it intersects with the near plane. You should see something like this:

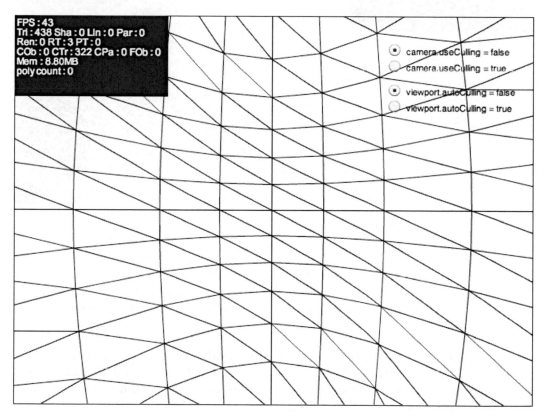

Notice that when the screenshot was taken, the **CTr** value shows that **322** triangles were culled. Therefore, even when both `camera.useCulling` and `viewport.autoCulling` are set to `false`, triangles are culled when they pass the near plane.

When a triangle intersects with the near plane, it will always be culled, even when camera-based culling and viewport culling are not applied. When the positions of one or more vertices of a triangle are behind the near plane, Papervision3D will not project them on the 2D plane, let stand alone draw the triangle.

Now move the camera backward again until the sphere is entirely visible and then move the camera to the left until the sphere is only partially visible. Select `viewport.autoCulling = true`.

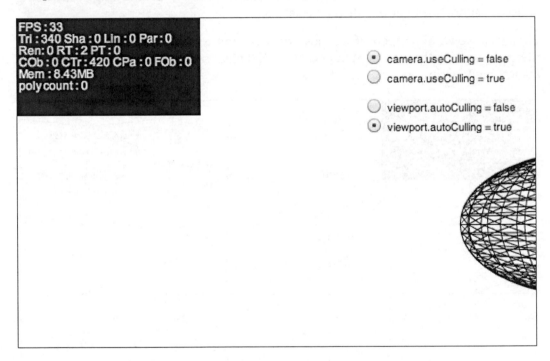

The **CTr** value in the statistics indicates that **420** triangles are culled. Apparently this was the number of triangles that were outside the viewport when the screenshot was taken.

Now move the camera even further to the left so that the entire sphere is outside the viewport and the frustum. Set `camera.useCulling` to `true`. You should see an empty viewport. The statistics now report that no triangles are culled. This is because the entire sphere has been culled, which is indicated by the **COb** value.

At the time of writing, **COb** indicated an incorrect number of culled objects due to a minor flaw in Papervision3D. You should divide it by 2 to get the correct value.

When moving the sphere around, also take a look at the first line of the statistics. **FPS** displays the frames per second, as executed by the Flash player. This is a good indicator of how well the demo performs. Notice that the more triangles are culled, the higher the frame rate will be.

Although culling is a common way to improve performance, it can also bring problems along. Let's see what they are and how we can deal with them.

Clipping

Clipping is a technique that solves a problem you may have seen before in 3D applications or demos, and that exists due to culling — an object comes too close to the camera, and because triangles are partially outside the frustum, they are culled and disappear. The following screenshot shows a sphere in Papervision3D that is very close to the camera. At the left side of the screenshot you can see that triangles have disappeared because of culling.

Clipping solves this problem by dividing the triangles that are too close to the camera into new triangles.

 Clipping is the process of dividing triangles of objects that are partially inside the frustum. Triangles that are divided into smaller ones will be rendered, whereas triangles that are outside the frustum will be thrown away.

Papervision3D includes the `FrustumClipping` class, which takes care of the clipping process described above.

Clipping in Papervision3D with FrustumClipping

The `FrustumClipping` class clips triangles that intersect with the side(s) of the frustum that you specify. But it does more than that:

- It makes sure that triangles outside the frustum are not drawn
- The vertices of these triangles are not projected, saving on performance

This may sound very promising, but `FrustumClipping` also has a drawback. The process of dividing triangles can get quite heavy, especially when all the triangles that intersect with the top, bottom, left, and right side of the frustum are being clipped. Fortunately, the class lets you specify the sides of the frustum that you want to include in the clipping process. The fewer sides you clip triangles against, the better your performance will be. Suppose you have only unwanted culling at the left side of the frustum because objects intersect with the left frustum plane, passing `FrustumClipping.LEFT` could be enough to fix these problems.

You need only the following line of code to put the class to work:

```
renderer.clipping = new FrustumClipping(FrustumClipping.NEAR);
```

You can add this line, for instance, at the top of your `init()` method. The constructor takes only one parameter, which is a static constant that specifies the planes or sides of the frustum you want the triangles to clip against. The following constants are available:

- `FrustumClipping.ALL`—all sides are included in the clipping process
- `FrustumClipping.NEAR`—only the near plane is clipped against
- `FrustumClipping.TOP`—only the top plane is clipped against
- `FrustumClipping.BOTTOM`—only the bottom plane is clipped against
- `FrustumClipping.LEFT`—only the left plane is clipped against
- `FrustumClipping.RIGHT`—only the right plane is clipped against

As said, including all planes in the clipping process is quite expensive. And generally spoken you won't need that. The most common situation that requires clipping is when an object comes too close to the near plane, so passing the `FrustumClipping.NEAR` constant will do for most clipping problems.

You can exclude an object from the clipping process as follows:

```
do3D.useClipping = false;
```

It keeps the object from being tested for clipping, which saves on calculations. Therefore, performance wise it's a good idea to set this property to `false` for objects that do not leave the frustum. However, the latter action is superfluous when `camera.useCulling` is set to `true`.

Seeing frustum clipping at work

To see frustum clipping at work, open the `FrustumClippingDemo.swf` in the download section. It shows a very simple scene, consisting of one plane that refers to a floor. The plane has a composite material applied to it, made up of color material and wireframe material so that we can see how the triangles are being divided when clipping is taking place. By default, the demo has no frustum clipping. Moving the camera by using the arrow keys shows a result that is not desired at all—triangles being culled too early. When you select `FrustumClipping.NEAR`, you see a much better result. Triangles do not disappear when coming close to the camera—instead they are divided into new ones. The following sequence of two screenshots shows two camera views that are very close to each other. In the left screenshot there is no clipping yet, whereas in the right screenshot the camera has moved a little more towards the plane and one of the triangles is divided.

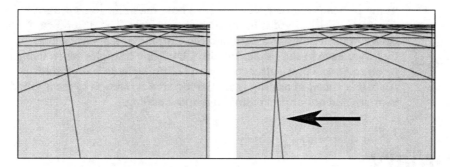

The third option in the demo, `FrustumClipping.ALL`, shows how triangles that intersect with the left and right plane are also clipped. Keep in mind that this is more costly than just near plane clipping.

Culling and clipping in the rendering pipeline

When using culling and clipping, every object is being tested to see if it needs to be culled and clipped. Let's take a look at the place of culling and clipping in the flow of each render:

```
Initialization
      v
   Culling
      v
  Clipping
      v
 Projection
      v
 Rendering
```

As you can see culling precedes clipping. But what does this mean? Suppose you have set `camera.useCulling` to `true` and also apply frustum clipping. After an object is tested on culling and Papervision3D decides that it needs to be culled, there is no need anymore to test it for clipping. However, if an object is not culled, it will be tested for clipping. Only the vertices that have stood both tests will be projected and finally drawn on the screen.

Use frustum clipping in conjunction with `camera.useCulling`. Setting this property to `true` has two benefits:

- Because objects outside the frustum are already culled, they will not be tested for clipping
- Objects entirely inside the frustum will not be tested for clipping

In the previous chapter we have seen how the `precise` property of materials also divides triangles into new ones. The difference between what `precise` does and the clipping process is the place that they have in the render pipeline. Dividing triangles when using `precise` takes place after culling and clipping have been tested. Also, it is aimed at adding more perspective correction to the applied textures and not at preventing unwanted culling.

Summary

The camera in Papervision3D represents a virtual point from which we view our scene. Because the `Camera3D` class inherits from `DisplayObject3D`, cameras have properties such as x, y, and z, and you can rotate them just like any other do3D.

The frustum is the 3D region that is rendered. Because it is cut off by the near and the far plane, which are imaginary planes perpendicular to the camera, the frustum is shaped like a truncated pyramid.

Zoom, focus, and field of view should be set while keeping in mind that they are inter-related. Focus is the equivalent of the `near` property and is defined by the distance from the camera to the near plane. Field of view is the vertical angle defined by the height of the viewport and the focus. The distance of the far plane to the camera can be set with the `far` property.

Papervision3D offers four types of camera—target, free, debug, and spring. The first two are the most commonly used types. The target camera is looking at a target, whereas the free camera is not. The debug camera provides built-in navigation and information about the settings of the camera. The spring camera is a special camera that smoothly follows an object, as if the camera is connected to the object by a spring.

The `lookAt()` method is an alternative for setting the target. You can make a camera look at a 3D object and vice versa. A 3D object can also have another 3D object as its target.

Six methods from `DisplayObject3D` have been discussed, which can be used for cameras as well as other do3Ds:

- `moveForward(),`
- `moveBackward()`
- `moveLeft()`
- `moveRight()`
- `moveUp();`
- `moveDown();`

We have seen several demonstrations of the features of different camera types and we have gone through some examples. We have also built some basic navigation to move an object or a camera.

Culling is the process of identifying what is totally or partially inside the frustum; what is outside will not be rendered. Papervision3D applies culling on two levels:

- Frustum culling per object
- Viewport culling per triangle

Frustum culling is set by the `camera.useCulling` property, viewport culling by `viewport.autoCulling`. Back-face culling does not render triangles that face away from the camera and is done automatically in Papervision3D.

Although culling saves a lot on performance, it also has a drawback. Triangles that intersect with one of the frustum planes may not be rendered correctly because culling takes place.

Clipping is the process of dividing triangles of objects that are partially inside the frustum and solves this culling problem. We have discussed how to use the `FrustumClipping` class, which enables us to clip triangles at the near, bottom, top, and side planes of the frustum.

In the next chapter, we will have a deeper look at how to animate cameras and 3D objects. We will discuss several tips and tricks and will examine how to use a **tweening engine** to create smooth transitions.

6
Moving Things Around

Animation is the illusion of motion and has always been an essential part of working with Flash. From web sites with animated menus, to games with advanced mouse interaction, Flash applications that have no animation at all are pretty rare. Animation keeps us, as users of the application or web site, interested, especially when we can move things on the screen ourselves.

Papervision3D has a lot to offer when it comes to user interaction. Although you could create predefined animation that the user cannot interact with, one of the great things about Papervision3D is that it is real-time. The user can freely interact with the objects in your scene because it has not been prerendered.

Although this chapter is mainly about moving things in your scene from one place to another, keep in mind that not all animation has to be in motion. Animation is also changing shapes, transparency, or color.

This chapter will cover the following topics:

- What can we move around and how
- Rotating objects
- Mouse interaction
- Animation using a tweening engine
- Keyboard interaction
- Camera perspectives

First, we will have a closer look at what kind of objects we can move around, and then briefly discuss *how* we can move things around. Next, we will walk through some examples that demonstrate how you can let the camera and 3D objects respond to the mouse. After that we will discuss a tweening engine, which enables you to create tweens in an easy way. The chapter will be concluded by a more elaborate example in which we will create advanced keyboard navigation. The example also demonstrates how you can implement multiple camera perspectives in your application.

What can we move around?

The first thing that may come to mind when discussing animation is moving the 3D objects that you can see in your scene. We have done that in previous chapters by using the local rotation properties. However, moving the camera is at least as powerful in enhancing the user's 3D experience and we can achieve pretty amazing effects by doing so. The third element that should not be overlooked is the point light, which also can be animated. Basically there are three types of objects we can move:

- The 3D objects that have a visual representation in the scene
- The camera
- The point light

The point light enables us to apply shading to objects and will be discussed in chapter 7. Now that we know *what* we're about to move, let's take a look at *how* we can move them.

How can we move things around?

We can think of animation as *change over time*. This can include not only motion, but also changing color, transparency, or even the shape of an object. There are two kinds of animation:

- Predefined animation
- Dynamic animation

Predefined animation is always the same, like a pre-rendered cartoon that you see on television or an animation you would make by creating frames on the timeline in the Flash IDE. Dynamic animation can be different every time you see it, either by implementing randomness (for example, changing the color of an object randomly every five seconds) or by user interaction (for example, scaling an object by clicking on it). Dynamic animation is created by code instead of using the timeline.

Animation by user interaction is always dynamic, but dynamic animation is not always triggered by user interaction. It can also be a predefined sequence of animations with some randomness that was built in by the developer of the program. The categorization into predefined and dynamic does not completely cover the range of possibilities. What if a user clicks on an object and then the object is doing a predefined animation? You could say that this is a predefined animation—the object always behaves the same—but it was triggered by user interaction.

Another distinction that can be made when discussing animation is the following:

- **Frame-based animation**
- **Time-based animation**

Frame-based animation means that the animation is dependent on the frame rate of the movie. In Chapter 2, we saw that if the frame rate is set to a higher value, animation will go smoother; and if the frame rate is set to a lower value, the animation may get jerky. A higher frame rate will also lead to a faster animation and a slower frame rate to a slower animation. Keep in mind that performance in Papervision3D is closely related to frame rate and to the capacity of the user's computer.

In **time-based animation**, the speed of the animation is dependent more on time and much less on frame rate. This type of animation can be accomplished by using the ActionScript 3.0 `Timer` class or a tween engine. Working with tween engines will be discussed in the *Animating with Tweener* section in this chapter. The benefit of time-based animation is that it will play at a more constant speed than frame-based animation, and relatively independent from the capacity of the user's computer. Suppose you create a multi-player game and use frame-based animation. Chances are that some users will see the animations in the game play faster than others, which may result in undesired differences between players. For example, when moving a player's avatar in a frame-based animation, some players would be able to move their avatar faster than others.

A user can interact with a Flash application in several ways. The two most common ones are:

- Mouse interaction
- Keyboard interaction

We have already seen some animation in previous chapters, for instance by using the aforementioned local rotation properties. By adding them in the render method, we incremented or decremented the rotation with a certain value at every frame, resulting in a predefined animation. The object was always turning in the same direction at a constant speed. So, it's about time we take a broader look at how to animate objects, cameras, and light, especially in interactions with the user. Before we do so, let's summarize the properties and methods we have used so far in order to animate objects, and explore some new ones and alternatives.

Rotating objects

In previous chapters, several methods and properties have been introduced to move and rotate objects. We have used the x, y, and z properties to set the position of objects and we have discussed the `moveForward()`, `moveBackward()`, `moveLeft()`, `moveRight()`, `moveUp()`, and `moveDown()` methods, which move an object in relation to its own axes. We also discussed the `lookAt()` method to make an object look at another object.

In many examples, we have set the `localRotationX`, `localRotationY`, and `localRotationZ` properties to rotate objects around their own x, y, and z-axis. However, when it comes to rotating objects, Papervision3D has more to offer.

Alternatives for local rotation—pitch(), yaw(), and roll()

The local rotation properties have their counterparts in the next three methods:

- `pitch()`: Rotates the object around its own x-axis (`localRotationX`)
- `yaw()`: Rotates the object around its own y-axis (`localRotationY`)
- `roll()`: Rotates the object around its own z-axis (`localRotationZ`)

Each method requires one argument that defines the rotation angle in degrees. Besides `pitch()`, `yaw()`, and `roll()` being methods instead of properties, there is another significant difference with local rotation.

Every time you set one of the local rotation properties to a new value, the *absolute* rotation is being set. Suppose you want to rotate a do3D around its y-axis. After the Flash player has run through the next two lines, the rotation will only be 10 degrees and not 45:

```
do3D.localRotationY = 35;
do3D.localRotationY = 10;
```

However, setting the value of the `localRotationY` counterpart `yaw()` sets the rotation of the object relative to its current rotation. If you add the next two lines in the `init()` method, the do3D would show a rotation of 45 degrees:

```
do3D.yaw(35);
do3D.yaw(10);
```

Mind you, adding the two lines after one another in the two previous examples would not make much sense in a real-world application. This was done only for demonstration purpose.

The `pitch()`, `yaw()`, and `roll()` methods can also be used inside the render method. For every frame, the value of the current rotation will be incremented or decremented by the angle that is passed as an argument. Putting the following line in the `render` method will show a do3D that is rotating around its own y-axis by one degree per frame:

```
do3D.yaw(1);
```

This results in the same rotation as placing the following line in the render method:

```
plane.localRotationY++;
```

The differences described above also hold good for `pitch()` as compared to `localRotationX` and `roll()` as compared to `localRotationZ`.

Another type of rotation—rotationX, rotationY, and rotationZ

Another way of rotating a do3D is setting the `rotationX`, `rotationY`, and `rotationZ` properties. They differ from local rotation in that they do not rotate the object around its own axes, but around the axes in local space (that is the axes of the parent's coordinate system):

- `rotationX`: Rotation of the object around the x-axis in local space
- `rotationY`: Rotation of the object around the y-axis in local space
- `rotationZ`: Rotation of the object around the z-axis in local space

 It is a common misconception to believe that the rotation properties define the rotation around the axes of the world space. However, they define the rotation around the axes in local space. Note that when an object is added directly to the scene, local space is equal to world space.

The `rotationX`, `rotationY`, and `rotationZ` properties are tricky to work with. Internally, Papervision3D uses **quaternions** for rotation, which are mathematical objects that contain a set of numbers. We will not discuss quaternions in detail. The good thing about them is that they can represent any rotation of a 3D object. The drawback is that they are quite hard to understand and read. In order to make it easier for users to work with rotation values, `rotationX`, `rotationY`, and `rotationZ` were added to the `DisplayObject3D` class. They are based on another way of representing rotation, called **Euler** angles, which again will not be discussed in detail. Just keep in mind that by using them you can simply set a rotation in degrees, which cannot be done when directly using quaternions. When you set a rotation, Papervision3D converts the Euler angles to a quaternion, which takes care of the rotation.

So far, so good. But the drawback of working with the rotation properties is that converting the quaternion back to Euler angles can lead to erroneous results. For instance, this leads to rotations that are returned as 180 instead of -180 degrees, resulting in objects or cameras that suddenly flip 180 degrees. Also, because Euler angles have a hierarchical structure, rotating an object around one axis after you have rotated it around another axis, may lead to unexpected results.

In order to stay on the safer side, it is best to avoid rotating around all of the three axes simultaneously, as that will easily lead to the problems described above.

The following URL shows a video, which explains what Euler angles are and the problems they can cause: `http://www.youtube.com/watch?v=zc8b2Jo7mno&feature=related`. The video also provides a solution to the **gimbal lock** problem by changing the hierarchy of axes, but this cannot be done in Papervision3D.

Quaternions can represent any rotation of a 3D object and allow objects to freely rotate over all of the axes without the problems described above. For more information on quaternions and Papervision3D, please visit `http://blog.zupko.info/?p=150`.

Let's take a closer look at the difference between rotation and local rotation by visualizing it.

Demonstrating the difference between rotation and local rotation

In order to see the difference between local rotation and rotation, open `RotationExample.swf`. You will see two small cubes that are both nested inside a bigger cube. You will also see visual representation of the axes of the cubes. Both small cubes (the children) are rotated around their own *x-axis* by 90 degrees.

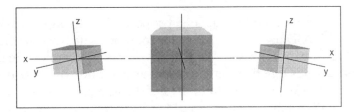

Clicking the left button shows what happens if we use `localRotationZ`. It starts and stops the rotation of the left cube around its own z-axis. Clicking on the right button rotates the right cube, not around its own z-axis but around the z-axis of the parent cube.

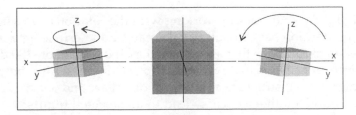

The naming of the local rotation properties is a little misleading, as local rotation of an object does not mean rotation in local space, but rotation around its own axes. The rotation properties refer to rotating in local space, relative to the coordinate system of the parent object.

We have discussed some new methods and properties that can be used to rotate objects. Let's move on to where the action is by studying two types of user interaction—mouse interaction and keyboard interaction.

Mouse interaction

There are several ways one can interact with Flash and Papervision3D applications. In this chapter, we will focus on mouse interaction and keyboard interaction. We will deal with keyboard interaction in the example at the end of this chapter. However, in this section, we will discuss some mouse interaction tricks—short pieces of code that you simply can put in the render method. When the user moves the mouse, this code will animate the camera or the object(s) in your scene. We will also take a look at how to orbit the camera around an object. **Orbiting** is moving the camera around an object over spherical coordinates, while keeping a constant distance to the object.

In order to demonstrate a sample of mouse interaction techniques, we will create a template class on which we will base the examples. Because we will make the mouse interact with a grid of planes, we will first build a grid as shown in the following screenshot:

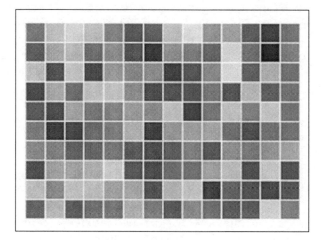

Place the following code in your document class, which we will use as the template:

```
package {
    import flash.events.Event;
    import flash.events.MouseEvent;
    import org.papervision3d.materials.ColorMaterial;
    import org.papervision3d.objects.DisplayObject3D;
    import org.papervision3d.objects.primitives.Plane;
    import org.papervision3d.view.BasicView;

    public class MouseInteractionTemplate extends BasicView
    {
        private var grid:DisplayObject3D;

        public function MouseInteractionTemplate()
        {
            stage.frameRate = 40;
            init();
            startRendering();
        }
        private function init():void
        {
            grid = new DisplayObject3D();
            scene.addChild(container);

            var numberOfColumns:int = 14;
            var numberOfRows:int = 10;
            var planeSize:int = 80;
            var planeSpacing:Number = 86;
            var centerOffsetX:Number = numberOfColumns  *
                            planeSpacing * 0.5 - planeSpacing * 0.5;
            var centerOffsetY:Number = numberOfRows * planeSpacing *
                                        0.5  - planeSpacing * 0.5 ;

            for(var i:uint = 0; i < numberOfColumns; i++)
            {
                for(var j:uint = 0; j < numberOfRows; j++)
                {
                    var plane:Plane = new Plane(new
                        ColorMaterial(Math.random() * 0xFFFFFF),
                        planeSize,planeSize);
                    plane.material.doubleSided = true;
                    plane.x = i * planeSpacing - centerOffsetX;
                    plane.y = j * planeSpacing - centerOffsetY;
                    grid.addChild(plane);
                }
            }
```

```
        }

        override protected function onRenderTick(e:Event=null):void
        {
            super.onRenderTick();
        }

    }
}
```

In the `init()` method, we create some local variables that define the attributes of the planes and the grid. We then create the grid in a nested `for` loop, which is an easy way to set the position of the planes. The center offset variables set the grid at the center of the viewport. The render method doesn't contain any animation code yet, so publishing this file shows the grid facing the camera frontally.

The first three examples will show how to add:

- Basic mouse interaction to move the camera
- Mouse interaction with easing to move the camera
- Mouse interaction with easing to rotate an object

Copy the code from the template we just created and paste it into the document class of a new project called `MouseInteractionExample`.

Because the explanation in the following examples assumes a stage size of 800 by 600 pixels, you need to set the stage to that size.

Getting the distance from the mouse to the center of the stage

Let's assume we want the position of the camera to respond to the position of the mouse. A common technique is to leave the camera at its initial position when the mouse is at the center of the stage and to change the position of the camera when the mouse moves away from the center. The farther the mouse moves from the center, the more the camera's position will alter. In order to create such an interaction, we need to know the distance from the x and y mouse positions to the center of the stage.

To keep track of the distances, we add two variables in the render method:

```
var xDist:Number = mouseX - stage.stageWidth * 0.5;
var yDist:Number = mouseY - stage.stageHeight * 0.5;
```

xDist keeps track of the distance between the x position of the mouse and the center of the stage, whereas yDist does this for the y mouse position. Let's take a closer look at the x distance. If mouseX is 0, the x distance will be the stage width divided by, which equals to -400 in our example class, as our stage width is 800. If the x position of the mouse is 800, the x distance will be 800 minus half the stage width, resulting in a value of 400.

Let's see how we can use this information when we want to move the camera on mouse movement.

Basic mouse interaction

In order to see basic mouse interaction, add the following after the line we just added to the onRenderTick() method:

```
camera.x = xDist;
```

Now publish the file. Moving the mouse to the left will move the camera to the left, moving it to the right will move the camera to the right. Let's analyze the line of code we just added with the explanation of xDist in the previous section in mind. Basically, it says that *the x position of the camera is the x position of the mouse minus half of the stage width*. So, the camera moves between -400 and 400, showing different perspectives of the grid.

Suppose we want to move the camera farther away from the grid. We can achieve this by increasing the range of the camera's x position. All we have to do is multiply the outcome by a positive number, for instance 2.

```
camera.x = xDist * 2;
```

Now, the range of the x position of the camera will be twice as big, from -800 to 800, resulting in the camera moving farther away from the grid. Because the grid is placed at the center of the scene — which is also the target for the camera — the camera will always look at the grid.

We can use similar code to move the camera in the y direction.

```
camera.y = yDist * 2;
```

If you publish the file now, the camera position will depend on the x and y position of the mouse. The following screenshot shows the grid and the mouse:

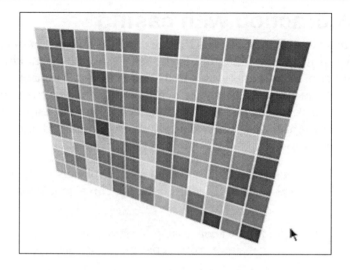

Keep two things in mind though. The first thing being minus and plus of the y-axis in Papervision3D are opposite to minus and plus of the y-axis in Flash. So, in order to make the camera respond to the mouse position the same way in the y direction, we have to inverse the calculated y value.

```
camera.y = -yDist * 2;
```

The other thing to keep in mind is that in our example, the stage height is smaller than the stage width. Therefore, the range covered by the y position of the mouse is also smaller—from zero to 600. This will result in a smaller range of the camera's y position. You could compensate for this by multiplying the original code by a higher number than 2. Having said that, the difference in camera range in the x and y direction is not a bad thing by definition. All the code we discuss in this section is highly dependent on personal preferences and needs. Playing around with some of the values can lead to outcomes that may or may not be to your liking.

The onRenderTick() method in our example should now look like the following:

```
override protected function onRenderTick(e:Event=null):void
{
    camera.x = xDist * 2;
    camera.y = -yDist * 2;
    super.onRenderTick();
}
```

The effect being achieved by this code is nice and can be quite useful, but it may need a little extra in order to make the camera motion look smoother. This is where **easing** comes into play.

Mouse interaction with easing

When you create a tween in the Flash IDE, you can add an **ease-in** or **ease-out** effect. **Easing out** is bringing an animation gradually to a standstill by making the object move slower and slower as it gets closer to its end position. You can also apply an ease-in equation at the start of a tween, which gradually makes the tween go faster until a given speed is reached. The well-known techniques of easing are by no means limited to object animation; you can also apply easing equations to changes in color, transparency, or shape.

When working with Papervision3D, we cannot put 3D objects in the timeline and tween them, let alone ease-in or out. Fortunately, we can also achieve easing by code.

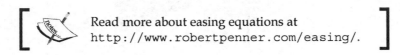

Read more about easing equations at
`http://www.robertpenner.com/easing/`.

Let's go back to our `MouseInteractionExample`. Comment the two lines you just added, and which updated the x and y coordinates of the camera. You can also remove them, but it may be a good idea to keep them for later reference.

Also, add the following class properties:

```
private var easeOut:Number = 0.3;
private var reachX:Number = 0.5;
private var reachY:Number = 0.5;
private var reachZ:Number = 0.05;
```

Add the following line in the `onRenderTick()` method:

```
camera.x += (xDist - camera.x * reachX) * easeOut;
```

Publish the file and you should see a much smoother camera motion, gradually slowing down when you don't move the mouse. We increment the x position of the camera in every frame with a value that, once we stop moving the mouse, gets smaller and smaller until it is 0, resulting in a camera that does not move anymore. Mind you, the incrementing value never becomes exactly 0, but for Flash it comes close enough to keep the camera within the same pixels. The higher you set the `reachX` class property, the lower the camera's reach in the x direction will be and the closer it will stay to the grid. The `easeOut` variable defines the strength of the ease-out equation—the higher you set it, the sooner the camera will come to a standstill.

We can apply the same type of easing for the y direction of the mouse and camera.

```
camera.y += (yDist- camera.y * reachY) * easeOut;
```

We haven't yet looked at making the z position of the camera respond to the mouse position. In combination with the previous line of code, the following line strongly enhances the 3D experience when moving the mouse in the y direction:

```
camera.z += (-mouseY * 2 - camera.z ) * reachZ;
```

The closer the y position of the mouse is to the viewport center, the closer the camera moves to the grid, again using an ease-out.

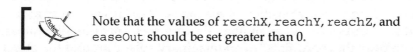 Note that the values of reachX, reachY, reachZ, and easeOut should be set greater than 0.

We have seen two examples of mouse interaction, one with and the other without an ease-out. Another popular mouse interaction technique is orbiting the camera around an object. Before we discuss orbiting, we will first take a look at how to rotate an object by moving the mouse.

Using mouse interaction to rotate an object

Suppose you do not want the mouse to interact with the camera, but with an object in your scene, for instance, rotate the grid in our example when the mouse moves. First, we add the following two class properties that define the amount of rotation of the grid around the x and y axis:

```
private var rotX:Number = 0.5;
private var rotY:Number = 0.5;
```

Comment the lines that you added in the previous section, which updated the x, y, and z coordinate of the camera. Now, add the following lines:

```
grid.rotationX = yDist * rotX;
grid.rotationY = xDist * rotY;
```

Publish the project. You should see the grid rotating based on the mouse position. Replacing the above two lines with the following code results in a rotation that eases out:

```
grid.rotationX += (yDist * rotX - grid.rotationX) * easeOut;
grid.rotationY += (xDist * rotY - grid.rotationY) * easeOut;
```

The current values of rotX and rotY enable you to rotate the grid multiple times. Changing them to a lower value such as 0.1 will rotate the grid, but won't show its backside. The given values are illustrative, so feel free to experiment. When you use the above code, the easeOut value should stay between 0 and 1.

This rotation example uses `rotationX` and `rotationY` values, meaning that the grid rotates around the axes in local space, which in this case is the equivalent of world space. In order to make the grid rotate around its own axes, you can replace the rotation properties with their local rotation counterparts.

Orbiting the camera around an object

So far we have moved the camera in the x and y direction, and in one example in the z direction depending on the y position of the mouse. We also saw how to rotate an object around its x and y axes when moving the mouse. By **orbiting** the camera, we mean moving it over the coordinates of an imaginary sphere around the object. This is a popular technique that can be achieved by using the `camera.orbit()` method. In order to demonstrate this method, we will build two examples:

- Orbiting by moving the mouse
- Orbiting by dragging the mouse

While the first example is pretty straightforward, the second one is a little more elaborate. Both examples will have code with and without easing. We will create a new project called `OrbitExample` and again use the code from `MouseInteractionTemplate` as a starting point.

Orbiting the camera by moving the mouse

First, let's add some class properties:

```
private var rotX:Number = 0.3;
private var rotY:Number = 0.3;
private var camPitch:Number = 90;
private var camYaw:Number = 270;
```

In order to define the mouse distance between the x and y mouse position and the stage center, we add the following two lines in the render method:

```
var xDist:Number = mouseX - stage.stageWidth * 0.5;
var yDist:Number = mouseY - stage.stageHeight * 0.5;
```

Add the following code right after the previous two lines of code, which adds basic orbiting:

```
camPitch = yDist * rotX + 90;
camYaw = xDist * rotY + 270;
camera.orbit(camPitch,camYaw);
```

`camPitch` and `camYaw` set the rotation around the x and y-axis respectively. The value `90` is added to `camPitch` and value `270` to `camYaw` so that the camera faces the grid frontally when the mouse is at the center of the stage. Setting `rotX` and `rotY` to a higher value results in more rotation around the x and y-axis respectively.

When the camera orbits around the object, its distance to the object is the initial distance between the two. In our example, the camera initially has the default z value of -1000 and the grid is positioned at the origin (0, 0, 0), resulting in a distance of 1000 units. Publishing the file should result in the camera responding to the mouse position, orbiting around the grid.

The `orbit()` method takes four parameters as shown in the next table:

	Parameter	Data type	Default value	Description
1	`pitch`	`Number`	—	Rotation around the x-axis.
2	`yaw`	`Number`		Rotation around the y-axis.
3	`useDegrees`	`Boolean`	`true`	Whether to use degrees or radians for `pitch` and `yaw`.
4	`target`	`DisplayObject3D`	`null`	An optional target to orbit around. If no target is passed, the camera target is used. If `camera.target` equals `null`, the camera will orbit around the origin of the scene (0, 0, 0).

We did not need to pass the grid as the target in our example because it is centered at the origin of the scene.

In order to add an ease-out to the orbiting camera, replace the lines that set `camPitch` and `camYaw` with the following:

```
camPitch += ((yDist  * rotX) - camPitch + 90) * easeOut ;
camYaw += ((xDist  * rotY) - camYaw + 270) * easeOut ;
```

Again, setting `rotX` and `rotY` to a higher value results in more rotation of the camera, and `easeOut` defines the strength of the easing effect. Keep the `easeOut` value between `0` and `1`.

Orbiting the camera by dragging the mouse

The code in the previous section orbits the camera around the grid by simply moving the mouse. Another popular way to orbit the camera is dragging the mouse, but the code to accomplish this is a little more advanced.

We will continue to work in `OrbitExample`. Comment the code you have added to the render method in the previous section, leave the existing class properties untouched, and add the following class properties to them:

```
private var isOrbiting:Boolean;
private var previousMouseX:Number;
private var previousMouseY:Number;
private var easePitch:Number = 90;
private var easeYaw:Number = 270;
private var easeOut:Number = 0.1;
```

Dragging the mouse implies that we want the stage to listen to mouse events. Therefore, add the following code at the top of the `init()` method:

```
stage.addEventListener(MouseEvent.MOUSE_DOWN,onMouseDown);
stage.addEventListener(MouseEvent.MOUSE_MOVE,onMouseMove);
stage.addEventListener(MouseEvent.MOUSE_UP,onMouseUp);
```

The mouse down handler looks like the following:

```
private function onMouseDown(e:MouseEvent):void
{
    isOrbiting = true;
    previousMouseX = e.stageX;
    previousMouseY = e.stageY;
}
```

`isOrbiting` will serve as a flag to keep track of whether the mouse is down or up, as we want to orbit the camera only when the mouse is down. `previousMouseX` and `previousMouseY` are set to the x and y mouse position and will be used in the mouse move handler to constantly store the mouse positions from the previous frame.

Next, we add the mouse up handler, which simply sets the flag back to `false` so that the camera will stop orbiting.

```
private function onMouseUp(e:MouseEvent):void
{
    isOrbiting = false;
}
```

The `onMouseMove()` event handler looks like the following:

```
private function onMouseMove(e:MouseEvent):void
{
    var differenceX:Number = e.stageX - previousMouseX;
    var differenceY:Number = e.stageY - previousMouseY;

    if(isOrbiting){
        camPitch += differenceY;
        camYaw += differenceX;

        previousMouseX = e.stageX;
        previousMouseY = e.stageY;
    }
}
```

Let's take a closer look at what this event handler does. First of all, two variables are set to store the difference between the current and the previous mouse position for every frame. Then an `if` statement evaluates whether the mouse is down or not. If it is, then we increment the value of two variables, `camPitch` and `camYaw`, with the difference that we just stored. For example, when you move the mouse to the left, the difference in the x direction between the current and the previous mouse position will be negative, resulting in a lower `camYaw` value. At the end of the `if` statement, we set the previous mouse position to its current position so that in the next frame `previousMouseX` and `previousMouseY` will be up-to-date again.

To drag and orbit the camera without easing, we just need to add the following line to the render method:

```
camera.orbit(camPitch,camYaw);
```

In order to add easing, replace the previous line with the following code:

```
easePitch += (camPitch - easePitch) * easeOut;
easeYaw += (camYaw - easeYaw) * easeOut;
camera.orbit(easePitch,easeYaw);
```

Change the value of `easeOut` in order to define the strength of the ease-out; setting it lower leads to a stronger easing effect.

Clamping the camera rotation

You may have noticed that when you orbit around the x axis, the scene seems to flip every now and then. However, it is not the scene or the grid that flips, but the camera. What is happening here is that the camera passes the top or the bottom of the grid, and because it is upside down from that moment on, it flips back to its normal orientation This actually is an expected result caused by the `lookAt()` method, which keeps the camera looking at the origin of the scene. The following illustration shows a side view of the grid and the path that the camera follows when the mouse is moved upward in the y direction. When the camera passes the top of the grid, it flips back to its normal orientation.

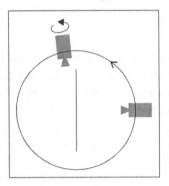

If you don't want the camera to pass the object, as you don't want to show the camera flip or for other reasons, you can clamp it. **Clamping** means that you build in a limit, keeping the camera within a certain angle and position, and hence preventing it from passing a certain point. The next illustration shows a camera that orbits upward or downward in the y direction, but never passes the top or bottom of the grid:

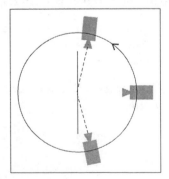

When the camera orbits, its rotation and position are related. So, by limiting the rotation you also limit the camera's position. In order to prevent the x rotation from getting higher than, for instance 85 degrees and lower than -85 degrees, we need to limit the value of camPitch in the if statement inside the onMouseMove() handler as follows:

```
if(camPitch < 5) camPitch = 5;
if(camPitch > 175) camPitch = 175;
```

With these settings, dragging the camera downward in the y direction will rotate it no less than -85 degrees, as shown in the following screenshot:

Dragging it upward in the y direction will keep the x rotation of the camera within 85 degrees.

In the examples we have just seen, we discussed how you can use mouse interaction to move the camera and how to rotate a 3D object, by adding code inside the render method. The following section of this chapter will discuss another approach—animation with a tweening engine.

Animating with Tweener

Tweening engines are sets of libraries that make it easy to do animation by code, including all kinds of easing in and out. With only a couple lines of code (or even a single line as we will see), a tweening engine lets you move objects around with smooth transitions. Tweening engines are used widely in 2D Flash applications. Fortunately, they can also be used in combination with libraries such as Papervision3D.

There are many open source tweening engines on the Internet and even more discussions about which one is the best, the fastest, the lightest, or the most convenient to work with. A list of some of the more popular engines is as follows:

- gTween: It has some nice features such as smart rotation, rotating objects in the shortest direction, even in 3D. It is developed by Grant Skinner. See http://www.gskinner.com/libraries/gtween/.
- TweenLite: It is small in kilobytes and known to be very fast. It is developed by Jack Doyle. See http://blog.greensock.com/tweenliteas3/.

- TweenMax: It is very versatile, but has a relatively steep learning curve. It is also developed by Jack Doyle. See `http://blog.greensock.com/tweenmaxas3/`.
- Tweener: It has easy-to-use syntax and is widely used in the Flash community. It is developed by Zeh Fernando. See `http://code.google.com/p/tweener/`.

In this book, we will use Tweener, which was developed by Zeh Fernando. It has gained a lot of credibility in the Flash community and the code is very simple to use. Tweener is not per se better or faster than any of the other engines, as all of them are well built and will run smoothly for every animation you have in mind. The subtle differences between the engines can mainly be found in the syntax that they use and the extra features that they offer, making the choice for a tweening engine a matter of personal preferences and taste.

Downloading Tweener

In Chapter 1, we walked through the process of getting started with Papervision3D and discussed several ways to download the source code. Tweener also offers an SVN download, a ZIP file, and an SWC file. We will only walk through the process of downloading and working with the ZIP file, but using SVN and downloading the SWC are also valid options and the process is similar to what we have done in Chapter 1.

Let's get started:

- Create a folder somewhere on your computer. Give it a name that refers to the Tweener library, we will name it `tweener_source`.
- Go to `http://code.google.com/p/tweener/`.
- Look for **Featured Downloads** and download the as3 ZIP file. This book uses the `tweener_1_33_74_as3.zip` file.
- Extract the ZIP file; inside is a folder called `caurina`. Save this folder inside the `tweener_source` folder we just created.
- In Flash, set the global path to the `tweener_source` folder the same way as you have set the global path to the Papervision3D `src` folder. The following screenshot shows the path set in Flash CS3 on the left and in Flash CS4 on the right:

Classpath:	Source path:
Macintosh HD:papervision3d_source:src	/papervision3d_source/src
Macintosh HD:tweener_source	/tweener_source

- In Flex Builder and Flash Builder, every time you create a new project or import an existing one, you must set the path to the `tweener_source` folder the same way as you set the path to the Papervision3D `src` folder. Your list of additional source folders in both authoring tools should look like the following:

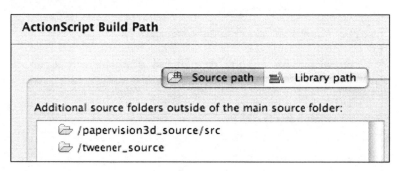

Similar to what we have seen in animating within the render method, we can tween all kinds of objects with a tweening engine — cameras, light sources, 3D objects and their properties such as transparency and scale. We will look at two examples:

- Tweening 3D objects
- Tweening the camera

Let's see what it takes to tween a 3D object in Papervision3D.

Tweening 3D objects

We will create an example that demonstrates how to use Tweener to tween a cube's rotation. The cube has bitmap file materials applied to its front, back, left, and right side. When you click the cube, it will rotate 90 degrees counter clockwise so that the adjacent left side is shown. Our aim is to create a smooth transition with easing and to get familiar with how Tweener works.

If we want to tween a cube we first need to create one. The following example is called `TweenerCubeExample` and creates a cube with bitmap textures applied to four of its sides. It assumes that you have an `assets` folder inside your `src` folder with four images named as `pic1.jpg`, `pic2.jpg`, `pic3.jpg`, and `pic4.jpg`.

```
package {
    import caurina.transitions.Tweener;
    import flash.events.Event;
    import org.papervision3d.events.InteractiveScene3DEvent;
    import org.papervision3d.materials.BitmapFileMaterial;
```

```
import org.papervision3d.materials.utils.MaterialsList;
import org.papervision3d.objects.primitives.Cube;
import org.papervision3d.view.BasicView;

public class TweenerCubeExample extends BasicView
{
    private var cube:Cube;

    public function TweenerCubeExample()
    {
        super(stage.stageWidth,stage.stageHeight,true,true);
        stage.frameRate = 40;

        init();
        startRendering();
    }

    private function init():void
    {
        var frontMat:BitmapFileMaterial = new BitmapFileMaterial
                                        ("assets/pic1.jpg");
        frontMat.interactive = true;
        var backMat:BitmapFileMaterial = new BitmapFileMaterial
                                        ("assets/pic2.jpg");
        backMat.interactive = true;
        var leftMat:BitmapFileMaterial = new BitmapFileMaterial
                                        ("assets/pic3.jpg");
        leftMat.interactive = true;
        var rightMat:BitmapFileMaterial = new BitmapFileMaterial
                                        ("assets/pic4.jpg");
        rightMat.interactive = true;

        var materialsList:MaterialsList = new MaterialsList();
        materialsList.addMaterial(frontMat,"front");
        materialsList.addMaterial(backMat,"back" );
        materialsList.addMaterial(leftMat,"left" );
        materialsList.addMaterial(rightMat,"right" );

        cube = new Cube(materialsList,320,320,240,4,4,4);
        cube.addEventListener(InteractiveScene3DEvent.
                        OBJECT_CLICK,onClick);
        scene.addChild(cube);

        camera.z = -700;
    }

    private function onClick(e:InteractiveScene3DEvent):void
    {
        //code to be added here
    }
```

```
override protected function onRenderTick(e:Event=null):void
{
    super.onRenderTick();
}
    }
}
```

There is nothing new here, so the code should look familiar. Notice that we do not apply materials to the top and the bottom as the cube will face the camera frontally and we will see only the front, back, left, and right side. We already added an interactive scene event listener to the cube that listens for mouse clicks, but the accompanying handler method is still empty. This is where Tweener will be put into service.

In order to use the Tweener library, we need to import it.

```
import caurina.transitions.Tweener;
```

In the onClick() method, add the following code. Don't forget to import DisplayObject3D.

```
var tweenObject:DisplayObject3D = e.displayObject3D;

Tweener.addTween(tweenObject, {localRotationY:tweenObject.
                          localRotationY + 90, time:1});
```

Publishing the file and clicking the cube should animate the cube 90 degrees counter clockwise with an ease-out transition applied to it. The following screenshot was taken in the middle of a tween:

Looking at the line of code, there are a couple of things worth mentioning.

Tweener knows only static methods, so we don't need to create new instances in order to tween an object. We use this syntax to call a tween:

```
Tweener.addTween(the object that should be tweened,
                {the Tweener parameters that you want
                 to set, as well as the properties that
                 should be tweened and their values});
```

As you can see, we basically pass two arguments in the `addTween()` method. The first is the object that should be tweened. This parameter is of the `Object` type where all classes inherit from.

The second argument is also of the `Object` type, and defines Tweener parameters —such as time and transition type—as well as the properties that you want to tween, along with their values. To specify parameters you use the in-line object notation, for example: `{rotationY:90, alpha:1}`.

Let's take a look at the first argument, defining the object we want to tween, which in our example is the cube. We could have just passed `cube`, as we defined our cube as a class property, and thus have access to it outside the method where it was instantiated. But we can also use the parameter that is passed from the event listener to the event handler, something we have done in our example.

Now, let's look at the second argument we pass in the `addTween()` method. Enclosed within curly brackets, we pass one Papervision3D property (`localRotationY`) and one parameter that Tweener has (`time`):

- `localRotationY:tweenObject.localRotationY + 90`: Sets the local y rotation of the cube. Just passing `localRotationY:90` will not do. Every time you set a local rotation, it is being set as an absolute value. Therefore, every time we tween the cube, we add 90 degrees to its current local rotation.
- `time:1`: The duration of the tween in seconds.

You may wonder how we can pass the `localRotationY` property into an external class that knows nothing about Papervision3D. Tweener was built in such a way that you can tween any numeric public property of any class, allowing us to tween Flash's `DisplayObject` properties such as `alpha`, `x`, and `y`, as well as properties specific to Papervision3D such as `z` and local rotation properties.

When you click the cube while it is still tweening, our example reveals a bug. The cube will start the next tween before the current one is finished. Suppose the cube is in the middle of a tween and the rotation at that moment is 30 degrees. Clicking the cube will start a new tween and when this tween is complete, the cube will be rotated 120 degrees (30 + 90), resulting in a cube that is not facing the camera frontally anymore when the last tween is complete.

In order to prevent Tweener from starting a new tween before the current tween is finished, we can call a Tweener method, `isTweening()`, which returns whether an object is tweening or not. The method requires one argument, which is the object that you want to check. It returns `true` when the object is tweening and `false` otherwise. The syntax looks like the following:

```
Tweener.isTweening(target);
```

So, let's put the method that calls the tween inside an `if` statement as follows:

```
if (!Tweener.isTweening(e.displayObject3D))
{
    var tweenObject:DisplayObject3D = e.displayObject3D;
    Tweener.addTween(tweenObject,{
        localRotationY:tweenObject.localRotationY + 90,
        time:1
    });
}
```

Now, when the user clicks the cube, we first check whether the cube is tweening, and if it is not, we execute the tween call.

 Tweener has many methods and properties which are handy and easy-to-use. They are described in the online documentation: `http://hosted.zeh.com.br/tweener/docs/en-us/`.

Our next example will implement more features of Tweener, this time to animate the camera.

TweenerCube

Tweening the camera over a curved path

Tweening the camera often leads to interesting results that keep the user focused on your application. In the next example, we create two cylinders. When the user clicks on the stage, the camera , which initially looks at the scene from one side, tweens to a new position and looks at the scene from the other side. Clicking on the stage again moves the camera back to the initial position, again with an easing tween. The paths that the camera follows are not straight, but curved.

Let's first create a new project named `TweenerCameraExample` and its accompanying document class. The class does the following:

- Instantiates a point light and two cylinders with flat shade material
- Adds the cylinders to the scene
- Positions the camera

The point light and flat shade material are new. Flat shade material is a material type that enables you to apply shading to an object. The point light defines the origin of the light source. Both will be discussed in detail in Chapter 7, along with other type of shading materials. For now, we will not go into how they work, as this example is about tweening the camera and not so much about the cylinders. The flat shade materials result in one cylinder that looks yellow and another that looks red.

```
package {

    import caurina.transitions.Tweener;

    import flash.events.Event;
    import flash.events.MouseEvent;

    import org.papervision3d.lights.PointLight3D;
    import org.papervision3d.materials.shadematerials.
                                    FlatShadeMaterial;
    import org.papervision3d.objects.primitives.Cylinder;
    import org.papervision3d.view.BasicView;

    public class TweenerCameraExample extends BasicView
    {
        public function TweenerCameraExample()
        {
            super(stage.stageWidth, stage.stageHeight);
            stage.frameRate = 40;

            init();
            startRendering();
        }

        private function init():void
        {
            stage.addEventListener(MouseEvent.CLICK,
                            stageClickHandler);

            var light:PointLight3D = new PointLight3D();
            light.y = 1000;

            var yellowCylinder:Cylinder = new Cylinder(new
                        FlatShadeMaterial(light,0xFFCC00,0x000000)
                        ,20,120,20,20);
            yellowCylinder.z = -100;
```

```
var redCylinder:Cylinder = new Cylinder(new
    FlatShadeMaterial(light,0xFF0000,0x000000)
    ,30,120,20,20);
redCylinder.z = 100;

scene.addChild(yellowCylinder);
scene.addChild(redCylinder);

camera.x = -50;
camera.y = 100;
camera.z = -300;
}

private function stageClickHandler(e:MouseEvent):void
{
    //code to be added here
}

override protected function onRenderTick(e:Event=null):void
{
    super.onRenderTick();
}

    }
}
```

We added the stage event listener but left the event handler blank. Before we fill it up with some code, let's first add a class property to our class:

```
private var pointOfView:String = "yellow";
```

This variable will be used to check on which side of the scene the camera is when the user clicks on the stage. Initially, the camera is set at the side where the yellow cylinder is located.

We also add a method that sets this property, which we will be calling from within the stage event click handler.

```
private function setPointOfView(view:String):void
{
    pointOfView = view;
}
```

Now, we are ready to add code to the `stageClickHandler()` method, which handles the stage click events. Again, we use the `isTweening()` method, because we don't want the camera to start a new tween when it is still tweening. So let's start by adding an `if` statement that checks this:

```
if (!Tweener.isTweening(camera))
{

}
```

Inside the `if` statement, we add a `switch` statement that evaluates on which side of the scene the camera is.

```
switch(pointOfView)
{
    case "yellow":
        //first Tweener call to be added here
        break;
    case "red":
        //second Tweener call to be added here
        break;
}
```

Before we add the first tween that is executed when the stage is clicked and the value of `pointOfView` is `yellow`, we need to add the following line to our `init()` method:

```
CurveModifiers.init();
```

It allows us to set a curved path for the camera. In order to use it, we need to import:

```
import caurina.transitions.properties.CurveModifiers;
```

The tween, which is significantly longer than the one we wrote in the previous example is highlighted in the following code that shows the updated `stageClickHandler()` method:

```
private function stageClickHandler(e:MouseEvent):void
{
    if (!Tweener.isTweening(camera)){
        switch(pointOfView){
            case "yellow":
                Tweener.addTween(camera,{
                    x:-80,
                    y:150,
                    z:300,
                    _bezier:{x:-1000, y:800, z:1000},
                    time:2,
                    transition:"easeInOutQuad",
                    onComplete:setPointOfView,
                    onCompleteParams:["red"]
                });
                break;

            case "red":
            //second Tweener call to be added here
            break;
        }
    }
}
```

Publishing the project should show you two cylinders with the camera at the side of the yellow cylinder, and clicking on the stage moves the camera to the other side. Note that the camera is always looking at the origin of the world axis (0, 0, 0) as we did not set a camera target.

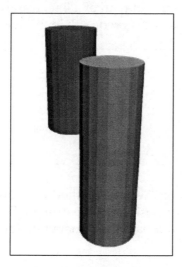

The transition takes places over a curved path and it is easing in and out. Let's examine the Tweener method to find out how this is achieved. First, we pass the object we want to tween, which in this example is the camera. Then, a set of parameters along with their values are passed:

- `x,y,z`: Define the coordinates where we want the camera to be when the tween is complete.

- `_bezier`: Defines the curved path that the camera follows during the tween. We will take a closer look at this in a bit. Notice the underscore.

- `time`: As in the previous example, the duration of the tween in seconds. The value type is `Number` and it defaults to `0` when not defined.

- `transition`: Defines the type of transition. The value is a string. An overview of all transition types can be found in the Tweener's documentation under **Transition Types**. The default value is `easeOutExpo`.

- `onComplete`: Calls the method passed as the value immediately after the tween is complete. In our example, `setPointOfView()` is called.

- `onCompleteParams`: Passes a list of parameters to the `onComplete` method; you can pass one or multiple parameters as an array. In our example, we pass `red` as the sole argument. The syntax is `onCompleteParams :[arg1,arg2,arg3]`.

Let's take a closer look at how the curved path of the camera tween is accomplished. In order to enable objects to move along a curved path, Tweener makes use of quadratic Bézier curves. If you are familiar with drawing software programs such as Illustrator, you have probably used quadratic Bézier curves a lot. They are handy equations that determine the curved path of a line, using one or more **control points**. The following illustration shows a curved path in 2D space, using one control point:

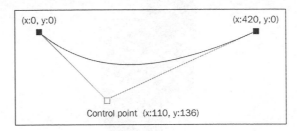

Looking back at the code in our Tweener method you can see that we added an x, y, and z coordinate to set the end position of the camera. We also set a control point in 3D space that defines the curved path the camera will follow.

```
x:-80
y:150
z:300
_bezier:{x:-1000, y:800, z:1000}
```

Although, it's quite hard to visualize exactly what a curved 3D path will look like when you define it, setting the Bézier control point parameters and experimenting with them allow you to create complex tweens with all kinds of curved paths. The following is a graphical representation of the control point we just set and the curved camera path that is defined by it:

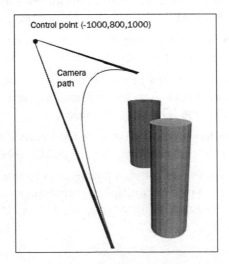

In order to finish the example, we add the other tween call inside the `switch` statement, executed when the point of view is evaluated to be `red`, in other words when the camera is on the side where it faces the red cylinder:

```
Tweener.addTween(camera,{
                          x:-50,
                          y:100,
                          z:-300,
                          _bezier:{x:600, y:2000, z:-1000},
                          time:2,
                          transition:"easeInOutExpo",
                          onComplete:setPointOfView,
                          onCompleteParams:["yellow"]
                          }
              );
```

This tween sends the camera back to the side where the yellow cylinder is located, by passing the initial camera settings of x, y, and z. Again, we added a Bézier control point to define the curved path for the camera to follow. This time we used another type of transition, which gives us a different kind of ease.

For more information about Bézier curves, see `http://en.wikipedia.org/wiki/Bézier_curve`.

For more information about Bézier curves in Tweener, see `http://zehfernando.com/2007/the-search-for-the-perfect-bezier-tweening-solution/`.

{Ex.} TweenerCamera {Ex.}

Example—the galaxy extended

In the previous chapter, we built a basic keyboard navigation to fly around a paper plane, demonstrating the spring camera. What goes for mouse interaction also goes for keyboard interaction—you can make it as smooth as you like. The navigation we created wasn't particularly smooth, although the spring effect helped. But the spring camera is built into Papervision3D and using it has some limitations, unless you were to tweak or extend the code.

In the next couple of paragraphs, we will not only build keyboard navigation that runs more fluently, we will also demonstrate how to implement several camera perspectives as seen in games.

We will build an application based on the example from Chapter 5 in which we created a galaxy of planes, a sphere that represents the earth, and a paper plane that we can fly around. The application will have the following features:

- Advanced keyboard navigation for the paper plane
- Dynamic zoom
- Multiple camera perspectives

Although the example will demonstrate some aspects relevant to gaming applications, it will by no means be a "game", as that would easily go outside the scope of this book. The intention of the example is merely to illustrate the features mentioned above, which are closely related to working with Papervision3D.

In previous examples, we have written all of our code in the document class. This is fine for small projects and quite handy when you want to demonstrate something quickly. But when your application gets more complicated, it is good practice to keep your document class as clean as possible and use extra classes to represent several aspects of the application.

In our example, we will write a separate class for:

- User input
- The galaxy of planes
- The player (paper plane)
- Controlling the camera

The user input class will handle the input from the user. This can be clicking the mouse or pressing keys on the keyboard. Inside the galaxy class, the galaxy along with the earth sphere will be created. The player class creates a paper plane and updates its position and rotation. Finally, we need a class to control the camera.

But first, let's create a new project called `GalaxyExample`. Copy and paste the code from `BookExampleTemplate` into your document class and rename the class definition name and the constructor. For now, this will do; we will finish the document class later in this section in order to initialize our application.

Creating a class for user input

We will start by creating a class that handles the user input and name it `UserInputHandler`. It will be based on the code that we wrote for our basic navigation of the paper plane. Remember that we added two event listeners to check *whether* there was input from the keyboard and two accompanying handler methods—`keyDownHandler` and `keyUpHandler`—to check *which* keys were pressed and released. In the handlers we used the flags `keyRight`, `keyLeft`, `keyForward` and `keyBackward` to set the state of each key.

If we take that code from `SpringCameraExample` in Chapter 5 and put it in a separate class named `UserInputHandler`, it would look like this:

```
package {
    import flash.display.Stage;
    import flash.events.KeyboardEvent;
    import flash.ui.Keyboard;

    public class UserInputHandler
    {
        public static var keyRight:Boolean;
        public static var keyLeft:Boolean;
        public static var keyForward:Boolean;
        public static var keyBackward:Boolean;

        public function UserInputHandler(stage:Stage)
        {
            stage.addEventListener(KeyboardEvent.KEY_DOWN,
                                   keyDownHandler);
            stage.addEventListener(KeyboardEvent.KEY_UP,
                                   keyUpHandler);
        }

        private function keyDownHandler(e:KeyboardEvent):void
        {
            switch(e.keyCode)
            {
                case "W".charCodeAt():
                case Keyboard.UP:
                    UserInputHandler.keyForward = true;
                    UserInputHandler.keyBackward= false;
                    break;

                case "S".charCodeAt():
                case Keyboard.DOWN:
                    UserInputHandler.keyBackward = true;
                    UserInputHandler.keyForward = false;
                    break;

                case "A".charCodeAt():
                case Keyboard.LEFT:
                    UserInputHandler.keyLeft = true;
                    UserInputHandler.keyRight = false;
                    break;

                case "D".charCodeAt():
```

```
                    case Keyboard.RIGHT:
                        UserInputHandler.keyRight = true;
                        UserInputHandler.keyLeft = false;
                        break;
                }
            }

            private function keyUpHandler(e:KeyboardEvent):void
            {
                switch(e.keyCode)
                {
                    case "W".charCodeAt():
                    case Keyboard.UP:
                        UserInputHandler.keyForward = false;
                        break;

                    case "S".charCodeAt():
                    case Keyboard.DOWN:
                        UserInputHandler.keyBackward = false;
                        break;

                    case "A".charCodeAt():
                    case Keyboard.LEFT:
                        UserInputHandler.keyLeft = false;
                        break;

                    case "D".charCodeAt():
                    case Keyboard.RIGHT:

                        UserInputHandler.keyRight = false;
                        break;
                }
            }
        }
    }
```

Save the class in the src folder of your project, which is the same folder that holds the document class. Before we add more code to the class, notice that the constructor holds a parameter of the Stage type. This will be passed from our document class so that we gain access to the stage. For this purpose, we also imported the Stage class.

The class we have created listens only to the keyboard changes. If we want it to handle mouse clicks as well, we need to import the MouseEvent class and add the following two event listeners to the constructor:

```
stage.addEventListener(MouseEvent.MOUSE_DOWN,mouseDownHandler);
stage.addEventListener(MouseEvent.MOUSE_UP,mouseUpHandler);
```

The accompanying event handlers look like the following:

```
private function mouseDownHandler (e:MouseEvent):void
{
    mouseDown = true;
}

private function mouseUpHandler (e:MouseEvent):void
{
    mouseDown = false;
}
```

They set a variable `mouseDown`, which we have not yet defined. Add the following line right after the other class properties:

```
public static var mouseDown:Boolean;
```

Notice that we are using public static variables for all of the flags in this class. This makes it easy for us to access them from within other classes, which we will see in a bit. Our `UserInputHandler` class is fine for now, so let's go to the next one.

Creating a class for the galaxy

The class that holds the properties and methods to create the galaxy of planes and the Earth sphere is named `Galaxy`. It should also be saved in the `src` folder and looks like the following:

```
package
{
    import org.papervision3d.events.FileLoadEvent;
    import org.papervision3d.lights.PointLight3D;
    import org.papervision3d.materials.BitmapFileMaterial;
    import org.papervision3d.materials.ColorMaterial;
    import org.papervision3d.objects.primitives.Plane;
    import org.papervision3d.objects.primitives.Sphere;
    import org.papervision3d.objects.DisplayObject3D;

    public class Galaxy extends DisplayObject3D
    {
        private var earthSphere:Sphere;

        public function Galaxy()
        {
            init();
        }

        private function init():void
```

```
    {
        var material:BitmapFileMaterial = new
            BitmapFileMaterial("assets/earth.jpg");
        material.precise = true;

        earthSphere = new Sphere(material,200,24,16);
        addChild(earthSphere);

        for(var i:uint = 0; i <  150; i++)
        {
            var plane:Plane = new Plane(new
                ColorMaterial(Math.random() * 0xFFFFFF),
                50,50, 1,1);
            plane.material.doubleSided = true;
            addChild(plane);
            plane.x = Math.random()*20000 - 10000;
            plane.y = Math.random()*1500 - 750;
            plane.z = Math.random()*20000 -10000;
            plane.localRotationY = Math.random() * 180 - 90;
        }
    }

    public function update():void
    {

        earthSphere.localRotationY += 0.2;
    }

  }
}
```

The code should look familiar, as it is quite similar to what we have seen in the examples of the debug and spring camera. There are three things worth mentioning though.

First of all, there should be a folder named assets in your src folder with earth.jpg. We have used the earth.jpg already in the examples of the debug and spring camera, but it can also be found in the download section, in the assets folder of the project with the same name.

Secondly, the class extends DisplayObject3D. We add the Earth sphere (and after that the galaxy planes) by using:

```
addChild(earthSphere);
```

So, we are not adding the sphere to the scene directly, but to this class, which actually is a do3D object. When we later instantiate the Galaxy class in the document class, we create an instance of this class that has the Earth sphere and the galaxy planes as its children. This way we do not need to have access to the scene.

Finally, we have added an `update()` method in which the local rotation of the Earth sphere is updated. Making this method public allows us to access it from the document class. Let's continue by creating a separate class for our paper plane.

Creating a class for the paper plane

The class that will create the paper plane is called `Player`. Save it like the other classes in the `src` folder.

```
package
{
    import org.papervision3d.materials.shadematerials.
                                        FlatShadeMaterial;
    import org.papervision3d.objects.DisplayObject3D;
    import org.papervision3d.objects.primitives.PaperPlane;
    import org.papervision3d.lights.PointLight3D;

    public class Player extends DisplayObject3D
    {
        private var paperPlane:PaperPlane;

        public function Player()
        {
            init();
        }

        private function init():void
        {
            var light:PointLight3D = new PointLight3D();

            var paperPlaneMat:FlatShadeMaterial = new
                FlatShadeMaterial(light,0xFFFFFF,0x848484);
            paperPlaneMat.doubleSided = true;
            paperPlane = new PaperPlane(paperPlaneMat);

            addChild(paperPlane);

            z= -1000;
            y = 300;
        }

        public function update():void
        {
        }

    }
}
```

Again, the code should look familiar. All we have to do is create a paper plane and apply a flat shade material to it. As mentioned earlier, chapter 7 will discuss this material type in detail, along with the `PointLight3D` class.

In the example we made for the spring camera, we called a `moveObject()` method from within our render method, checking at every frame the state of the `keyForward`, `keyBackward`, `keyRight`, and `keyLeft` flags. If a state was true, we acted upon it by moving or steering the flying object. In our current example, we will be doing something similar, but we will add two things:

- When the paper plane stops moving, it will do so with an ease-out transition
- When the user steers it, the paper plane will roll or rotate a little over its own z-axis, giving the steering animation a smooth and realistic touch.

The following screenshot shows the paper plane taking a right turn while rotating a little over its z-axis:

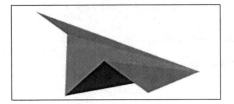

First, let's take care of moving the paper plane forward and backward by adding the following code in the `update()` method of our newly-created `Player` class:

```
if(UserInputHandler.keyForward)
{
    topSpeed = 50;
}
else if(UserInputHandler.keyBackward)
{
    topSpeed = -30;
}
else
{
    topSpeed = 0;
}

speed -= (speed - topSpeed) * 0.1;
moveForward(speed);
```

In order to make this code work, we have to declare two variables at the top of the class.

```
private var topSpeed:Number = 0;
private var speed:Number = 0;
```

The speed variable stands for the actual speed that the paper plane has at any moment. It is passed into the moveForward() method, which moves the Player object forward in the direction of its own z-axis. Notice that we do not use a moveBackward() method. If you pass a negative number to moveForward(), the object will move backward.

The topSpeed variable is set to 50 when the up arrow key is pressed, to -30 when the down arrow key is pressed, and to 0 when neither of the two keys is pressed. It is the speed that the Player object will eventually have when the accompanying state is true.

For example, if the speed at a given moment is 50 and the user releases the up arrow key, the topSpeed is set to 0. In the next frame, the speed will be 45 because it decrements by a value of 5:

$(50 - 0) * 0.1 = 5$

In the frame after that, the speed will be 40.5 because it decrements by a value of 4.5:

$(45 - 0) * 0.1 = 4.5$

In the frame after that, the speed will be 36.45.

You can see that the speed value diminishes in steps that get smaller and smaller, resulting in an ease-out. Remember that the values in this example are idealized for demonstration purpose. The speed value will never be exactly the same as the topSpeed value because of the paradox that is essential for this kind of easing equation. In the example of setting the topSpeed value to 0, the speed will never get there because in every new frame we multiply the speed by 0.1.

The equation used here also results in a gradual acceleration when the paper plane starts to move, but it is not what one would call a classical ease-in. That would require more code and would lead to very small steps at the start of the motion that get bigger with every frame, until the desired value has been reached. The equation we use gives us steps that get smaller at every frame until the desired value has been reached (again, actually we never really get there), but it serves us well enough as we will see when we are ready to publish the project.

You may have noticed that the conditions evaluated in the if statements start with UserInputHandler, followed by the Boolean variable that we created in the UserInputHandler class. Defining variables as public static allows us to access them from any other class. Both the Player class and the class that will control our camera (to be built in the next section) need to constantly know what the user input is. An easy solution to achieve this is to make use of public static variables.

Let's continue with the code that handles the steering of the paper plane. Add the following lines in the update() method right after the code we have just discussed:

```
if (UserInputHandler.keyRight)
{
    if (topSteer < 30)
    {
        topSteer = 30;
    }
}
else if (UserInputHandler.keyLeft)
{
    if (topSteer > -30)
    {
        topSteer = -30;
    }
}
else
{
    topSteer -= topSteer * 0.1;
}
steer -= (steer - topSteer) * 0.1;
yaw(speed * steer * 0.002);
paperPlane.localRotationZ = steer;
```

In order to make use of the variables topSteer and steer, we define them at the top of the class.

```
private var topSteer:Number = 0;
private var steer:Number = 0;
```

But what happens in the code we added? First, we check whether the right or left key is being pressed. If the right key is pressed and if the topSteer value is below 30, we set it to 30, which will be the maximum local z rotation of the paper plane. Vice versa, we set this value to -30 when the left arrow key is pressed. If neither of the two is pressed, we lower the topSteer value in steps that get smaller and smaller, resulting again in an ease-out animation.

The steer value is used both for the roll effect—the paper plane rotating around its own z-axis when steering—and for steering the paper plane to the left and right. The roll is caused by adjusting the localRotationZ property of the paper plane, while the steering is handled by the yaw() method on the parent of the paper plane.

This is interesting. Why would we use the moveForward() and yaw() method of the parent of the paper plane, but not the localRotationZ property of the paper plane itself? Couldn't we just use all of the three on the paper plane or on its parent? Why does the paper plane need a parent anyway?

What we want to achieve in this example is that the paper plane should be able to keep flying on the same imaginary horizontal plane, not changing its y position relative to the global scene, but at the same time we should have the freedom to:

- Move it forward and backward
- Steer it left and right
- Roll it over its z-axis

If you would try to do all this by using only one object that is not nested into a parent object, you would then be out of luck or into a lot of coding.

In order to illustrate this problem, open NestingDemo.swf. The paper plane that you see is added to a blank do3D. Think of this blank do3D—the parent—as the equivalent of the Player object in our example. The axes that you see represent the coordinate system of the local space of the paper plane—the child.

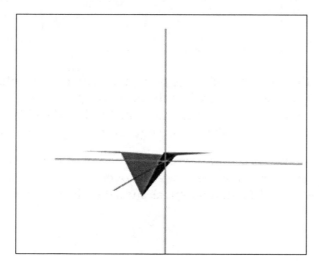

The parent is rotating around its y-axis using the `yaw()` method and the paper plane, being the child, seems to rotate along according to its local space. Selecting the buttons sets either the `localRotationZ` of the paper plane or the `localRotationZ` of its parent to `30`. Although this value is arbitrary, it is also the maximum roll that we want the player object to have in our example. Selecting the parent to perform the local z rotation results in two things:

- The parent rotates locally around its z-axis
- The parent's y-axis also changes relative to world space. It was pointing perpendicular to the world's x-axis, but now clearly has an angle greater than 0.

The following screenshot illustrates this result:

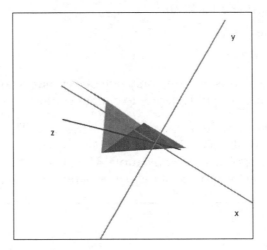

As a consequence, the paper plane's nose now points up or down most of the time. The previous screenshot was taken when the nose was pointing down. You can imagine that if we now use the `moveForward()` method on the object, it would fly downward, which is something that we do not want to happen in our example.

Setting the local z rotation of the paper plane instead of its parent solves the problem. Now, we have a paper plane that has a rotation over its own z-axis, while the axes of the parent still have their default rotation, as shown in the following illustration:

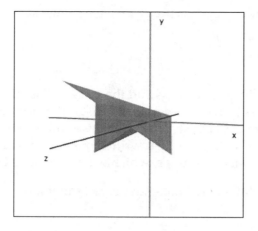

This gives us the freedom to work with rotation on two levels. While we can set the local z rotation of the paper plane to achieve the desired roll effect, we are also free to move the parent forward and backward and steer it (rotating around the y axis) without messing things up. This is why our Player class extends DisplayObject3D, and not the PaperPlane class directly. Instantiating a Player object will give us a parent object that we can fly and steer. It also gives a child object—the paper plane itself—to add the roll effect to without changing the y position of our player object relative to world space.

Now that we have completed our Player class, let's see what things look like so far and initialize the application by adjusting the document class.

Initializing the application in our document class

We have already created the document class at the beginning of this walkthrough. Now, add the following two class properties:

```
private var galaxy:Galaxy;
private var player:Player;
```

Add the following code in the init() method:

```
galaxy = new Galaxy();
scene.addChild(galaxy);

player = new Player();
scene.addChild(player);
```

```
var userInput:UserInputHandler = new UserInputHandler(stage);

camera.target = player;
camera.z = -1500;
camera.y = 400;
```

This code instantiates the `Galaxy` class and the `Player` class that we just created and adds both instances to the scene. Also, we instantiate the `UserInputHandler` class and pass the stage to its constructor so that we can use the stage event listeners that we have added. As we have not yet written our camera controller class, we temporarily add some camera settings, which we will remove later on.

Finally, add these two lines in the `onRenderTick()` method:

```
galaxy.update();
player.update();
```

The first line calls the `update()` method in the `Galaxy` class. This method is responsible for rotating the Earth sphere. The second line calls the `update()` method in the `Player` class, which takes care of moving and steering our player object.

Publishing our application should give a view of the galaxy, the Earth sphere, and the paper plane. We should now be able to fly the paper plane by using the arrow keys, see the easing when stopping the object, and the roll effect when we steer it.

You will also notice that the paper plane quite easily moves away from the camera, a result that may not be very useful when building a game with a 3D object that you want to fly or drive. This is where our camera controller class comes in.

Controlling the camera

The `CameraController` class will take care of setting some initial camera properties and updating the camera position when the user presses certain keys that we will define in a while. We will add five features as follows:

- A **dynamic zoom** to smoothly zoom in and out on the player object
- A **3D person camera** to place the camera right behind the player object and follows it

- A **first-person camera** to replace the player object by the camera, as if the player object represents the user's eyes
- An option to generate random perspectives from different angles
- An option to return to the initial target camera

The initial CameraController class should be saved in the src folder together with the other classes and looks like the following:

```
package
{
    import org.papervision3d.core.proto.CameraObject3D;

    public class CameraController
    {
        private var camera:CameraObject3D;
        private var player:Player;
        public function
            CameraController(camera3D:CameraObject3D,player3D:Player)
        {
            camera = camera3D;
            player = player3D;
            init();
        }
        private function init():void
        {
            camera.z = -1500;
            camera.y = 400;
            camera.focus = 20;
            camera.far = 20000;
            camera.target = player;
        }
        public function update():void
        {
        }
    }
}
```

The two parameters that the constructor takes and that will be passed from the document class are the player and the camera, enabling us to access both. We will see in a bit why we also want to have access to the player in this class.

In the init() method, we have added some basic camera settings. You can now remove the temporary camera settings that we added earlier in the init() method of the document class. The update() method is still empty and will be called from within the render method in the document class just like we called the update() methods in the Galaxy and Player classes. Let's add some code to create our first feature—the dynamic zoom.

Adding dynamic zoom

Add the following lines in the update() method of the CameraController class:

```
var cameraZoom:Number;
if(UserInputHandler.mouseDown)
{
    cameraZoom =  200;
}
else
{
    cameraZoom =  40;
}
camera.zoom -= (camera.zoom - cameraZoom) * 0.1;
```

We have already added mouse down and mouse up listeners in our UserInputHandler class and we make use of them here. The local cameraZoom variable defines the desired zoom value, 200 when the mouse is being pressed and 40 when the mouse is released. The line that follows the if-else statement makes the camera zoom in and out smoothly. The zoom in consists of steps that get smaller until the desired zoom is reached. The zoom out is a classical ease-out and provides steps that get smaller at every frame and end up around 40.

In order to see the dynamic zoom in action, we first need to complete the document class. To be able to use the camera controller class from within the render method, we assign an object to a class property:

```
private var cameraController:CameraController;
```

Add a new line to the init() method, which should look like the following:

```
private function init():void
{
    galaxy = new Galaxy();
    scene.addChild(galaxy);

    player = new Player();
    scene.addChild(player);

    var userInput:UserInputHandler = new
    UserInputHandler(stage);

    cameraController = new CameraController(camera,player);
}
```

The line we added creates our camera controller and passes the camera and the player to the constructor in order to have access to both of them in the `CameraController` class. That is why the new line should be placed *after* the instantiation of the camera and the player.

Our finished `render` method is shown in the following screenshot. By calling the camera controllers `update()` method we will update the zoom of the camera.

```
override protected function onRenderTick(e:Event=null):void
{
    galaxy.update();
    player.update();
    cameraController.update();
    super.onRenderTick();
}
```

If you now publish the project, you should be able to fly the paper plane and at the same time use your left mouse button to dynamically zoom in and out.

 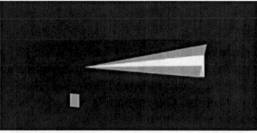

Although we can zoom in to the paper plane whenever we want, it still tends to move away from the camera quite easily. Obviously, this is a result of the camera not moving. Let's see how we can make the camera follow the paper plane.

Adding a third-person camera

The third-person camera perspective is used a lot in games. It places the camera right behind the player's avatar, which can be a visual representation of almost anything, from warriors or aliens to cars or spaceships, or a paper plane as in our example.

We will be pressing the *1* key on the keyboard in order to tell our application that we want to switch to the third-person perspective. Add the following right after the other public static variables in the `UserInputHandler` class, which in the `update()` method of `CameraController`:

```
public static var camMode:String;
```

Add the following to the `keyDownHandler()` method:

```
case "1".charCodeAt():
    camMode = "thirdPerson";
    break;
```

As we will implement multiple camera modes, the `CameraController` class continuously needs to know the current mode. This can be achieved by adding a `switch` statement in the `update()` method. The `switch` statement will be extended later, when we add other perspectives. But first, add the following right after the zoom code in the `update()` method of `CameraController`:

```
switch(UserInputHandler.camMode)
{
    case "thirdPerson":
        camera.copyTransform(player);
        camera.moveBackward(400);
        camera.moveUp(100);
        player.visible = true;
        break;
}
```

Before we take a closer look at what happens in the code that we just added, let's publish the project. You should still be able to fly the object around. Pressing the *1* key on your keyboard however, changes the view to the third-person camera perspective. The camera is placed behind the paper plane and will follow it, no matter where you are heading.

Take a look at the code inside the `switch` statement we just added. It evaluates the camera mode and when the mode is set to `thirdPerson`, the following happens:

The camera copies the position as well as the rotation of the `Player` instance, using the `copyTransform()` method, which copies not only the position of another do3D, but also its rotation and scale.

After the camera copies the position and rotation of the `Player` instance, it moves backward by `400` and upward by `100` units. This gives us the actual third-person view. With the third-person camera, the object remains visible, unlike the first-person camera where we will set the `visible` property to `false`. Let's see why.

Adding a first-person camera

In the world of gaming, the first-person camera is used just as often as the third-person camera. Many games offer the option to switch between the two, making the game more interesting, and that is exactly what we will do. The process we will walk through is similar to how we added the code for the third-person perspective.

Add the following to the `keyDownHandler()` method in the `UserInputHandler` class:

```
case "2".charCodeAt():
    camMode = "firstPerson";
    break;
```

This time we will use the 2 key on the keyboard to switch to the first-person perspective. Now, open the `CameraController` class and add the following code inside the `switch` statement that is part of the `update()` method:

```
case "firstPerson":
    camera.copyTransform(player);
    camera.moveBackward(1);
    player.visible = false;
    break;
```

Let's first see what this code does by publishing the project. If all went well, you can now fly around the paper plane, zoom in and out, select the third-person perspective, and by pressing the 2 key on your keyboard, select the first-person perspective. You can also switch between the third and the first-person camera perspectives.

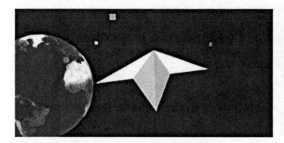 

The code that handles the first-person perspective is quite similar to that of the third-person perspective, so let's see what the similarities and differences are. Again, the camera copies the position, rotation, and the scale of the `Player` instance. This time however, we do not want the camera to see the object. Think of the first-person perspective as if it replaces the player's avatar or as being the player's eyes. However, we do move the camera a little backward, to prevent a `lookAt` error that Papervision3D throws when you make an object look at another object that is on the exact same position. Finally, we turn off the visibility of the `Player` instance, so we will not see it.

Adding random camera perspectives

Another known trick that can give a compelling effect is switching to a random perspective. The effect can be enhanced by adding a slow motion to the camera, in its x, y, or z direction.

When the user presses the keyboard key that generates the new random perspective (in this case the 3 key), we want to make sure only one perspective is being shown instead of switching to a new perspective at every frame, which would be an unwanted result. In the UserInputHandler class, we need a flag to keep track of this:

```
public static var randomCamActive:Boolean;
```

Inside the switch statement in the keyDownHandler() method, we add the code that sets the camera mode to the random camera perspective:

```
case "3".charCodeAt():
        camMode = "randomCam";
        break;
```

The switch statement in the keyUpHandler() also needs to be extended, by adding the following:

```
case "3".charCodeAt():
        randomCamActive = true;
        break;
```

When the user releases the 3 key, the flag we created is set to true.

Now, let's go to the CameraController class and add two class properties:

```
private var axes:Array = ["x","y","z"];
private var axis:String = axes[0];
```

Add the following code inside the switch statement of the update() method in the CameraController class:

```
case "randomCam":
        if(UserInputHandler.randomCamActive)
        {
            camera.x = player.x + (Math.random() * 1000 - 500);
            camera.y = player.y + (Math.random() * 1000 - 500);
            camera.z = player.z + (Math.random() * 1000 - 500);

            axis= axes[Math.floor(Math.random() * 3)];
            UserInputHandler.randomCamActive = false;
            player.visible = true;
        }
        else
        {
            camera[axis] += 2;
        }
        break;
```

Before we examine the code, publish the project and see what it leads to. All of the features we have implemented still work, and on top of that we can create random camera perspectives by using the 3 key on the keyboard.

Switching between the 1, 2, and 3 keys (and also using the zoom feature) can be fun, resulting in compelling changes of view and an instant feeling of being in the middle of a game. Also notice that when we select a new random perspective, the camera slowly moves over its x, y, or z-axis, contributing to the effect of switching perspectives.

Let's run through the code that handles the random perspective. A new perspective will only be shown if the `randomCamActive` Boolean is `true`. The x, y, and z coordinate of the camera are set by creating a random number between -500 and 500 and by adding this number to the x, y, and z coordinates of the player.

In order to move the camera slowly over one of the axes, we randomly select one of the strings in the `axes` array. Suppose the first node of the array is selected, which is the x string. By using the array access operator, we increment the value of the camera's x property in order to move the camera by 2 units per frame over the x-axis:

```
camera["x"] +=2;
```

Switching back to the default view

We have implemented several camera perspectives and a zoom feature. It would be nice though if we could return to our default camera perspective, set the camera to its initial position, and make the paper plane visible again, in case we are switching back from the first-person perspective. Open up the `UserInputHandler` class and add the following lines inside the `switch` statement in the `keyDownHandler()` method to achieve this:

```
case "4".charCodeAt():
    camMode = "defaultCam";
    break;
```

The user will have to press the 4 key on the keyboard in order to return to the default camera mode, which we have named `defaultCam`.

In the `update()` method of the `CameraController` class, we add the following inside the `switch` statement:

```
case "defaultCam":
        player.visible = true;
        camera.z = -1500;
        camera.y = 400;
        break;
```

Now, when the user presses the 4 key, the camera will switch to its initial position.

We have just finished our application. As said, it is not a complete game, but the intention is to demonstrate how to create a more sophisticated keyboard navigation to drive or fly an object, how to work with different camera perspectives, and how to create a dynamic zoom; features that you could implement in games and other types of applications built with Papervision3D. The complete project can be found in the download section of this book.

[Ex.] GalaxyExample [Ex.]

Summary

Animation is the illusion of motion. It can be predefined, meaning the user cannot interact with it; or it could be dynamic, which is created by code and allows users to interact with the animation. You can move around 3D objects, the camera, and the light source. But animation is not only about moving things; changing the color, transparency, or shape of an object is also animation.

We have walked through several pieces of code that you can add in the render method and that enables the user to interact with the scene. In these examples, the concept of easing was introduced.

We have discussed Tweener, one of the available open source tweening engines, which can be used in combination with Papervision3D. A tweening engine lets you create and control tweens in an easy way. Tweener allows you to use quadratic Bézier curves, which are equations that define curved paths, meaning that we can tween the camera (or other objects) over a predefined curved path.

We have extended the basic keyboard navigation for the paper plane, adding advanced keyboard navigation with easing equations. Also, a roll effect was added when steering the paper plane. In the same example, we implemented a dynamic zoom and several camera perspectives that are widely used in gaming applications.

In the next chapter, we will learn about shading, which is the process of adding levels of shade to the materials on an object, giving the object a better illusion of depth and reality.

7

Shading

In Chapter 4, we've learned how to use materials on objects. By choosing the right material, we can make a simple object appear very detailed. Shading adds several levels of shade to the materials on an object, giving a better illusion of depth and reality. There are a number of shading types built into Papervision3D that make use of shading. These types are known as **shaders**.

This chapter covers the following topics:

- Introduction to shading
- Basic shading and lighting
- Bumping your materials
- Reflection mapping

Introduction to shading

Shading is the process used to simulate the interaction of light with a material on a 3D object. With the presence of light, lighter and darker areas on an object can be calculated. Imagine a cube, made of one single color. When all sides use the same color, your object is barely recognizable as a cube, just like the following screenshot illustrates:

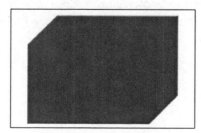

Because you were just told that it is supposed to be a cube, you can see that it is with some imagination. However, if you were to see this image outside the context of this book, chances are that you wouldn't have recognized it as a cube. Have a look at what happens when we apply a shader to the cube's materials:

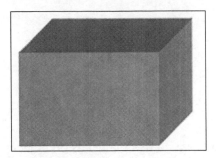

That looks more like a cube, right? Depending on the angle between each side of the object and a light source, the color used on the side brightens or darkens. To achieve this you could define a different material color for each side of the cube. Depending on your situation, that might be good enough. However, materials with real-time shading applied can add more realism to your objects. This is especially true when the parameters that define the look of an object change, due to an animated light source, object, or camera. Depending on its changed position or rotation, the appearance of a shaded object changes.

The cube in the above image has a solid fill color on each side. Colors are ideally determined per pixel of each triangle, resulting in perfect and very smooth shading. Unfortunately, doing this at real time for every pixel is very CPU intensive. Therefore, more efficient shaders were invented. These are less precise, but still add a certain level of realism to your object.

Shading also includes bump maps and environment maps. Bump maps can be used for adding the illusion of relief to your 3D objects and environment maps for reflection of the environment on a 3D object.

In order to better understand the parameters of each shading type, a demo has been included in the download of the book, named ShadingTypesDemo.swf. This demo shows each shading type, including a simple interface that allows you to adjust its parameters.

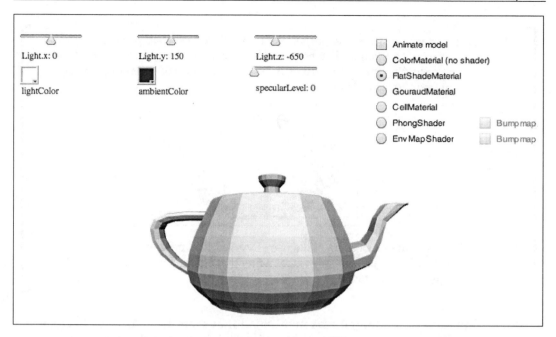

The famous Utah teapot has been added as the model in this demo. Besides being a standard object to explain 3D concepts, its sub objects form several types of 3D shapes. This makes the Utah teapot a good 3D object to see how each shader affects the way your object looks. It is a good idea to play around with the settings of each shading type while they are discussed in the following paragraphs.

There are two ways shading can be added:

- By a shade material to shade an object completely based on lighting
- By a shader to apply shading on an existing material

These concepts will be explained in more detail in the following section

Flat shading

Flat shading is the most basic and lightweight type of shading. By default, the `ShadingTypesDemo.swf` opens with **FlatShadeMaterial** selected. With flat shading, each triangle of an object will be shaded by using a color fill. The color is determined by the angle between a triangle's **surface normal** and the position of the light. As there's no interpolation between the colors used on a triangle and the triangle next to it, this will result in hard edges and a very blocked look and feel, which seems even stronger because of the 3D model that we use. The model has pairs of triangles, which share the same surface normal. This also gives the incorrect impression that flat shading is based on polygons instead of triangles.

A surface normal is the perpendicular vector of a surface, which in this example is a triangle. The normal determines the orientation of a surface. The following image illustrates the surface normals of six triangle pairs that seem to form a polygon together:

More advanced shaders make use of **vertex normals**, which is an averaged triangle surface normal value that is based on the neighboring triangles of a vertex.

In the introduction to shading, it was mentioned that there are two ways to create a shader. The differences and usage can best be explained with the help of the following example that uses flat shading:

- When you want to flat shade your object based on a color, you should use a `FlatShadeMaterial` instance. This type can be applied directly as a material for any 3D object, and is completely defined by lighting parameters. Therefore, we call this a color-based shader.

- In case you want to flat shade an instance of `BitmapMaterial`, you should use a `FlatShader` instance in combination with a `ShadedMaterial` instance. A `ShadedMaterial` instance applies a flat shader to a bitmap material. The `ShadedMaterial` instance can then be applied as your object's material. The appearance of the object is defined by a combination of lighting and a bitmap, which makes this material type bitmap based.

Movie materials are bitmap materials too

Note that all materials that inherit from BitmapMaterial are bitmap materials. This means that instances of MovieMaterial, MovieAssetMaterial, BitmapAssetMaterial, and VideoStreamMaterial can have shading applied to them. Due to a bug in Papervision3D at the time of writing this book, instances of BitmapFileMaterial can't be shaded.

To keep this chapter consistent, we'll use a bitmap for all our shaded materials in each example. Feel free to replace that with the material types of your choice. As long as they inherit from BitmapMaterial, you should not have any problems (except when working with BitmapFileMaterial instances)

Note that all other shading types, which will be explained later in this chapter, have similar color-based and bitmap-based shaders available.

To show the usage of both flat shading types, we will create two spheres—one with color-based shading, and the other with bitmap-based shading. A circular moving light will demonstrate how the changing light source affects the appearance of the two spheres.

FlatShadeMaterial for color-based shading

This example has quite a few extra classes that need to be imported. We will discuss each new class as soon as we instantiate it.

```
import flash.display.Bitmap;
import flash.display.Loader;
import flash.events.Event;
import flash.net.URLRequest;

import org.papervision3d.lights.PointLight3D;
import org.papervision3d.materials.BitmapMaterial;
import org.papervision3d.materials.shadematerials.FlatShadeMaterial;
import org.papervision3d.materials.shaders.FlatShader;
import org.papervision3d.materials.shaders.ShadedMaterial;
import org.papervision3d.objects.primitives.Sphere;
```

A light and an angle value are needed as class properties so that we can have access to them when we animate the light in circles on enter frame.

```
private var light:PointLight3D;
private var angle:Number = 0;
```

The only available light object in Papervision3D is a **point light**. This basically is a point somewhere in 3D space that defines the origin of a light source. Each shader in Papervision3D requires a point light. Papervision3D does not provide other types of lights such as spotlights and directional light. To add a point light we need to create an instance of `PointLight3D`. We'll do this inside the `init()` method.

```
private function init():void
{
    light = new PointLight3D(true);
    light.z = 0;
    light.y = 300;
    scene.addChild(light);
```

As you can see, we set the first parameter, a Boolean `showLight`, to `true`. By doing this, we add a do3D to the `PointLight3D` instance, representing the light, which allows us to add a visual representation of the light to the scene, just like we add any other do3D. This is especially useful for debugging purposes, as we can see where the light is positioned in 3D space. The `PointLight3D` inherits from `DisplayObject3D`, so a point light has `DisplayObject3D` properties and methods such as `localRotationX`, `yaw`, `lookAt()`. This is a bit misleading, as changing most of these properties will not affect the behavior of your light on the shader. Keep in mind that only the position of the point light is relevant for shading. This means that only methods and properties that relate to the position of the light—such as `x`, `y`, and `z`—affect the manner in which the shader is applied.

With the light defined, we can continue creating a color-based flat shading material, by instantiating `FlatShadeMaterial`, which has four parameters available at instantiation. Let's take a look at what they stand for.

	Parameter	Data type	Default value	Description
1	light	LightObject3D	—	A reference to a `PointLight3D` instance.
2	lightColor	uint	0xFFFFFF	A 32-bit hexadecimal color value, which will be used as the light source color.

	Parameter	Data type	Default value	Description
3	ambientColor	uint	0x000000	A 32-bit hexadecimal color value, which defines the ambient color. This adds constant non-directional lighting and is best visible on triangles that don't reflect light coming from a point light, which is when a triangle is not facing the light source.
4	specularLevel	uint	0	A number between 0 and 255, defining shininess or specularity of the material. The higher this value, the more light will be absorbed by your object. By default, this is set to 0, which results in reflecting as much light as possible.

 Both lightColor and ambientColor can be specified as 32-bit colors. Most of the time these are specified as 24-bit colors, as you can't really use alpha on a light. In some rare situations, you might want to set one of these to using 32-bit colors.

At instantiation of FlatShadeMaterial, we pass our light instance, give it a white color, a red ambient color, and a specular level of 100.

```
var shadeMaterial:FlatShadeMaterial = new FlatShadeMaterial
                            (light,0xFFFFFF,0xFF0000,100);
```

To get familiar with how light color, ambient color, and specular level affect the look of your object, you can open ShadingTypesDemo.swf and play around with these values.

 In Papervision3D you can have only one light object as the source for a shader. Although it is possible to add multiple lights to a scene, only one light is used per shader.

An instance of `FlatShadeMaterial` can be applied the same way as you would apply a regular material. The logical next step is to create a 3D object and add `shadeMaterial` to it as the material.

```
var sphere:Sphere = new Sphere(shadeMaterial,250,10,10);
sphere.x = -300;
scene.addChild(sphere);
```

FlatShader for bitmap-based shading

As mentioned earlier, there are two ways to add flat shading. We've now successfully created a flat-shaded sphere, completely based on lighting information. The second part of this example is to create a bitmap-based shaded material. To use the bitmap, we first need to load it manually.

```
var imgLoader:Loader = new Loader();
imgLoader.contentLoaderInfo.addEventListener(Event.
                        COMPLETE,loadComplete);
imgLoader.load(new URLRequest("assets/mill.jpg"));
}
```

Once the bitmap is loaded, we can create a `BitmapMaterial` instance just as usual.

```
private function loadComplete(e:Event):void
{
    var bitmap:Bitmap = e.target.content as Bitmap;

    var bitmapMaterial:BitmapMaterial = new BitmapMaterial
                                (bitmap.bitmapData);
```

Instead of creating a `FlatShadeMaterial` instance, we now create a `FlatShader` instance. This object takes exactly the same parameters as the `FlatShadeMaterial` constructor.

```
var shader:FlatShader = new FlatShader(light,0xFFFFFF,0x000000,
                    100);
```

For this shader, we pass a black ambient light color instead of the red color used in the example with `FlatShadeMaterial`.

We can't assign this newly-created `FlatShader` instance as a material yet, as we could with `FlatShadeMaterial`. First, we need to apply the shader to the previously created bitmap material. This can be achieved by instantiating `ShadedMaterial` with the bitmap material and shader as the parameters:

```
var shadedMaterial:ShadedMaterial = new ShadedMaterial
                            (bitmapMaterial,shader);
```

The newly-created instance of ShadedMaterial can be used as the material for your objects. Therefore, let's create another sphere, passing the shaded material and add it to the scene.

```
var sphere:Sphere = new Sphere(shadedMaterial,250,10,10);
sphere.x = 300;
scene.addChild(sphere);
}
```

As the final step we will animate the position of our light in a circular movement. This can be achieved by drawing a sine and a cosine function.

```
override protected function onRenderTick(e:Event=null):void
{
    light.z = Math.sin(angle) * 400;
    light.x = Math.cos(angle) * 600;
    angle +=0.01;
    super.onRenderTick();
}
```

{Ex.} FlatShadingExample {Ex.}

When you publish this code you should see something similar to this:

Gouraud shading

Gouraud shading is a more advanced shading technique compared to flat shading. Instead of using a single color fill on each triangle, the Gouraud shader draws a gradient on each triangle. The colors of the gradient are determined by the ambient color and a calculated color per vertex normal. These can then be interpolated by drawing a gradient.

Determining the color per vertex normal is similar to calculating the color of each triangle using flat shading. Gouraud shading calculates the angle between a vertex normal and a light source.

Because there are more vertex normals than triangle normals to be calculated and drawing a gradient is more CPU intensive than drawing a regular fill, this shader is a bit heavier on the CPU than flat shading.

Have a look at the following three spheres. The sphere on the left uses a flat shader. The sphere in the middle shows eight vertices that form six triangles. Based on the calculated color value of each vertex and the ambient color, a gradient is drawn on the six triangles in the illustration. The flat shading is purely illustrative so that we still can see all triangle pairs forming a sphere. The third image shows how these gradients look for all triangles.

The image shows that Gouraud shading does a relatively good job. It isn't as blocky as with flat shading. On the contrary, the shading is very smooth. However, Gouraud shading has some issues as well. Take a look at the `ShadingTypesDemo.swf` tool, select **GouraudMaterial**, and slide to a high **specularLevel**, 200 for example. This will result in the following render of the teapot. For the sake of comprehensiveness, a render of a sphere with the same settings is added as well.

Because lighting is calculated at vertex level, highlights will concentrate around the vertices. As you can see, this will give less smooth results.

Now, have a look at how we can use the Gouraud shader. Because using a Gouraud shader is very similar to using a flat shader, we can copy our previous example and change it slightly.

First, we'll change the instantiation of `FlatShadeMaterial` into the instantiation of `GouraudMaterial`. See the following code:

```
var shadeMaterial:FlatShadeMaterial = new FlatShadeMaterial(light,
                          0xFFFFFF,0xFF0000,100);
```

We will replace it with this code:

```
var shadeMaterial:GouraudMaterial = new GouraudMaterial
                              (light,0xFFFFFF,0xFF0000,100);
```

The code change for applying a Gouraud shader on a bitmap material is just as easy. Instead of instantiating `FlatShader` as shown next:

```
var bitmapMaterial:BitmapMaterial = new BitmapMaterial
                              (bitmap.bitmapData);
var shader:FlatShader = new FlatShader(light,0xFFFFFF,0x000000,100);
var shadedMaterial:ShadedMaterial = new ShadedMaterial
                              (bitmapMaterial,shader);
```

You can instantiate `GouraudShader` as shown next:

```
var bitmapMaterial:BitmapMaterial = new BitmapMaterial
                              (bitmap.bitmapData);
var shader:GouraudShader = new GouraudShader(light,0xFFFFFF,
                        0x000000,100);
var shadedMaterial:ShadedMaterial = new ShadedMaterial
                              (bitmapMaterial,shader);
```

In both cases, the only difference is the class name. Each parameter is exactly the same as with flat shading. The final step is changing the imports at the top of the class. First, we'll remove the ones related to flat shading.

```
import org.papervision3d.materials.shadematerials.FlatShadeMaterial;
import org.papervision3d.materials.shaders.FlatShader;
```

Then we add the following to use Gouraud shading:

```
import org.papervision3d.materials.shadematerials.GouraudMaterial;
import org.papervision3d.materials.shaders.GouraudShader;
```

{Ex.} GouraudShadingExample {Ex.}

The published code will result in an image like this:

Cell shading

Cell shading is a type of shading for non-photorealistic rendering, used to render 3D objects in a cartoon style. Therefore this shading type is also known as **toon shading**. Lighting on objects is applied as if they have been hand drawn. In most 3D modeling programs, cell shading supports a **silhouette outline** of the object, to give even a better illusion of a hand-drawn image. Because **silhouette rendering** has been considered too CPU intensive, it is not implemented in Papervision3D. The following image on the left shows a cell-shaded teapot that was created with Papervision3D. The image on the right is a cell-shaded and silhouette-rendered teapot that you can make with a 3D modeling program.

A trick to fake outline rendering is to apply a glow filter to your object. Filters and effects will be discussed in Chapter 10.

Again we have two ways to apply cell shading to our material. We can instantiate a `CellMaterial` instance, or we can instantiate a `CellShader` instance and use it in combination with a bitmap material and a shaded material. Both `CellMaterial` and `CellShader` take the same parameters at instantiation:

	Parameter	Data type	Default value	Description
1	light	LightObject3D	—	A reference to a `PointLight3D` object.
2	color_1	int	0xFFFFFF	Sets a 32-bit hexadecimal value that will be used as the color for the highlights.
3	color_2	int	0x000000	Sets a 32-bit hexadecimal value that defines the surface color that is not reflecting any light. This could be considered as the ambient light color for cell shading.
4	steps	int	3	Defines the amount of steps to interpolate from `color_1` to `color_2`. You should keep this quite low to get a good cell shading effect.

The `ShadingTypesDemo.swf` demo demonstrates cell shading. Play around with these values to get familiar with the available parameters.

Working with this class is pretty much the same as working with flat shading and Gouraud shading. Let's take the flat shading example as the base class for this example. Create a new project and copy the code from that example.

First, we need to switch to the right imports to use cell shading:

```
import org.papervision3d.materials.shadematerials.CellMaterial;
import org.papervision3d.materials.shaders.CellShader;
```

Next, we replace the instantiation of the shader inside the `init()` method. Remove the following:

```
var shadeMaterial:FlatShadeMaterial = new FlatShadeMaterial
                                    (light,0xFFFFFF,0xFF0000,100);
```

Now replace it with:

```
var shadeMaterial:CellMaterial = new CellMaterial
                              (light,0xFFFFFF,0xFF0000,5);
```

This will create a cell-shaded material, which interpolates from color `0xFFFFFF` to `0xFF0000` in five steps.

The next and final step replaces the instantiation of `FlatShader` inside the `loadComplete()` method. Replace the following line:

```
var shader:FlatShader = new FlatShader(light,0xFFFFFF,0x000000,100);
```

with this line:

```
var shader:CellShader = new CellShader(light,0xFFFFFF,0x000000,5);
```

{Ex.} CellShadingExample {Ex.}

After you publish this code, you'll see two cell-shaded spheres that look as follows:

Phong shading

Phong shading is a very precise shading technique. Instead of calculating lighting per triangle as with flat shading or per vertex as with Gouraud shading, it calculates lighting per pixel. Because lighting is calculated per pixel, it results in very smooth and accurate shading.

In Papervision3D, per pixel shading has been approximated — it doesn't entirely match real Phong shading. It shades objects based on an ambient color and specular lighting, instead of ambient and diffuse colors as in Gouraud shading. This results in a major difference between how both shade an object; a Phong-shaded object has a dominant ambient color.

Take a look at the `ShadingTypesDemo.swf` demo again. Play with the specular level and see how realistic the lighting is. The image on the left shows a low specularity level and the image on the right has a very high specularity level:

Note that the teapot in this demo has some z-sorting problems. Chapter 9 will address these problems in detail.

The only disadvantage of Phong shading is that it consumes a lot of CPU power. You simply can't have a scene full of Phong-shaded objects. With this heavy shading type, the speed limitations of the Flash player are reached even sooner.

Usage of this shader works the same as the other shaders we've seen so far. Therefore, we'll base this example on the previously made examples, starting off by defining the imports at the top of the class:

```
import org.papervision3d.materials.shadematerials.PhongMaterial;
import org.papervision3d.materials.shaders.PhongShader;
```

The instantiation of `PhongMaterial` takes the same parameters as the instantiation of `FlatShadeMaterial` and `GouraudMaterial`. However, unlike the other shaders, there are no default parameters when you instantiate `PhongMaterial`.

In the `init()` method we change the shader definition into the following:

```
var shadeMaterial:PhongMaterial = new PhongMaterial(light,0xFFFFFF,
                                    0xFF0000,100);
```

Changing the shader definition inside the `loadComplete()` method goes like this:

```
var shader:PhongShader = new PhongShader(light,0xFFFFFF,0x000000,100);
```

Note that the second argument that you pass to the constructor, which defines the light color, has no default value.

{Ex.} PhongShadingExample {Ex.}

After publishing this code, you'll see the following two shaded spheres:

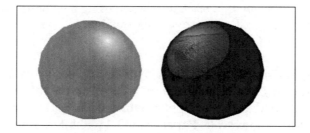

In the next two sections, we'll look at special functionalities that some shaders offer in order to add even more detail to 3D objects. We will learn how to bump materials and apply reflection mapping using shaders.

Bumping your materials

A common trick to make an object look more realistic is to use a bump map. A **bump map** allows relief to be added to the surface of the object without the need to add extra triangles.

In `ShadingTypesDemo.swf`, an example of bumping has been implemented. Select **PhongShader** and check the **Bumpmap** checkbox. See how this changes the details of your object.

At the time of writing, Papervision3D has some problems regarding bump maps and external models. This issue is visible in the shading types demo when the model is rotating. Around the **UV seams** (these are visible as very thin black lines when using the **PhongShader** without bump map), you'll notice some dark smudge.

A bump map in Papervision3D works with an ordinary bitmap as the source and can be used to apply bumping to a bitmap material. Based on the information found in the image, each pixel is shaded darker or lighter, which adds the bumpy effect. The image can be in normal colors or grayscale. Papervision3D will internally detect where the bumps are as it detects the edges of the shapes in the image. Technically this differs from using bump maps in a 3D modeling program, where a bump map must be a grayscale image. However, the result is about the same.

Depending on the bumps that you need, you could use the same image that serves as the bitmap material, or choose a separate bitmap containing a separate pattern.

The only shading type we've seen so far that supports bump maps is a bitmap-based Phong shader. We can take the previous example as the starting point to see how to add bump mapping. In this example we use a randomly generated **Perlin noise** bitmap as the bump map.

Here's what a randomly generated Perlin noise bitmap looks like:

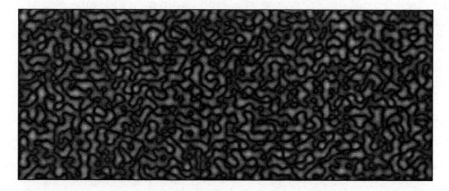

Creating a Perlin noise image can be done with a method of the BitmapData class, which needs to be imported first.

```
import flash.display.BitmapData;
```

As bump maps work only with a bitmap-based Phong shader, we need to remove the instantiation of PhongMaterial and Sphere from the init() method. Your altered init() method will look like this:

```
private function init():void
{
    light = new PointLight3D(true);
    light.z = -400;
    light.y = 300;
    light.x = 0;
    scene.addChild(light);

    var imgLoader:Loader = new Loader();
    imgLoader.contentLoaderInfo.addEventListener
                              (Event.COMPLETE,loadComplete);
    imgLoader.load(new URLRequest("assets/mill.jpg"));
}
```

We will keep the loader for our external bitmap, as we will bump map this image once it's loaded.

The loadComplete() method starts off unchanged, assigning the loaded bitmap to the bitmap variable.

```
private function loadComplete(e:Event):void
{
    var bitmap:Bitmap = e.target.content as Bitmap;
```

Then we create a **Perlin noise** bitmap, which we'll use as the bump map. Although it's not necessary, we make the bump map the same size as our loaded image.

```
var bumpmap:BitmapData = new BitmapData
                         (bitmap.width,bitmap.height);
bumpmap.perlinNoise(10,10,1,Math.random() *
                    100,true,false,1,true);
```

Next, a normal `BitmapMaterial` instance is created, which we'll use as the material to be shaded.

```
var bitmapMaterial:BitmapMaterial = new BitmapMaterial
                                    (bitmap.bitmapData);
```

The following part does the trick for bump mapping, where we apply the Perlin noise `BitmapData` as the fifth parameter when we instantiate `PhongShader`. To have a good look at how the object is bump mapped, we set the specular level to 0, so it will reflect the maximum amount of light.

```
var shader:PhongShader = new PhongShader
                         (light,0xFFFFFF, 0x000000,0,bumpmap);
```

Notice that the fifth parameter is of the `BitmapData` type, which is `null` by default, meaning no bump map.

Finally, we create a shaded material, pass it to a sphere that we instantiate, and add the sphere to the scene.

```
var shadedMaterial:ShadedMaterial = new ShadedMaterial
                                    (bitmapMaterial,shader);

var sphere:Sphere = new Sphere(shadedMaterial,250,10,10);
scene.addChild(sphere);
}
```

Notice that we have not changed the position of our sphere, as we did in previous examples when we worked with two spheres in the scene.

[Ex.] PhongShadingBumpExample [Ex.]

Publishing this code will show clearly that we've applied a bump map and how that affects lighting on the sphere:

You may want to experiment with different bump maps. For example, try applying the bitmap used for the bitmap material as your bump map or try loading an image containing a pattern.

Reflection mapping

The technique of simulating a reflection of the environment on a surface is called **reflection mapping**. You basically take a pre-rendered image of an environment and use this as the source for reflection mapping. In fact, it doesn't really reflect the environment around the object, it is just a simulation. For this technique, believability is more important than accuracy.

Because this feature has some serious issues in combination with an external model and UV mapping, we used a sphere in our demo application instead. At the time of writing, it is not recommended to apply this technique on external UV mapped models. Take a look at **EnvMapShader** in the demo and see how the sphere seems to reflect an image of a desert. Select the **bumpmap** checkbox and see how this gives an even better illusion of reflection caused by the surface which isn't perfectly flat anymore. Also, have a look at how changing the light position changes the reflected image. The following image on the left is without a bump map and the image on the right is with a bump map.

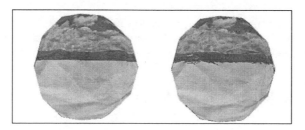

Because the printed version of this book is in grayscale, it's a good idea to examine the difference in the `ShadingTypesDemo.swf`, which will give a stronger illusion of reflection.

 Due to problems with Papervision3D and bump mapping, some darkness will concentrate around the edges of the rendered sphere. At the time of writing this is an unsolved issue.

As for our example, we'll create an illusion of reflection, which is even stronger than you've seen in the shading types demo. By adding the reflected image to the stage, we get the illusion of a reflected environment. To see clearly how the object seems to reflect the environment map, we'll rotate the sphere around its local y-axis instead of animating the light. The example uses the same methods and class properties as the previous examples in this chapter. We only need to apply some changes to the methods and import two extra classes:

```
import org.papervision3d.materials.utils.BitmapMaterialTools;
import org.papervision3d.materials.shaders.EnvMapShader;
```

To rotate the sphere in the `onRenderTick()` method, we need to create the following sphere class property:

```
private var sphere:Sphere;
```

Another small change is removing the `startRendering()` method call inside the constructor. As we'll rotate the sphere inside the `onRenderTick()` method, we don't want to call this method before the sphere is instantiated.

Next, we change the `init()` method. We position the light and load a new image.

```
private function init():void
{
    light = new PointLight3D(true);
    light.z = -400;
    light.y = 0;
    light.x = 0;
    scene.addChild(light);

    var imgLoader:Loader = new Loader();
    imgLoader.contentLoaderInfo.addEventListener
                            (Event.COMPLETE,loadComplete);
    imgLoader.load(newURLRequest("assets/sky.jpg"));
}
```

So far nothing new, so let's look at how to apply an environment map as soon as the image is loaded.

Instead of using the loaded bitmap as the source image for instantiating a
`BitmapMaterial`, we'll now use a randomly generated Perlin noise bitmap,
at a size of 512 by 512 pixels.

```
private function loadComplete(e:Event):void
{
    var materialBitmapData:BitmapData = new BitmapData(512,512);
    materialBitmapData.perlinNoise(100,100,10,Math.random() *
                            100,true,true,1,true);
    var bitmapMaterial:BitmapMaterial = new BitmapMaterial
                            (materialBitmapData);
```

Note that this Perlin noise is created passing other values as arguments than the one
in the previous example.

The loaded image will serve as the environment map. Because Papervision3D flips
environment maps over the y-axis, we need to flip the loaded image manually so
that it will reflect as expected. The same image will be added to the stage as the
background for our movie. Therefore, we need to flip the environment image by
using a copy instance of it. If we don't do this, the environment image on the stage
will be mirrored.

```
var envBitmap:Bitmap = e.target.content as Bitmap;
var flippedEnvMap:BitmapData = new BitmapData
                            (envBitmap.width,envBitmap.height);
flippedEnvMap.draw(envBitmap);
BitmapMaterialTools.mirrorBitmapY(flippedEnvMap);
```

Based on the flipped environment bitmap, we instantiate `EnvMapShader`. This class
takes a light object as the first parameter and two `BitmapData` instances as the
second and third parameters.

```
var shader:EnvMapShader = new EnvMapShader(light,flippedEnvMap,
                        flippedEnvMap);
```

The first bitmap data object is the environment bitmap used by all triangles that are
facing the light. The second bitmap data object is used for all triangles that are back
facing the light.

For this example, the illusion of reflection works well enough using the same image
for front-facing and back-facing triangles.

The light object is only passed to the `EnvMapShader` to determine if a triangle
needs to use the front environment map or the back environment map. It does not
apply lighting on your object like we have seen with other shaders. When you play
with the shading types demo, you will see how changing the light affects how the
refection is mapped to the sphere.

Next, we create a `ShadedMaterial` instance and a sphere instance.

```
var shadedMaterial:ShadedMaterial = new ShadedMaterial
                                (bitmapMaterial,shader);

sphere = new Sphere(shadedMaterial,250,10,10);
scene.addChild(sphere);
```

To fake the presence of an environment in the background, we add the environment bitmap to the stage, using the same width and height of the stage.

```
envBitmap.width = stage.stageWidth;
envBitmap.height = stage.stageHeight;
addChildAt(envBitmap,0);
```

Now that the sphere is defined, we can start rendering the scene.

```
        startRendering();
    }
```

To rotate the sphere around its local y-axis we need to alter the `onRenderTick()` method. Replace the code that's inside by the following:

```
sphere.localRotationY++;
super.onRenderTick();
```

{Ex.} EnvironmentShadingExample {Ex.}

After publishing this code, you should see an image similar to this one:

In this example we've seen how we can instantiate an `EnvMapShader`. Although two notes need to be added.

Firstly, the fourth parameter at instantiation of this class defines the ambient color. However, at the time of this writing, Papervision3D ignores this color value.

Secondly, we can provide a bump map as the fifth parameter of this class. This works and you could try to apply the bump map that we created in the previous section.

Example—shading the Earth in our galaxy

In the previous chapters, we have created a galaxy made of planes, the Earth, a flat-shaded paper plane, and several camera types. With what we have learned in this chapter, we can extend the example and apply shading. We can add more realism to the Earth by adding a shader and a bump map to it. This way we can simulate the presence of the sun and add some relief to the Earth.

Let's take the galaxy example from Chapter 6 as the starting point for this example. There we made use of several classes to create the galaxy. Let's fresh up our memory by summing them up:

- `Galaxy` creates a visual representation of the galaxy. It adds the Earth and planes that are used as stars.
- `Player` is responsible for creating a flat-shaded paper plane instance as the visual representation of the player.
- `UserInputHandler` takes care of handling the user's keyboard input in order to move our player.
- `CameraController` is used in order to switch between several camera types and point of views.
- A document class wraps all classes together as an application.

For this example we only need to work in the `Galaxy` class. All other classes can be left intact.

Adding a shader and a bump map

In this example we need to use bitmap based Phong shading in order to add a shader and a bump map to the sphere. Just like we did in the other shading examples, we need to load a bitmap and add a load complete listener, before we can start shading the Earth. For this we need to change the `init()` method so that it will load only the bitmap texture that will be used as material on the Earth. It may be a good idea to copy or comment the code that is inside the method before applying the following change:

```
private function init():void
{
    var imgLoader:Loader = new Loader();
    imgLoader.contentLoaderInfo.addEventListener
                            (Event.COMPLETE,loadComplete);
    imgLoader.load(new URLRequest("assets/earth.jpg"));
}
```

Once the bitmap has been loaded, we can create a `PointLight3D` instance and a Phong-shaded material with a bump map applied to it.

```
private function loadComplete(e:Event):void
{
    var light:PointLight3D = new PointLight3D();
    light.y = 5000;
    light.x = 6000;
    light.z = -6000;

    var bitmap:Bitmap = e.target.content as Bitmap;

    var bitmapMaterial:BitmapMaterial = new BitmapMaterial
                                (bitmap.bitmapData);
    var shader:PhongShader = new PhongShader(light,0xFFFFFF,
                        0x00000022,0,bitmap.bitmapData);
    var shadedMaterial:ShadedMaterial = new ShadedMaterial
                                (bitmapMaterial,shader);
```

Note that the instantiation of `PhongShader` also uses the loaded image as the bump map and that it has a 32-bit color provided as ambient color. This is because we do not want to make the Earth completely black on triangles that face away from the light source.

Next, we instantiate and add a Sphere with the `ShadedMaterial` instance as material to the scene, followed by creating the galaxy of planes that was originally done in the `init()` method.

```
earthSphere = new Sphere(shadedMaterial,200,24,16);
addChild(earthSphere);

for(var i:uint = 0; i < 150; i++)
{
        var plane:Plane = new Plane(new ColorMaterial
                        (Math.random() * 0xFFFFFF),50,50,1,1);
        plane.material.doubleSided = true;
        addChild(plane);
        plane.x = Math.random()*20000 - 10000;
        plane.y = Math.random()*1500 - 750;
        plane.z = Math.random()*20000 -10000;
        plane.localRotationY = Math.random() * 180 - 90;
}
```

In order not to break our code, we need to prevent that the current `update()` method rotates the Earth on every enter frame while its not yet been instantiated. Rotating it without this change will result in a runtime error, as the Earth sphere is only instantiated once its material has been loaded. Therefore, we add a new private class property that is named `isReady` and holds a `Boolean` value of `false` by default. At the end of the `loadComplete()` method, we set this value to `true`.

```
        isReady = true;
    }
```

The final step is changing the `update()` method, so it will only start rotating the Earth sphere once `isReady` is set to `true`.

```
    public function update():void
    {
        if(isReady)
        {
                earthSphere.localRotationY += 0.2;
        }
    }
```

ShadedGalaxyExample

This project can be published and will result in a render that looks as follows:

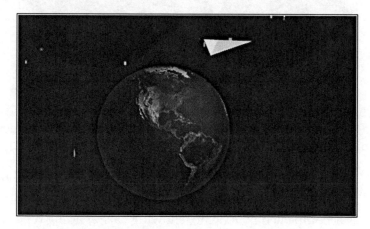

Summary

Shading is a technique that adds more realism to the appearance of your objects. Generally speaking this is done by calculating lighting for each triangle in one of the following ways:

- A single color per triangle using flat shading
- A gradient fill per triangle when using Gouraud shading
- Per pixel on a triangle's surface giving the object a cartoonish look with cell shading
- Approximately per pixel on a triangle's surface as the most realistic shading with Phong shading

While discussing the more advanced shading types, we've seen how we can add bump maps to a Phong shader and how we can add the illusion of reflection using environment mapping.

Phong shading and a bump map have been used to extend the existing galaxy example and shade the Earth.

This chapter was accompanied by a demo, showing each shading type and its parameters. The famous Utah teapot was used to apply shaded materials to. In the next chapter, we'll see how we can export 3D models—such as the Utah teapot—from several 3D modeling tools, and import them into Papervision3D.

8
External Models

In the previous chapter, the Utah teapot was introduced to demonstrate several shaders. Of course, we did not create the teapot by manually defining each triangle to form the shape of a teapot. Papervision3D allows us to work with models that are created and exported by a **3D modeling program**, which adds many possibilities, especially when the shape of the default primitives doesn't fit your needs.

With Papervision3D we can load several types of 3D models. Some of them support animations that have been created in the 3D modeling program. There are many programs that support the model formats Papervision3D reads, more than what we can cover in this book. We will have a look at the following three:

- **Autodesk 3ds Max**: One of the widely-known commercial 3D programs, which runs only on Windows
- **Sketchup**: A free 3D modeling program provided by Google. Designed to be a more intuitive 3D program, which runs on Max OS X and Windows
- **Blender**: An open source, platform-independent 3D modeling tool

The main focus of this chapter will be on how to get models from these programs into Papervision3D. The process of creating models in general is too program-specific and out-of-scope for this book. Therefore, only the creation of a simple 3D object per program will be discussed. However, some more complex preconfigured models are also provided.

This chapter covers the following:

- Modeling for Papervision3D
- Preparing for loading models
- Creating and loading models using Autodesk 3ds Max
- Loading an animation from Autodesk 3ds Max

- Creating and loading models using SketchUp
- Creating and loading models using Blender
- Controlling loaded materials

Let's start off by having a look at some general practices to keep in mind when modeling for Papervision3D.

Modeling for Papervision3D

As mentioned in the introduction, this chapter will not describe in detail how to create models. Each tool works differently and requires a different approach for creating suitable models.

In this section, we will discuss several techniques that relate to modeling for Papervision3D. As Papervision3D is commonly used for web-based projects, modeling requires a different mindset than modeling for an animated movie, visualization, or game. Most of the techniques discussed relate to improving performance. This section is especially useful for modelers who need to create models for Papervision3D.

Papervision3D Previewer

Papervision3D Previewer is a small program that should be part of every modeller's toolbox. This tool comes in handy for testing purposes. It allows a modeler to render an exported model in Papervision3D, and it displays some statistics that show how the model performs. At the time of writing, this tool was not compatible with Papervision3D 2.1, which could result in small problems when loading external models.

Papervision3D Previewer can be downloaded from `http://code.google.com/p/mrdoob/wiki/pv3dpreviewer`

Keep your polygon count low

Papervision3D is a cutting edge technology that brings 3D to the Flash Player. It does this at an amazing speed relative to the capabilities of the Flash player. However, performance of Papervision3D is just a fraction of the performance that can be achieved with hardware-accelerated engines such as used by console games. Even with hardware-accelerated games there is a limit to the number of polygons that can be rendered, meaning there is always a compromise between detail and performance. This counts even more for Papervision3D, so always try to model using as few polygons as possible.

Papervision3D users often wonder what the maximum number of triangles is that the Flash player can handle. There is no generic answer to this question, as performance depends on more factors than just the number of triangles. On average, the total triangle count should be no more than 3000, which equals 1500 polygons (remember that one polygon is made of two triangles).

[Unlike most 3D modeling programs, Papervision3D is triangle based and not polygon based.]

Add polygons to resolve artifacts

Although this seems to contradict the previous suggestion to keep your polygon count low, sometimes you need more polygons to get rid of texture distortion or to reduce z-sorting artifacts. z-sorting artifacts will often occur in areas where objects intersect or closely intersect each other. Subdividing polygons in those areas can make z-sorting more accurate. Often this needs to be done by creating new polygons for the intersecting triangles of approximately the same size.

There are several approaches to prevent z-sorting problems. The next chapter will discuss these in detail. Depending on the object you're using, it can be very time consuming to tweak and find the optimal amount and location of polygons. The amount of polygons you add in order to solve the problem should still be kept as low as possible. Finding the optimal values for your model will often result in switching a lot between Papervision3D and the 3D modeling program.

Keep your textures small

Textures used in the 3D modeling tool can be exported along with the model to a format that is readable for Papervision3D. This is a valuable feature as the texture will automatically be loaded by Papervision3D. However, the image, which was defined in the 3D authoring tool, will be used exactly as provided by Papervision3D. If you choose a 1024 by 1024 pixels image as the texture, for example the wheels of a car, Papervision3D loads the entire image and draws it on the wheel of a car that appears on screen at a size of 50 by 50 pixels for example. There are several problems related to this:

- It's a waste of bandwidth to load such a large image. Loading any image takes time, which should be kept as short as possible.
- It's a waste of capacity. Papervision3D needs to resize the image from 1024 by 1024 pixels to an image, which will be, for example, maximal 50 by 50 pixels on screen.

Always choose texture dimensions that make sense for the application using it, and keep in mind that they have to be power of two. This will enable mipmapping and smoothing, which come without extra performance costs.

Use textures that Flash can read

3D modeling programs usually read a variety of image sources. Some even support reading Adobe Photoshop's native file-format PSD. Flash can load only GIF, JPG, or PNG files at run time. Therefore, stick to these formats in your model so that you do not have to convert the textures when the model needs to be exported to Papervision3D.

Use UV maps

If your model is made up of several objects and textures, it's a good idea to use **UV mapping**, which is the process of unwrapping the model and defining all its textures into one single image. This way we can speed up initial loading of an application by making one request from Flash to load this image instead of loading dozens of images. UV mapping can also be used to tile or reuse parts of the image. The more parts of the UV-mapped image you can reuse, the more bandwidth you'll save. Always try to keep your UV-mapped image as small as possible, just as with keeping your normal textures small. In case you have a lot of objects sharing the same UV map and you need a large canvas to unwrap the UV map, be aware of the fact that the maximum image size supported by Flash Player 9 is 2880x2880 pixels. With the benefits of power of two textures in mind, the maximum width and height is 2048x2048 pixels.

Baking textures

Baking textures is the process of integrating shadows, lighting, reflection, or entire 3D objects into a single image. Most 3D modeling tools support this.

This contradicts what has been said about tiling images in UV maps, as baking results in images that usually can only be used once because of the baked information on the texture. However, it can increase the level of realism of your application, just like shading does, but without the loss of performance caused by calculating shading in real time.

Never use them in combination with a tiling image, as repeated shading, for instance, will result in unnatural looking renders. Therefore, each texture needs to be unique, which will cause longer loading times before you can show a scene.

Use recognizable names for objects and materials

It is always a good convention to use recognizable names for all your objects. This counts for the classes, methods, and properties in your code, and also for the names of the 3D objects in your modeling tool.

Always think twice before renaming an object that is used by an application. The application might use the name of an object as the identifier to do something with it—for example, making it clickable. When working in a team of modelers and programmers, you really need to make this clear to the modelers as changing the name of an object can easily break your application.

Size and positioning

Maintaining the same relative size for your modeled objects, as you would use for instantiating primitives in your scene, is a good convention. Although you could always adjust the scale property of a loaded 3D model, it is very convenient when both Papervision3D and your modeling tool use the same scale.

 Remember that Papervision3D doesn't have a metric system defining units of a certain value such as meters, yards, pixels, and so on. It just uses units.

Another convention is to position your object or objects at the origin of the 3D space in the modeling tool. Especially when exporting a single object from a 3D modeling tool, it is really helpful if it is located at a position of 0 on all axes. This way you can position the 3D object in Papervision3D by using absolute values, without needing to take the offset into account. You can compare this with adding movie clips to your library in Flash. In most cases, it is pretty useful when the elements of a movie clip are centered on their registration point.

Finding the balance between quality and performance

For each project you should try to find the balance between lightweight modeling and quality. Because each project is different in requirements, scale, and quality, there is no rule that applies for all. Keep the tips mentioned in the previous sections in mind and try to be creative with them. If you see a way to optimize your model, then do not hesitate to use it.

Before we have a look at how to create and export models for Papervision3D, we will create a basic application for this purpose.

Creating a template class to load models

In order to show an imported 3D model using Papervision3D, we will create a basic application. Remember the example in chapter 6, in which we made the camera orbit around a grid of planes by moving the mouse? We will use the same code to rotate around the models, which we are going to create and load later in this chapter.

Based on the orbit example we create the following class. Each time we load a new model we just have to alter the init() method. First, have a look at the following base code for this example:

```
package {

    import flash.events.Event;

    import org.papervision3d.materials.WireframeMaterial;
    import org.papervision3d.materials.utils.MaterialsList;
    import org.papervision3d.objects.DisplayObject3D;
    import org.papervision3d.objects.primitives.Cube;
    import org.papervision3d.view.BasicView;

    public class ExternalModelsExample extends BasicView
    {
        private var model:DisplayObject3D;
        private var rotX:Number = 0.1;
        private var rotY:Number = 0.1;
        private var camPitch:Number = 90;
        private var camYaw:Number = 270;
        private var easeOut:Number = 0.1;

        public function ExternalModelsExample()
        {
            stage.frameRate = 40;

            init();
            startRendering();
        }

        private function init():void
        {
            model = new Plane();
            scene.addChild(model);
        }
```

```
private function modelLoaded(e:FileLoadEvent):void
{
        //To be added
}

override protected function onRenderTick(e:Event=null):void
{
        var xDist:Number = mouseX - stage.stageWidth * 0.5;
        var yDist:Number = mouseY - stage.stageHeight * 0.5;

        camPitch += ((yDist * rotX) - camPitch + 90)
                        * easeOut;
        camYaw += ((xDist * rotY) - camYaw + 270) * easeOut;

        camera.orbit(camPitch, camYaw);

        super.onRenderTick();
}
    }
}
```

We have created a new plane using a wireframe as its material. The plane is assigned to a class property named model, which is of the DisplayObject3D type. In fact, any external model is a do3D. No matter what type of model we load in the following examples, we can always assign it to the model property. The classes that we'll use for loading 3D models all inherit from DisplayObject3D.

Now that we have created a default application, we are ready to create our first model in 3D Studio Max, export it, and then import it into Papervison3D.

Creating models in Autodesk 3ds Max and loading them into Papervision3D

Autodesk 3ds Max (also known as **3D Studio Max** or **3ds Max**) is one of the widely-known commercial 3D modeling and animation programs. This is a good authoring tool to start with, as it can save to two of the file formats Papervision3D can handle. These are:

- **COLLADA** (extension *.dae): An open source 3D file type, which is supported by Papervision3D. This is the most advanced format and has been supported since Papervision3D's first release. It also supports animations and is actually just a plain text XML file.
- **3D Studio** (extension *.3ds): As the name suggests, this is one of the formats that 3ds Max natively supports. Generally speaking it is also one of the most common formats to save 3D models in.

As of 3ds Max version 9, there is a built-in exporter plugin available that supports exporting to COLLADA. However, you should avoid using this, as at the time of writing, the models it exports are not suitable for Papervision3D.

 Don't have a license of 3ds Max and want to get along with the following examples? Go to www.autodesk.com to download a 30-day trial.

Installing COLLADA Max

An exporter that does support COLLADA files suitable for Papervision3D is called **COLLADA Max**. This is a free and open source exporter that works with all versions of 3ds Max 7 and higher.

Installing this exporter is easy. Just follow the steps mentioned below:

1. Make sure you have installed 3ds Max version 7 or higher.
2. Go to http://sourceforge.net/projects/colladamaya/.
3. Click on **View all files** and select the latest COLLADA Max version. (At the time of writing this is **COLLADA Max NextGen 0.9.5**, which is still in beta, but is the only version that works with 3ds Max 2010).
4. Save the download somewhere on your computer.
5. Run the installer.
6. Click **Next**, until the installer confirms that the exporter is installed.
7. Start 3ds Max and double check if we can export using the **COLLADA** or **COLLADA NextGen** filetype, as shown in the following screenshot:

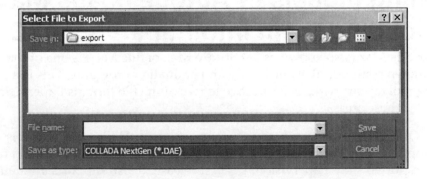

If the only COLLADA export option is **Autodesk Collada**, then something went wrong during the installation of COLLADA Max, as this is not the exporter that works with Papervision3D.

Now that 3ds Max is configured correctly for exporting a file format that can be read by Papervision3D, we will have a look at how to create a basic textured model in 3ds Max and export it to Papervision3D.

Creating the Utah teapot and export it for Papervision3D

If you already know how to work with 3ds Max, this step is quite easy. All we need to do is create the Utah teapot, add UV mapping, add a material to it, and export it as COLLADA. However, if you are new to 3ds Max, the following steps needs to be clarified.

1. First, we start 3ds Max and create a new scene. The creation of a new scene happens by default on startup.

2. The Utah teapot is one of the objects that comes as a standard primitive in 3ds Max. This means you can select it from the default primitives menu and draw it in one of the viewports. Draw it in the top viewport so that the teapot will not appear rotated over one of its axes.

3. Give it a **Radius** of **250** in the properties panel on the right, in order to make it match with the units that we'll use in Papervision3D.

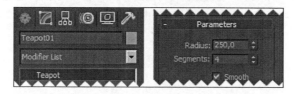

4. Position the teapot at the origin of the scene. You can do this by selecting it and changing the **x**, **y**, and **z** properties at the bottom of your screen. You would expect that you need to set all axes to 0, although this is not the case. In this respect, the teapot differs from other primitives in 3ds Max, as the pivot point is located at the bottom of the teapot. Therefore, we need to define a different value for the teapot on the z-axis. Setting it to approximately **-175** is a good value.

5. To map a material to the teapot, we need to define a UV map first.

 UV mapping is also known as **UVW mapping**. Some call it UV mapping and others call it UVW mapping. 3ds Max uses the term UVW mapping.

6. While having the teapot still selected, go to modify and then select **UVW Mapping** from the modifier list. Select **Shrink Wrap** and click **Fit** in the **Alignment** section. This will create a UVW map for us.

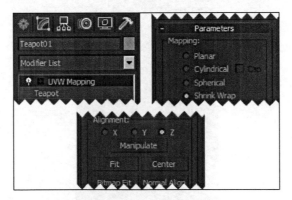

7. Open the material editor using keyboard shortcut *m*. Here we define the materials that we use in 3ds Max.

8. Give the new material a name. Replace **01 – Default** with a material name of your choice—for example, **teapotMaterial**.

9. Provide a bitmap as the diffuse material. You can do this by clicking on the square button, at the right of the **Diffuse** value within **Blinn Basic Parameters** section.

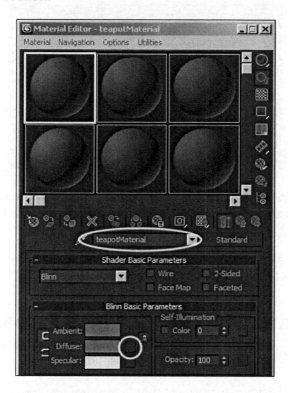

10. A new window called **Material/Map Browser** will open. Double-click **Bitmap** to load an external image. Select an image of your choice. We will use `teapotMaterial.jpg`, which has been provided as a file in the folder of this chapter.

11. The material editor will now update and show the selected material on an illustrative sphere. This is your newly-created material, which you need to drag on the created teapot.

12. The teapot model can now be exported. Depending on the version of the installed COLLADA exporter, select **COLLADA** or **COLLADA NextGen**. Note that you should not export using **Autodesk Collada**, as this exporter doesn't work properly for Papervision3D.

13. Give it a filename of your choice, for example **teapot**, and hit **Save**.

14. The exporter window will pop up. The default settings are fine for exporting to Papervision3D, so click **OK** to save the file.

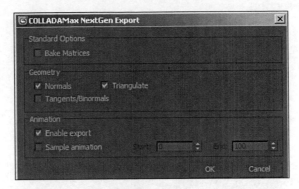

Save the model in the default 3ds Max file format (.max) somewhere on your local disk, so we can use it later when discussing other ways to export this model to Papervision3D.

The model that we have created and exported is now ready to be imported by Papervision3D. Let's take a look at how this works.

Importing the Utah teapot into Papervision3D

To work with the exported Utah teapot, we will use the ExternalModelsExample project that we created previously in this chapter.

Browse to the folder inside your project where you have saved your document class. Create a new folder called assets and copy to this folder, the created COLLADA file along with the image used as the material of the teapot.

The class used to load an external COLLADA file is called DAE, so let's import it.

```
import org.papervision3d.objects.parsers.DAE;
```

This type of class is also known as a parser, as it parses the model from a loaded file.

When you have a closer look at the source files of Papervision3D and its model parsers, you will probably find out about the Collada class. This might be a little confusing as we use the DAE parser to load a COLLADA file and we do not use the Collada parser. Although you could use either, this book uses the DAE parser exclusively, as it is a more recent class, supporting more features such as animation. There is no feature that is supported by the Collada parser, and is not supported by the DAE parser.

Replace all code inside the `init()` method with the following code that loads a COLLADA file:

```
model = new DAE();
model.addEventListener(FileLoadEvent.LOAD_COMPLETE,modelLoaded);
DAE(model).load("assets/teapot.DAE");
```

Because `model` is defined as a `DisplayObject3D` class type, we need to cast it to `DAE` to make use of its methods so that we can call the `load()` method.

An event listener is defined, waiting for the model to be completely loaded and parsed. Once it is loaded, the `modelLoaded()` method will be triggered. It is a good convention to add models only to the scene once the model is completely loaded. Add the following line of code to the `modelLoaded()` method:

```
scene.addChild(model);
```

{Ex.} COLLADA Utah Teapot Example {Ex.}

Publishing this code will result in the teapot with the texture as created in 3ds Max.

In real-world applications it is good practice to keep your models in one folder and your textures in another. You might want to organize the files similar to the following structure:

- Models in `/assets/models/`
- Textures in `/assets/textures/`

By default, textures are loaded from the same folder as the model is loaded from, or optionally from the location as specified in the COLLADA file. To include the `/assets/textures/` folder we can add a file search path, which defines to have a look in the specified folder, to see if the file is located there, in case none can be found on the default paths. This can be defined as follows:

```
daeModel.addFileSearchPath("assets/textures");
```

You can call this method multiple times, in order to have multiple folders defined. Internally, in Papervision3D, it will loop through an array of file paths.

Exporting and importing the Utah teapot in 3ds format

Now that we have seen how to get an object from 3ds Max into a Papervision3D project, we have a look at another format that is supported by both 3ds Max and Papervision3D. This format is called **3D Studio**, using a **3ds** extension. It is one of the established 3D file formats that are supported by most 3D modeling tools.

Exporting and importing is very similar to COLLADA. Let's first export the file to the 3D Studio format.

1. Open the Utah teapot, which we've modeled earlier in this chapter.

2. Leave the model as it is, and go straight to export. This time we select **3D Studio (*.3DS)** as the file type. Save it into your project folder and name it **teapot**.

3. Click **OK** when asked whether to preserve Max's texture coordinates.

4. If your model uses `teapotMaterial.jpg` from the book downloads as material, or an image with more than eight characters in its filename, the exporter will output a warning.

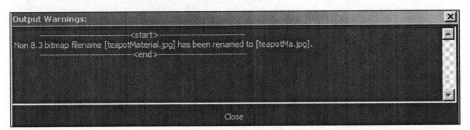

You can close this warning, but you need to be aware of the output message. It says that the bitmap filename is a non-8.3 filename, that is, a maximum amount of 8 characters for the filename and a 3-character extension. The 3D Studio file is an old format, released at the time when there was a DOS version of 3ds Max. Back then it was an OS naming convention to use short filenames, known as 8.3 filenames. This convention still applies to the 3D Studio format, for the sake of backward compatibility. Therefore, the reference to the bitmap has been renamed inside the exported 3D Studio file.

5. Because the exported 3D Studio file changed only the reference to the bitmap filename internally and it did not affect the file it refers to, we need to create a file using this renamed file reference. Otherwise, it won't be able to find the image. In this case we need to create a version of the image called `teapotMa.jpg`. Save this file in the same folder as the exported 3D Studio file.

As you can see, it is very easy to export a model from 3ds Max to a format Papervision3D can read. Modeling the 3D object is definitely the hardest and most time consuming part, simply because creating models takes a lot of time. Loading the model into Papervision3D is just as easy as exporting it.

First, copy the 3D Studio file plus the renamed image to the `assets` folder of your project. We can then alter the document class in order to load the 3ds file. The class that is used to parse a 3D Studio file is called `Max3DS` and needs to be imported.

```
import org.papervision3d.objects.parsers.Max3DS;
```

In the `init()` method you should replace or comment the code that loads the COLLADA model from our previous example, with the following:

```
model = new Max3DS();
model.addEventListener(FileLoadEvent.LOAD_COMPLETE,modelLoaded);
Max3DS(model).load("assets/teapot.3ds", null, "./assets/");
```

As the first parameter of the `load` method, we pass a file reference to the model we want to load. The second parameter defines a materials list, which we will not use for this example. The third and final parameter defines the texture folder. This folder is relative to the location of the published SWF. Note that this works slightly different than the DAE parser, which loads referenced images from the path relative to the folder in which the COLLADA file is located or loads images as specified by the `addFileSearchPath()` method.

{Ex.} ExternalModelsExample {Ex.}

Publish the code and you'll see the same teapot. However, this time it's using the 3D Studio file format as its source.

Importing animated models

The teapot is a static model that we exported from a 3D program and loaded into Papervision3D. It is also possible to load **animated models**, which contain one or multiple animations. 3ds Max is one of the programs in which you can create an animation for use in Papervision3D. Animating doesn't require any additional steps. You can just create the animation and export it. This also goes for other modeling tools that support exporting animations to COLLADA.

For the sake of simplicity, this example will make use of a model that is already animated in 3ds Max. The model contains two animations, which together make up one long animation on a shared timeline. We will export this model and its animation to COLLADA, load it into Papervision3D, and play the two animations.

1. Open **animatedMill.max** in 3ds Max. This file can be found in the book downloads.

2. You can see the animation of the model directly in 3ds Max by clicking the play button in the menu at the bottom right corner, which will animate the blades of the mill. The first 180 frames animate the blades from left to right. Frames 181 to 360 animate the blades from right to left.

3. As the model is already animated, we can go ahead with exporting, without making any changes to the model. Export it using the COLLADA filetype and save it somewhere on your computer.

4. When the COLLADA Max exporter settings window pops up, we need to check the **Sample animation** checkbox. By default **Start** and **End** are set to the length of the timeline as it is defined in 3ds Max. In case you just want to export a part of it, you can define the start and end frames you want to export. For this example we leave them as they are: **0** and **360**.

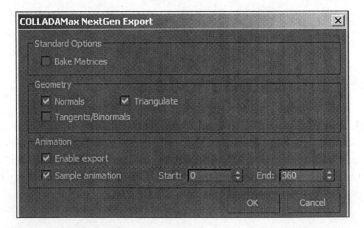

By completing these steps you have successfully exported an animation in the COLLADA format for Papervision3D. Now, have a look at how we can load the animated model into Papervision3D.

First, you need to copy the exported COLLADA and the applied material
— Blades.jpg, House.jpg, and Stand.jpg—to the assets folder of your project.

To load an animated COLLADA, we can use the DAE class again. We only need to
define some parameters at instantiation, so the animation will loop.

```
model = new DAE(true,null,true);
model.addEventListener(FileLoadEvent.LOAD_COMPLETE,modelLoaded);
DAE(model).load("assets/animatedMill.dae");
```

Take a look at what these parameters stand for.

	Parameter	Data type	Default value	Description
1	autoPlay	Boolean	true	When an animation is found in the COLLADA file and this value is set to true, Papervision3D will automatically play the animation. If a COLLADA contains multiple animations it will play all of them.
2	name	String	null	An optional name, which can be handy to find a reference to the model.
3	loop	Boolean	false	Defines whether or not to loop the animation that is found in the COLLADA file. When set to false it will play the animation only once.

Publish the project in order to see the mill with animated blades.

Animation clips

Once the project is published, you will notice that it is playing the two animations—left rotating blades and right rotating blades. This is because we have not defined the animation as two separate animation clips. Right now we just play the entire animation. In order to choose in which direction the blades rotate, we have to define the **animation clips** first. This is nothing more than splitting one long animation into two or more animations that make part of one animation timeline.

The `AnimationClip3D` class takes care of defining an animation clip. The following table lists its parameters at instantiation:

	Parameter	Data type	Default value	Description
1	name	String	—	A unique name for the animation clip. This is used as a reference to play an animation.
2	startTime	Number	0.0	Defines the start time of an animation. It should not be higher than the end time of the total animations. The total time of an animation can be found at the `daeModel.animation.endTime` animation property of a DAE instance.
3	endTime	Number	0.0	Defines the end time of an animation. It should not be higher than the end time of all animations.

 Exported animations are time based instead of frame based as in 3ds Max. All animations in 3ds max should be kept at 30 frames per second.

The `AnimationClip3D` class is imported as follows:

```
import org.papervision3d.core.animation.clip.AnimationClip3D;
```

In this example we want to define two animations—animation right and animation left. The right rotating animation is defined from frame 0 to frame 180, which is half the total animation length. The entire animation is 360 frames at 30 frames per second, which is 360 / 30 = 12 seconds. Therefore, the end time of our right rotating animation will be 6. This will be also the start time of the left rotating blades animation.

Defining the animation clips can be done only when the model is completely loaded, so let's add the following code to the `loadComplete()` method:

```
var animationRight:AnimationClip3D = new AnimationClip3D
                                     ("right",0,6);
var animationLeft:AnimationClip3D = new AnimationClip3D("left",6,12);
```

This defines the time span of the two animation clips, but it still doesn't have any link with the animation in the loaded model. The animation clips need to be registered as playable animation clips on the DAE instance:

```
DAE(model).animation.addClip(animationRight);
DAE(model).animation.addClip(animationLeft);
```

Now the animation clips are defined and ready to be played. Playing an animation makes use of the name that is provided as the first parameter at instantiation of the animation clip. For example, when we want to play the right rotating animation we can call the play method on a DAE instance.

```
DAE(model).play("right");
```

When you want to stop your animation, you can call:

```
DAE(model).stop();
```

{Ex.} ExternalModelsExample {Ex.}

That's easy, isn't it? The most difficult part is definitely making an animated model. There are a lot of online tutorials available that explain how to animate in 3ds Max.

It is important to note that we've exported our model in the COLLADA format. At the time of writing, it is not possible to load animations using the 3D Studio format. COLLADA and **MD2** (which will not be covered by this book) are the only formats for which Papervision3D supports animation.

Creating and loading models using SketchUp

SketchUp is a free 3D modeling program, which was acquired by Google in 2006. It has been designed as a 3D modeling program that's easier to use than other 3D modelling programs. A key to its success is its easy learning curve compared to other 3D tools.

Mac OS X, Windows XP, and Windows Vista operating systems are supported by this program that can be downloaded from http://sketchup.google.com/. Although there is a commercial SketchUp Pro version available, the free version works fine in conjunction with Papervision3D.

An interesting feature for non-3D modelers is the integration with Google's 3D Warehouse. This makes it possible to search for models that have been contributed by other SketchUp users. These models are free of any rights and can be used in commercial (Papervision3D) projects.

Exporting a model from Google's 3D Warehouse for Papervision3D

There are several ways to load a model, coming from Google 3D Warehouse, into Papervision3D. One of them is by downloading a SketchUp file and exporting it to a format Papervision3D works with. This approach will be explained.

The strength of Google 3D Warehouse is also its weakness. Anybody with a Google account can add models to the warehouse. This results in a variety of quality of the models. Some are very optimized and work fluently, whereas others reveal problems when you try to make them work in Papervision3D. Or they may not work at all, as they're made of too many polygons to run in Papervision3D. Take this into account while searching for a model in the 3D warehouse.

For our example we're going to export a picnic table that was found on Google 3D Warehouse.

1. Start Sketch Up.

2. Choose a template when prompted. This example uses **Simple Template – Meters**, although there shouldn't be a problem with using one of the other templates.

3. Go to **File | 3D Warehouse | Get models** to open 3D Warehouse inside SketchUp.

4. Enter a keyword to search for. In this example that will be **picnic table**.

5. Select a model of your choice. Keep in mind that it has to be low poly, which is something you usually find out by trial and error.

6. Click on **Download Model**, to import the model into SketchUp and click **OK** when asked if you want to load the model directly into your Google SketchUp model.

7. Place the model at the origin of the scene. To follow these steps, it doesn't have to be the exact origin, approximately is good enough.

8. By default, a 2D character called **Sang** appears in the scene, which you do not necessarily have to remove; it will be ignored during export.

9. Because the search returned a lot of picnic tables varying in quality, there is a SketchUp file provided with this book. This file has a picnic table already placed on the origin. Of course, you could also choose another picnic table, or any other object of your choice.

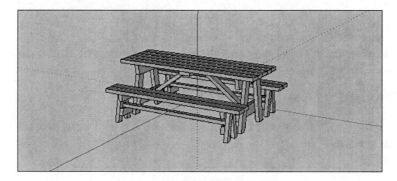

10. Leave the model as it is and export it. Go to **File | Export | 3D Model**. Export it using the **Google Earth** (*.kmz) format and save it in your assets folder.

The file format we're exporting to originally was meant to display 3D objects in Google Earth. The file ends with .kmz as its extension, and is actually a ZIP archive that contains a COLLADA file and the textures. In the early days of Papervision3D, it was a common trick to create a model using SketchUp and then get the COLLADA file out of the exported Google Earth file, as the Google Earth KMZ file format wasn't still supported then.

Importing a Google Earth model into Papervision3D

Now that we have successfully exported a model from SketchUp, we will import it into Papervision3D. This doesn't really differ from loading a COLLADA or 3D Studio file.

The class we use for parsing the created `PicnicTable.kmz` file is called `KMZ` and can be found in the `parsers` package. Add the following line to the import section of your document class:

```
import org.papervision3d.objects.parsers.KMZ;
```

Replace or comment the code that loads the animated COLLADA model and defines the animations from the previous example. In the `init()` method we can then instantiate the `KMZ` class, assign it to the `model` class property, and load the KMZ file. Make sure you have saved `PicnicTable.kmz` file into the `assets` folder of your project.

```
model = new KMZ();
model.addEventListener(FileLoadEvent.LOAD_COMPLETE,modelLoaded);
KMZ(model).load("assets/PicnicTable.kmz");
```

{Ex.} ExternalModelsExample {Ex.}

That looks familiar, right? Now let's publish the project and your model should appear on the screen.

Notice that in many cases, the downloaded and exported model from Google 3D Warehouse might appear very small on your screen in Papervision3D. This is because they are modeled with other metric units than we use in Papervision3D. Our example application places the camera at a 1000 units away from the origin of the scene. Many 3D Warehouse models are made using units that define meters or feet, which makes sense if you were to translate them to real-world units. When a model is, for example, 1 meter wide in SketchUp, this equals to 1 unit in Papervision3D. As you can imagine, a 1 unit wide object in Papervision3D will barely be visible when placing the camera at a distance of 1000. To solve this you could use one of the following options:

- Use other units in Papervision3D and place your camera at a distance of 5 instead of 1000. Usually you can do this at the beginning of your project, but not while the project is already in progress, as this might involve a lot of changes in your code due to other objects, animations, and calculations that are made with a different scale.

- Scale your model inside SketchUp to a value that matches the units as you use them in Papervision3D. When the first option can't be realized, this option is recommended.

- Scale the loaded model in Papervision3D by changing the scale property of your model.

  ```
  model.scale = 20;
  ```

  Although this is an option that works, it's not recommended. Papervision3D has some issues with scaled 3D objects at the time of writing. It is a good convention to use the same units in Papervision3D and your 3D modeling tool.

If you want to learn more about modeling with SketchUp, visit the support page on the SketchUp web site `http://sketchup.google.com/support`. You'll find help resources such as video tutorials and a help forum.

Creating and loading models using Blender

Blender is an open source, platform-independent 3D modeling tool, which was first released in 1998 as a shareware program. It went open source in 2002. Its features are similar to those in commercial tools such as 3ds Max, Maya, and Cinema4D. However, it has a reputation of having a difficult learning curve compared to other 3D modeling programs. Blender is strongly based on usage of keyboard shortcuts and not menus, which makes it hard for new users to find the options they're looking for. In the last few years, more menu-driven interfaces have been added.

It's not in the scope of this book to teach you everything about the modeling tools that can be used with Papervision3D. This also counts for Blender. There are many resources such as online tutorials and books that cover how to work with Blender.

Blender 3D — architecture, buildings, and scenery

Packt Publishing has released a book called *Blender 3D: Architecture, Buildings, and Scenery*, which is targeted at modeling for architecture — a good starting point for learning how to model in Blender . It describes the most important things you need to know about modeling for Papervision3D.

A link to the Blender installer download can be found on its web site: `www.blender.org`.

Exporting a textured cube from Blender into Papervision3D

In this example, we're going to create a textured and UV mapped cube to show how we can export a model from Blender to Papervision3D. The most recent versions of Blender have an integrated COLLADA exporter. Where the integrated exporter in 3ds Max has issues with Papervision3D, this exporter works fluently.

Let's see how we have to model and texture a cube in Blender:

1. Start Blender. By default it opens a minimal scene, made up of a camera, a 3D object, and a light source.

2. Go to **Add | Mesh | Cube** in the top menu. This will add a new cube to the scene.

3. Place the cube on the origin of the scene. You can do this by dragging the gizmo or by changing the transform properties. These can be opened by using the **Object** menu (located at the bottom of the viewports) and by going to **Transform Properties** (shortcut *n*). Set **LocX**, **LocY**, and **LocZ** to **0**, which will set the cube's position to zero on all axes. Double-clicking the current values makes them editable.

 Selecting objects

In case you lose the selection of an object in a Blender scene, you can re-select it by right-clicking it.

4. Scale the object, so it will match the units that we'll use in Papervision3D. This can be achieved in the **Transform Properties** panel. A dimension of 500 on all axes is a good value. You can set either the **Scale** values to 250 or the **Dim** values to 500. When you select the **Link Scale** button, you have to change these values only for one axis, as it will constrain its proportions.

5. Scroll your mouse wheel to zoom out and see the whole cube again.

6. Change from **Object Mode** to **Edit Mode**.

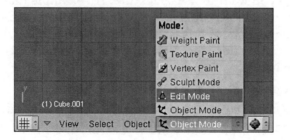

7. The **Object** menu will be replaced with **Mesh** menu. Collapse it and select **UV Unwrap** (shortcut *U* when in edit mode). Click the bottom option called **Unwrap (smart projections)** and click **OK** when a new window shows up. This will create a UV map for us.

8. The unwrapped map of the surface can be found in the **UV/Image Editor**. You can change your view from **3D View** to **UV/Image Editor** by clicking the window icon at the bottom left corner of the 3D view of the scene.

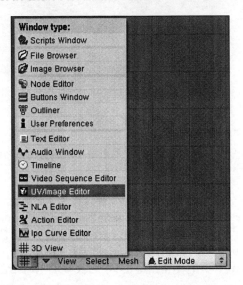

9. The UV/image editor will replace the 3D view and some new menu items show up. Go to the **Image** menu and select **Open** (shortcut *Alt + O*) to open up the image you want to use as texture. An example image can be found in the book downloads. In order to use relative paths in the exported model, we will save the model once it is finished to the same folder as the texture, which we have selected in this step. You might want to take this into account when selecting the image.

10. The selected image should appear on your screen.

11. Exit the UV/image editor by selecting the **3D View** window type.

12. Change the **Draw type** from **Solid** to **Textured**, using the button next to the Mode selection, which we've previously set to **Edit Mode**.

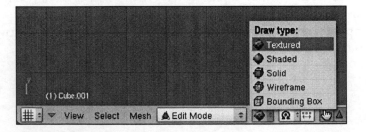

13. In the **Buttons Window**, which is the bottom window by default, select the **Shading** and **Material** button.

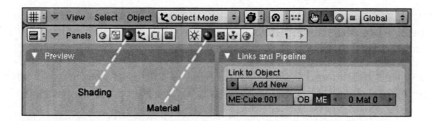

14. You will see the **Links and Pipeline** panel, as shown in the previous image, press **Add New** to link the material to the cube.

15. After linking the object, a new panel called **Material** will show up. Select the **TexFace** button.

16. Save your file in the Blender format into the same directory as you have saved the used texture. This enables us to export using relative paths.

17. Make sure you have the cube still selected and go to **File | Export | COLLADA 1.4 (.dae)**. This will open the COLLADA exporter.

18. Enter location to save the file and make sure you have selected:

    ° **Triangles**
    ° **Only Export Selection** because we do not want to export any other objects in the scene
    ° **Use Relative Paths**, so we do not have to change the path to the material manually in the COLLADA file
    ° **Use UV Image Mats**, so the model will make use of the UV map

19. Press **Export and Close** or just **Export**, to save the COLLADA.

Once these steps are completed successfully, the cube is ready for loading in Papervision3D. Loading this model works exactly the same as loading COLLADA, which is created by 3ds Max.

Copy the created model and texture to the `assets` folder of your project before loading the model. Loading requires you to have the DAE parser imported.

Change the `init()` method so that it will load the COLLADA model instead of the model from our previous example.

```
model = new DAE();
model.addEventListener(FileLoadEvent.LOAD_COMPLETE,modelLoaded);
DAE(model).load("assets/BlenderCube.dae");
```

{Ex.} ExternalModelsExample {Ex.}

Publish your project and you should see the cube we created in Blender.

Keeping control over your materials

It is very convenient that the materials defined inside a 3D modeling tool can be used in Papervision3D. On the other hand, there are situations where you want to have control over materials. To name a few:

- When you want to use another material type such as a movie clip or streaming video
- When you want to change a material property such as `interactive`, `precise`, and `smooth`
- When you want to apply a shader

The moment you call the `load()` method using any of the 3D model parsers, you can pass a material list, specifying the materials you want to use. This works in a similar way to specifying a material list at instantiation of a cube and looks as follows:

```
var materials:MaterialsList = new MaterialsList();
materials.addMaterial(new ColorMaterial(0x0000FF),
"materialDefinition");
var model:DAE = new DAE();
model.load("model.dae",materals);
```

The `materialDefinition` string in the materials list refers to the unique ID of a material that was automatically set during export of a model. As you do not have any control over setting the ID yourself, you have to find it either by opening the COLLADA file in a text editor or trace it once the model has been loaded. The latter approach will be explained in a while.

The final example in this chapter shows how to change properties of a material once the object and materials are loaded. We're going to make the material interactive and rotate the object on each click. The previous example with the Blender-created cube will be used as a starting point.

Create a new project out of the previous example. For this new project we will use Tweener, so add the Tweener library to your **Build Path** (Flex Builder), **Classpath** (Flash CS3) or **Source Path** (Flash CS4), like we've seen in Chapter 4.

In the `init()` method we can set viewport interactivity to `true` and add an event listener to the model, waiting for `FileLoadEvent.LOAD_COMPLETE` to be dispatched.

```
viewport.interactive = true;
model.addEventListener(FileLoadEvent.LOAD_COMPLETE, modelLoaded);
```

Next, we define the `modelLoaded()` method. Once this method is triggered, we will have full access to the loaded model and its child objects.

```
private function modelLoaded(e:FileLoadEvent):void
{
```

As we're going to change the materials applied to the model, it might be helpful to trace `model.materials`, to find out their name(s). Some exporters automatically define a material name or add a suffix to the name, which was defined in the modeling program.

```
trace("Used materials by this model: " + model.materials);
```

In our case this would trace `BlenderCube_jpg`. This string can be used to get an object's material, allowing you to set its properties.

```
model.getMaterialByName("BlenderCube_jpg").interactive = true;
```

 Note that if you want to set `BitmapMaterial`-specific properties such as smooth, you first need to cast the material to `BitmapMaterial`.

Next, we define a listener waiting for clicks on an object nested inside the model. This needs to be set for every child object you want to be clickable. Therefore, we use `model.getChildByName` and search for a nested object. You can set the second parameter recursive to `true`, in order to search for a nested object inside a nested object. In fact, the model is a child object of the DAE class that was used to load it.

```
model.getChildByName("Cube_001", true).addEventListener
                        (InteractiveScene3DEvent.OBJECT_CLICK, click);
}
```

The name `Cube_001` was automatically defined inside the modeling tool. You can also see this name when Papervision3D parses the object and traces its name in the output window.

INFO: DisplayObject3D: Cube_001

To see this you can publish the previous project that also loads the cube created in Blender.

In the final part of this example, we set up the `click()` method that will be triggered each time the cube is clicked. Tweener will be used to animate the cube.

```
private var targetRotationX:Number = 0;

private function click(e:InteractiveScene3DEvent):void
{
    targetRotationX+=90;
    Tweener.addTween(model, {localRotationX:targetRotationX, time:1.5,
transition:"easeOutElastic"});
}
```

{Ex.} ModelMaterialsExample {Ex.}

Publish this code and you will see the same cube as in the Blender example. However, clicking on it will rotate the cube over its local x-axis, with an elastic transition.

As this example shows, we can change material properties at run time. If you like, you can even change the material at run time, just like you would replace a material on primitive cube. As we have seen in previous chapters a primitive cube also works with a material list.

Summary

Modeling is a very broad topic as there are many 3D programs, each with numerous features. When you want to display custom objects besides the built-in primitives, you can load models created by 3D programs.

This chapter showed how to create basic models in 3ds Max, SketchUp, and Blender, and how to export them for Papervision3D. To do this we've used three different file formats:

- COLLADA (`.dae`): An open source 3D model file type, which has been supported since the early releases of Papervision3D. This is the most developed file type, which also supports animation and animation clips.
- 3D Studio (`.3ds`): An established 3D file format that is supported by most 3D modeling programs.
- SketchUp (`.kmz`): A format that is used by Google Earth, which can be created by a free program called SketchUp.

Creating models for use in Papervision3D has some requirements and conventions to take into account:

- Keep a low polygon count
- Add polygons to problematic parts of your model to prevent z-sorting artifacts or texture distortion
- Keep your texture small
- Use textures Flash can read
- Use UV maps
- Bake textures
- Use recognizable names for objects and materials
- Use the same metrics as in Papervision3D
- Find balance in optimization

Models that are loaded in Papervision3D automatically load images that are defined as materials in the 3D modeling program. At the end of this chapter we've seen how we can have access to these materials. The way we can access a model's material doesn't differ from accessing a material on a primitive cube.

The next chapter discusses z-sorting. We're going to have a look at how Papervision3D draws its renders to the viewport and the issues with determining which object should be drawn first. The mill that was used in this chapter will be part of an example on how to solve z-sorting issues.

9
Z-Sorting

Z-sorting issues are among the most common problems experienced when working with Papervision3D. But what is **z-sorting** and what are the problems that come with it? And most importantly—how do we get rid of them while maintaining good performance? This chapter discusses the following topics:

- What is z-sorting
- Layering scene renders
- Complex rendering using quadtrees

By the end of this chapter, you will know how to solve z-sorting issues and realize that beauty comes at a price. Therefore, we first need to know what exactly is z-sorting and what is causing the issues.

What is z-sorting

Chances are that you have already experienced issues with z-sorting while reading this book or seeing some demos made with Papervision3D. Especially in the previous chapter about modeling, which introduced situations that are bound to cause z-sorting problems. The more complex your model is, the sooner you will experience z-sorting problems.

The following image shows the teapot that was used in Chapter 7 as part of the shading types demo. It clearly shows what the z-sorting issue is about.

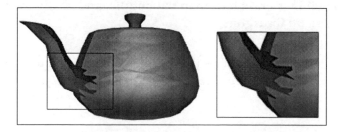

Notice that some of the triangles seem to be missing. The missing triangles of the spout are sorted behind triangles of the teapot body. This issue is an artifact of how z-sorting works in Papervision3D .

The painter's algorithm

Z-sorting is the process of determining the depth of each triangle that will be drawn on the screen. It defines the order in which the triangles are drawn on top of each other, based on their distance to the camera. The process of determining which triangle should be in front is CPU intensive. By default, Papervision3D uses a very fast but not very accurate algorithm to determine the sorting of each triangle. This algorithm is known as the **painter's algorithm**, whose name comes from a technique that is often used by painters, in which the distant parts of a scene are drawn before the nearer parts.

The painter's algorithm works as follows:

- First, all of the triangles that are positioned inside the camera frustum are sorted from the furthest to the closest, relative to the camera.

- Then, each triangle is drawn on your screen in the order in which they are sorted.

This means, drawing begins with the farthest and ends with the closest triangles. The following illustration shows this process, which can be found on the Wikipedia page about this subject:

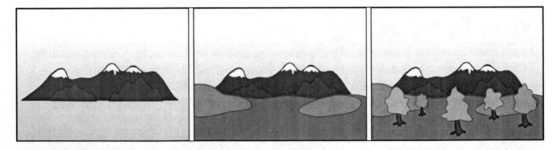

As you can see, the image on the left draws the mountains. These are farthest from the camera, followed by a grass terrain in the middle, and finally the trees that are closest to the camera on the right.

 More information about the painter's algorithm can be found on Wikipedia at: http://en.wikipedia.org/wiki/Painter's_algorithm.

Sorting triangles

To better understand the problems related to z-sorting, we need to know how the triangles are sorted. The following image shows two illustrative triangles and their distance to the camera:

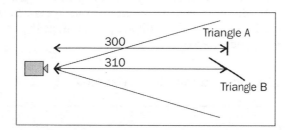

How do you think these triangles will be sorted and drawn on your screen? Keep in mind what was explained in the previous section about the painter's algorithm. To draw these triangles in correct order, triangle A should be drawn first followed by triangle B. However, the painter's algorithm draws the farthest triangle first, which is triangle B and then the closest triangle, which is triangle A.

The following image illustrates the expected render and the z-sorted render using the painter's algorithm, applied on two triangle pairs that are also known as polygons in 3D modeling programs:

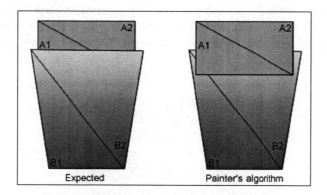

Depending on the situation, this can be solved by a variety of techniques, which will be discussed in this chapter. A very basic but effective solution for this situation would be to subdivide polygon B, so that you end up with triangles that are in front of the triangles of polygon A and triangles that are behind it. This adds more detail, and hence more accuracy in sorting the triangles.

In 3D modeling tools, subdividing is the process of splitting up one polygon into multiple polygons. This needs to be done with a modeling tool and cannot be achieved with Papervision3D.

When you are working with the built-in primitives, you can add more segments to your objects to get similar results. Note that this only adds extra triangles and doesn't subdivide polygons, as Papervision3D knows only about triangles.

The following image illustrates subdividing Triangle B:

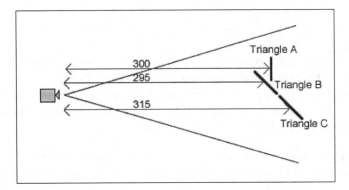

Triangle pair B has been subdivided into two new triangle pairs—B and C. Rendering this scene will result in drawing triangle pair C first, followed by triangle pair A, and finally triangle pair B in front. This will result in the following rendered image:

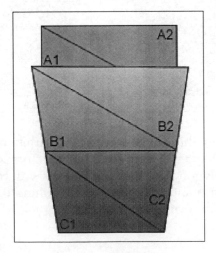

This works fine in this situation where we are looking at the object from a given point of view. Changing the point of view also changes the order in which triangles are sorted, and hence this might introduce new z-sorting issues. Have a look at the following image, which illustrates a new point of view for the same triangles as used previous:

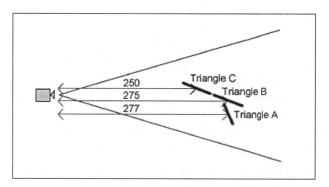

Because triangle pair A is farthest from this point of view, it will be drawn first, followed by triangle pair B, and then triangle pair C. This will cause triangle pair B to overlap triangle pair A, which is a z-sorting problem.

As you can see, z-sorting is a bit problematic with the default way in which Papervision3D works. Subdividing your 3D objects so that they have more triangles might be a solution. However, adjusting your models in a 3D modeling tool could become more time consuming as your project grows. Fortunately, there are alternative approaches to solve these issues.

Layering your renders

Performance wise, adding more triangles is not always the best solution. Each vertex of a triangle will be projected and the triangles need to be drawn on your screen. More triangles means more work for the CPU to render. An alternative to adding more triangles is to use **viewport layers**. Viewport layers are nested and extended sprites of a viewport. Essentially, these layers work the same as layers in programs such as Photoshop and Flash. In Photoshop, each layer can hold a single element or a composition of elements. With layers in Papervision3D, we can do the same. We can, for example, render a chair on one layer and a table on another. The order of each layer can either be defined manually or automatically, using the algorithms provided by Papervision3D.

To demonstrate each approach, we'll reuse the animated mill that was introduced in Chapter 8, *External Models*, and place it on a ground surface, which will immediately reveal serious z-sorting problems. Let's first create a template application for the examples in this chapter:

```
package {
    import flash.events.Event;
    import org.papervision3d.core.animation.clip.AnimationClip3D;
    import org.papervision3d.events.FileLoadEvent;
    import org.papervision3d.materials.ColorMaterial;
    import org.papervision3d.materials.WireframeMaterial;
    import org.papervision3d.materials.special.CompositeMaterial;
    import org.papervision3d.objects.parsers.DAE;
    import org.papervision3d.objects.primitives.Plane;
    import org.papervision3d.view.BasicView;

    private class ViewportLayersExample extends BasicView
    {
        private var mill:DAE;
        private var floor:Plane;
        private var rotX:Number = 0.1;
        private var rotY:Number = 0.1;
        private var camPitch:Number = 90;
        private var camYaw:Number = 270;
        private var easeOut:Number = 0.1;

        public function ViewportLayersExample()
        {
            stage.frameRate = 40;
            init();
        }

        private function init():void
        {
            mill = new DAE(true,null,true);
            mill.addEventListener(FileLoadEvent.LOAD_COMPLETE,
                modelLoaded);
            mill.load("assets/animatedMill.dae");

            var colorMat:ColorMaterial = new ColorMaterial(0x006600);
            var wireMat:WireframeMaterial = new WireframeMaterial();
            var floorMat:CompositeMaterial = new CompositeMaterial();
            floorMat.addMaterial(colorMat);
            floorMat.addMaterial(wireMat);
            floorMat.doubleSided = true;

            floor = new Plane(floorMat,1000,1000,1,1);
```

```
      floor.y = -410;
      scene.addChild(floor);
      floor.rotationX = 90;
    }

    private function modelLoaded(e:FileLoadEvent):void
    {
      scene.addChild(mill);
      var animationLeft:AnimationClip3D = new AnimationClip3D
                                    ("right",0,6);
      var animationRight:AnimationClip3D = new AnimationClip3D
                                    ("left",6,12);

      mill.animation.addClip(animationRight);
      mill.animation.addClip(animationLeft);

      mill.play("right");

      startRendering();
    }

    override protected function onRenderTick(e:Event=null):void
    {
      var xDist:Number = mouseX - stage.stageWidth * 0.5;
      var yDist:Number = mouseY - stage.stageHeight * 0.5;

      camPitch += ((yDist * rotX) - camPitch + 90) * easeOut;
      camYaw += ((xDist * rotY) - camYaw + 270) * easeOut;

      camera.orbit(camPitch, camYaw);

      super.onRenderTick();
    }
  }
}
```

By now, this class should look quite familiar, as it is based on previous examples. In the init() method, we first load the external model, add it to the scene, and wait for the FileLoadEvent.LOAD_COMPLETE event. This is followed by the creation of a composite material made of green color and a wireframe for the floor, which helps us to see how the triangles are sorted.

The rest of the code relates to mouse interaction, which orbits the camera around the origin of the scene, similar to what we have done in previous chapters.

Before we continue, let's see how the published application appears on screen. The floor introduces some z-sorting issues:

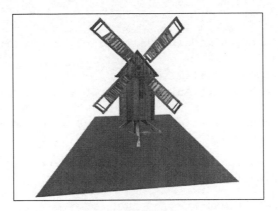

Notice how the bottom of the mill disappears behind the ground that it overlaps with. By using layers, we'll try to solve this.

Creating a viewport layer

The mill and the floor make a perfect scene to demonstrate viewport layers. When we look at the previous image, we can tell that the total surface of the floor should be drawn at the back as the bottom layer, and the mill at the front as the top layer. There are multiple ways to accomplish this.

Creating a viewport layer using useOwnContainer

The easiest way to create a layer is by setting the useOwnContainer property of do3D to true, which causes Papervision3D to add a new layer and draw the do3D onto it. You cannot add other objects to this layer. This approach is more CPU intensive than the other approaches that we will see.

 Because useOwnContainer is more CPU intensive than the other approaches, it is not advised to use it for purposes other than quickly prototyping an application.

First, have a look at how to draw the mill in a layer using the useOwnContainer property, which can be done by adding the following code to the modelLoaded() method:

```
mill.useOwnContainer = true;
```

Each object that is not defined to be rendered to a layer will be rendered to the viewport. All viewport layers lay on top of the viewport. In this example, where we have only added the mill to a layer using `useOwnContainer`, the floor will be rendered to the regular viewport with the mill on top, as it is a part of a viewport layer.

{Ex.} ViewportLayersExample {Ex.}

At first glance, publishing your code will already result in a better view of your scene:

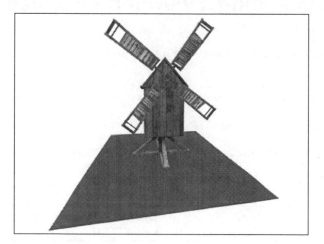

As said, initially this looks just like we want it to be rendered. No z-sorting problems between the floor and the mill can be found. However, when the camera moves to a lower point of view, you will notice a new issue, which is made clear by the two pictures in the following image:

Because the mill is always drawn on the front, this approach results in nonrealistic looking renders.

This is where sorting layers comes in handy. Papervision3D has several options to sort layers automatically. However, some situations require doing this by hand. Before we look at the sorting options, we will first discuss the other ways to create a viewport layer, which are more efficient performance wise. Use these two approaches instead of useOwnContainer in real-world applications.

Creating and sorting a viewport layer using getChildLayer

The second way to create a layer is to get a ViewportLayer instance from the viewport.

```
var millLayer:ViewportLayer = viewport.getChildLayer(mill);
```

In order to make this work, we also need to import the ViewportLayer class:

```
import org.papervision3d.view.layer.ViewportLayer;
```

The method getChildLayer() takes three parameters:

	Parameter	Data type	Default value	Description
1	do3d	DisplayObject3D		Defines a do3D whose layer you want to access or create by using the second parameter createNew.
2	createNew	Boolean	true	Defines whether or not to create a new viewport layer for the passed do3D, in case no viewport layer is found for the object.
3	recurse	Boolean	true	Defines whether the children of do3D also need to be added to the viewport layer.

Once you have a viewport layer instance, you can also register other 3D objects that need to be rendered in the same layer. So when we have, for example, multiple mills in a row, we can render them into just one layer. To demonstrate, we will add the floor to the previously created millLayer. This is not very practical, as the result will be equal to using no layers at all, but it gives you an idea of how it works:

```
millLayer.addDisplayObject3D(floor);
```

[Ex.] ViewportLayersExample [Ex.]

That brings us to the final approach on creating a viewport layer.

Creating a viewport layer by instantiating a new ViewportLayer

It is also possible to manually create a `ViewportLayer` instance. The following code demonstrates how to do this:

```
var millLayer:ViewportLayer = new ViewportLayer(viewport,null);
viewport.containerSprite.addLayer(millLayer);
millLayer.addDisplayObject3D(mill,true);
```

Instantiation of a `ViewportLayer` takes three parameters:

	Parameter	Data type	Default value	Description
1	viewport	Viewport3D	—	A `Viewport3D` instance in which the layer should be created.
2	do3d	DisplayObject3D	—	A do3D that needs to be added to the layer.
				In the `getChildLayer()` method we could set recurse to true in order to add all children to the layer. However, there is no recurse parameter to set when instantiating `ViewportLayer`, therefore this is set to null in the above example. The mill is added using the `addDisplayObject3D()` method, which supports a recurse parameter.
3	isDynamic	Boolean	false	Defines whether or not to remove the layer in the next render. This is used only internally by Papervision3D and should never be touched manually.

[Ex.] ViewportLayersExample [Ex.]

After instantiation of viewport, we registered the viewport layer. We also added the mill model to the layer with the recurse parameter set to `true`.

Sorting layers

The previous examples showed that creating a viewport layer helps preventing z-sorting problems. However, adding layers may result in sorting problems for the layers themselves. Papervision3D has three built-in sorting modes that solve these problems in some cases. The way Papervision3D sorts the layers is defined by the `sortMode` property of a viewport container sprite:

```
viewport.containerSprite.sortMode = ViewportLayerSortMode.Z_SORT;
```

Papervision3D supports three sorting algorithms for viewport layers, which are assigned by one of the three constants from `ViewportLayerSortMode`:

- `ViewportLayerSortMode.Z_SORT`
- `ViewportLayerSortMode.ORIGIN_SORT`
- `ViewportLayerSortMode.INDEX_SORT`

To define the sorting mode with one of the constants, you need to import `ViewportLayerSortMode`:

```
import org.papervision3d.view.layer.util.ViewportLayerSortMode;
```

Sorting layers with ViewportLayerSortMode.Z_SORT

By default, layers are z-sorted, which is based on the average z-distance of all vertices in a layer. The layer with the longest average z-distance to the camera is drawn first, followed by layers that are closer. You can see this is as z-sorting based on a do3D (or multiple do3Ds), instead of triangle.

So far, we have created only one layer for the mill. When we want to z-sort the floor and the mill, we also need to add the floor to a viewport layer.

```
var millLayer:ViewportLayer = viewport.getChildLayer(mill);
var floorLayer:ViewportLayer = viewport.getChildLayer(floor);
```

These lines create two viewport layers. When you publish this code and try to view the scene from the bottom, up to the 3D model and the floor, you'll notice that the layers automatically seem to have correct z-sorting. However, when you look carefully and position the camera just a little above the floor, you'll notice some z-sorting issues again, but this time the whole floor is drawn in front of the mill, instead of just a single triangle.

In some cases, you can help Papervision3D by setting a forced screen depth on certain layers. For example, if you know that the floor is always 2000 units away from the camera, you can force this value so that it sorts the viewport layers as if the floor is constantly 2000 units away from the camera.

```
floorLayer.forceDepth = true;
floorLayer.screenDepth = 2000;
```

This especially comes in handy when you have more than two viewport layers and want the floor to always be at the back and at the same time want to sort the other objects on their calculated z-distance to the camera. You may want to play around with these properties, but do not expect them to solve the z-sorting issues in our example.

Sorting layers with ViewportLayerSortMode. ORIGIN_SORT

The second sorting algorithm is based on the origin point of each do3D, which is useful when the default z-sorting mode isn't accurate enough. This could happen when you have a model that has a lot of vertices based on one side and fewer vertices on the other. When these positions are averaged, your object can get out of balance. Origin sorting prevents this by applying sorting based on an object's origin point, which is equal to x:0, y:0, and z:0 in the local space of an object.

When a layer contains multiple objects, the origin points are averaged.

Sorting layers with ViewportLayerSortMode.INDEX_ SORT

The third and last algorithm for z-sorting layers is based on an index number, which we define, allowing us to control the order manually.

```
var millLayer:ViewportLayer = viewport.getChildLayer(mill);
var floorLayer:ViewportLayer = viewport.getChildLayer(floor);
millLayer.layerIndex = 1;
floorLayer.layerIndex = 2;
viewport.containerSprite.sortMode = ViewportLayerSortMode.INDEX_SORT;
```

We set the layerIndex property of millLayer to 1 and floorLayer to 2, resulting in drawing the millLayer first and then the floorLayer on top. Although it is not very practical to render the floor on top, the above code demonstrates how to use the layerIndex property.

So far, we have seen some options to sort the viewport layers, but none resulted in correctly drawing the objects from all points of view in the demo application. An option for the floor is to make it one-sided, instead of double sided. This way, we will not draw the floor at all when we get beneath the floor surface. But for now, that's not what we want; we want to see the floor and mill correctly when the camera is above and below the surface. So, what if we were to use index sorting for the layers, and swap the layer index of the mill layer and floor layer once the camera is above or below the floor?

The `onRenderTick()` method is a good place to check and change these values:

```
if(camera.y<-410)
{
  viewport.getChildLayer(mill).layerIndex = 1;
  viewport.getChildLayer(floor).layerIndex = 2;
}
else
{
  viewport.getChildLayer(mill).layerIndex = 2;
  viewport.getChildLayer(floor).layerIndex = 1;
}
```

Don't forget to set the sort mode to index sorting, by adding the following line to the `modelLoaded()` method:

```
viewport.containerSprite.sortMode = ViewportLayerSortMode.INDEX_SORT;
```

{Ex.} ViewportLayersExample {Ex.}

The above code solves the problem in this example, but as each project is different, it will not work in every situation.

Creating and sorting sublayers

Viewports are not the only objects that support layers. Layers themselves can also contain layers and have their own sorting mode. This allows you to apply multiple ways of sorting within one scene, which is useful when several objects in your scene require a different approach to solving z-sorting issues.

The following image shows the hierarchy of an illustrative scene and viewport with nested viewport layers and different sort modes:

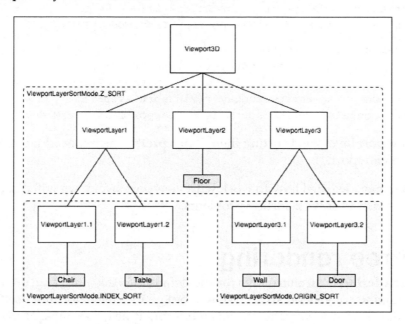

Creating a structure of layers and objects as illustrated in the previous figure could be done by using the following code:

 The following code is purely illustrative and is not part of an example.

```
//Create viewport layer 1 structure
var viewportLayer1:ViewportLayer = new ViewportLayer(viewport,null);
var viewportLayer1_1:ViewportLayer = new ViewportLayer(viewport,
                                    chair);
var viewportLayer1_2:ViewportLayer = new ViewportLayer(viewport,
                                    table);
viewportLayer1.addLayer(viewportLayer1_1);
viewportLayer1.addLayer(viewportLayer1_2);
viewportLayer1.sortMode = ViewportLayerSortMode.INDEX_SORT;

//Create a regular viewport layer 2
var viewportLayer2:ViewportLayer = new ViewportLayer(viewport,floor);

//Create viewport layer 3 structure
var viewportLayer3:ViewportLayer = new ViewportLayer(viewport,null);
var viewportLayer3_1:ViewportLayer = new ViewportLayer(viewport,wall);
```

```
var viewportLayer3_2:ViewportLayer = new ViewportLayer(viewport,door);
viewportLayer3.addLayer(viewportLayer3_1);
viewportLayer3.addLayer(viewportLayer3_2);
viewportLayer3.sortMode = ViewportLayerSortMode.ORIGIN_SORT;

//Add parent layers to the viewport
viewport.containerSprite.addLayer(viewportLayer1);
viewport.containerSprite.addLayer(viewportLayer2);
viewport.containerSprite.addLayer(viewportLayer3);
viewport.containerSprite.sortMode = ViewportLayerSortMode.Z_SORT;
```

Nesting viewport layers and sorting them looks pretty much like adding and sorting layers in the viewport.

Now that we have learned how to work with viewport layers, we will discuss another approach to solve z-sorting problems.

Quadtree rendering

Quadtree rendering is an alternative for the default `BasicRenderEngine`, which is the render engine we've used so far. We will not go into the algorithm used by this renderer. All we need to know about this rendering type is that most of the time it solves z-sorting issues. It's been mentioned earlier that quality often costs CPU power. That definitely counts for quadtree rendering as this is a real CPU killer. However, its use is very simple, so let's see how it works.

First we create a new project, based on the `ViewportLayersExample` class from the beginning of this chapter. Add the following import at the top of your document class:

```
import org.papervision3d.render.QuadrantRenderEngine;
```

Then, add the following to the `init()` method:

```
renderer = new QuadrantRenderEngine();
```

This code replaces the `BasicRenderEngine`, which was instantiated automatically by the `BasicView` class, with a `QuadrantRenderEngine` instance. That's all you have to do in order to render with the quadtree algorithm. Publishing the code shows that the floor and mill are both z-sorted in a correct manner immediately!

Instantiation of `QuadrantRenderEngine` takes one parameter, defining which type you want to use for corrective z-sorting. These types are static constant properties of the `QuadrantRenderEngine` class:

- `QuadrantRenderEngine.CORRECT_Z_FILTER`: This should be used for corrective z-sorting of all triangles that do not intersect with other triangles.

- `QuadrantRenderEngine.QUAD_SPLIT_FILTER`: For triangles that intersect other triangles, this type could be used. The render engine will automatically split the intersecting triangles for correct z-sorting on intersecting parts.

- `QuadrantRenderEngine.ALL_FILTERS`: This is a combination of the above filters. When you use `QuadrantRenderEngine.QUAD_SPLIT_FILTER`, you probably also want to have the correct z filter applied for the other triangles that do not intersect. This is the default type, when you do not provide the `QuadrantRenderEngine` with a type parameter at instantiation.

When you publish your code, you'll notice that its performance is horrible. Because we have a model that is made of quite a few triangles, the limits of quadtree rendering are already reached. Fortunately, there is an optimization at hand to run it a bit better.

The problem is that every triangle is sorted and rendered with the quadtree algorithm. However, it is not always necessary to render each triangle using this algorithm. We can exclude 3D objects from being rendered using quadtrees so that they will be rendered with the default render engine. This can be achieved by setting the `testQuad` property of a do3D to `false`.

The problem in our example is the z-sorting of the floor. It would be enough in this case to just render the floor using quadtrees and render the mill with the regular render engine.

```
mill.getChildByName("Blades",true).testQuad = false;
mill.getChildByName("Stand",true).testQuad = false;
mill.getChildByName("House",true).testQuad = false;
```

Because setting `mill.testQuad` to `false` doesn't work recursively for its children, we have to set the `testQuad` properties on all the children of the do3D.

{Ex.} QuadTreeRenderingExample {Ex.}

After publishing, you'll notice some increase in speed while still having correct z-sorting of the floor and the mill.

Summary

Z-sorting is about sorting triangles and deciding in which order the triangles need to be drawn on the viewport. Drawing a render happens from furthest triangles to the closest triangles, based on their position in relation to the camera. This is known as the painter's algorithm.

There are several ways to affect the order in which objects are rendered.

We learned about viewport layers, which are similar to layers in Photoshop, for example. These layers can be ordered in three ways:

- `ViewportLayerSortMode.Z_SORT`
- `ViewportLayerSortMode.ORIGIN_SORT`
- `ViewportLayerSortMode.INDEX_SORT`

The z-sorting issues we've seen with the mill and floor were solved by index sorting. Based on the position of the camera, we changed the layer index order. This is not the solution for all z-sorting problems. But for the example discussed in the chapter, it worked great.

Besides adding and sorting viewport layers as children of the viewport, we've also seen how we can nest viewport layers as children of other viewport layers. This way, you can even use several viewport sorting modes in one application.

At the end of the chapter, we had a look at quadtree rendering, which is an advanced algorithm that creates better renders in order to solve z-sorting issues. We learned how we can accomplish correct z-sorting for non-intersecting triangles using the `QuadrantRenderEngine.CORRECT_Z_FILTER` type. Sorting on intersecting triangles can be solved with `QuadrantRenderEngine.QUAD_SPLIT_FILTER`. Most of the time you also want to use the correct z-filter type together with the quad split filter. In those cases, you can set `QuadrantRenderEngine.ALL_FILTERS`.

As said earlier, beauty comes at a price. The price you pay is either a lower performance when using quadtree rendering, or more work and time on creative thinking when using viewport layers.

Adding objects to viewport layers can solve z-sorting problems. Another use of layers is when you want to apply effects. The next chapter will explain how you can add all kinds of effects to your scenes—from simple transparency, to glows, blurs, blend modes, and even fire.

10
Particles

Particles are 2D graphics, which are positioned relative to 3D coordinates without using perspective projection. In other words, particles always face the camera. Another characteristic of particles is that they are lightweight objects. As the performance of your 3D application is greatly affected by the number of triangles, their lightweightness makes particles a good partner to work with. In this chapter, we will discuss why to use particles and walk through some examples that demonstrate how to create them.

This chapter covers the following:

- What are particles and why to use them
- How to create particles and apply particle materials
- Adding interactivity to particles
- How to create particle fields
- Working with the Flint particle system

Before we examine how to create particles, let's see what they are and how we can use them.

What particles are and why to use them

If you have ever played 3D games, you must have seen particles in action. Many 3D games use particles to simulate all kinds of (mostly natural) phenomena such as explosions, falling leaves, and blood spatters.

In Papervision3D, a particle can be described as a 2D graphic that can be scaled and positioned relative to a 3D point. Think of it as a lightweight plane that always faces the camera. This chapter mainly discusses the following two aspects of working with particles:

- Billboarding, which is a technique used to cut down the number of triangles in your scene
- Creating natural phenomena, which is usually done with the help of a particle system

The two aspects do not exclude each other. However, this classification is a good starting point when discussing particles in Papervision3D.

Billboarding

Suppose you want a couple of trees in your scene. To create the trees you would probably need many polygons. However, depending on the other objects in the scene, rendering the trees could be quite hard for the user's computer. Or suppose you want to add 1000 reflective balls. Creating 1000 spheres with shading would also be very CPU consuming. A technique to deal with such situations is the use of particles.

Now, suppose we have a 2D graphic of a shiny ball. By positioning and scaling instances of the 2D graphic relative to 3D coordinates, you can give the illusion that it is a 3D object. This way you would cut down on the polygons immensely. The technique of replacing a 3D object with a 2D graphic that faces the camera is called **billboarding**.

Take a look at the following picture, which is a screenshot from a Papervision3D scene. It shows three shiny balls that seem to be 3D objects positioned in 3D space. But they are not spheres created in Papervision3D or in a modeling program. They are simply 2D graphics, created in a graphics editing program.

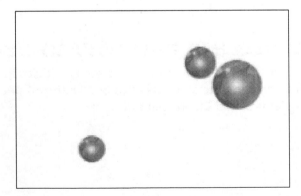

Billboarding has pros and cons. Using 2D graphics instead of 3D objects with a lot of triangles gives the renderer a much lighter workload. However, billboard particles may look less realistic than 3D objects for two reasons. Firstly, you cannot move the camera around a particle to get a view from a different angle, as you can with a 3D object. Secondly, the particles in the previous screenshot look like balls that reflect light. But the reflection will always look the same no matter where the camera is, which may lead to a less realistic result than a sphere with real-time shading.

Speaking of realism, particles do not necessarily have to be graphics with baked shading. In this chapter we will see particles that consist of just a circle or square. But generating, positioning, and scaling a lot of these particles in your scene can still create a pretty strong 3D experience and can, for instance, be used to suggest a star field. The following screenshot was also taken from a Papervision3D scene:

Creating a star field of particles as shown in the previous screenshot is fairly simple in Papervision3D as we will see in the examples. But creating phenomena such as explosions, falling snow, or fountains is more complicated and would require pretty advanced coding. This is where particle systems come in.

Particle systems

There are many ways to define what a particle system is. Let's summarize what all definitions seem to have in common:

- Particle systems simulate organic phenomena such as fireworks and falling leaves.
- A particle system generates and moves a collection of small objects (particles).
- The particles have attributes such as velocity and acceleration.

- There is a random element built-in to manipulate the attributes of the particles within certain limits that are usually set by the program.
- The particles have a lifecycle—they are created, move according to their characteristics, and then become extinct.

Usually the particles are generated by an **emitter**, which also initializes the attributes of each particle. The following screenshot shows a fountain that was created with the help of a particle system:

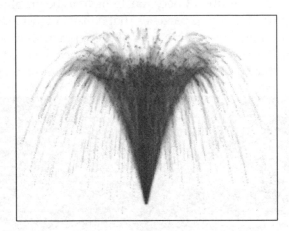

Papervision3D does not include a particle system, but at the end of this chapter we will take a look at an external, open source library called **Flint**, which can be easily used with Papervision3D.

We have discussed what particles are and what we can use them for. It's time to turn these thoughts into some practical examples and see how we create particles in Papervision3D.

Creating particles

The process of creating and displaying particles looks as follows:

- Create a particle material
- Create a `Particles` instance, which will be used to contain and render the particles
- Use the `Particle` class to instantiate a particle (or more likely, a whole bunch), and pass material, size, and position as parameters to it
- Use the `addParticle()` method to add the particle(s) to the `Particles` object

The order of the first two steps is interchangeable because the particle material and the `Particles` instance do not need each other.

Using a `Particles` class, as well as a `Particle` class may sound confusing. The `Particles` instance is solely used to hold and render the `Particle` instances and, in fact, is a do3D. But the `Particle` instances are the actual particles and the applied material defines the way they look.

To create particles in Papervision3D we need materials that define their appearance. You can apply three types of material to a particle:

- **ParticleMaterial**: The most basic material, which allows you to create particles in the shape of a circle or a rectangle.

- **BitmapParticleMaterial**: Material that uses a bitmap as the source. The bitmap can be drawn dynamically or loaded externally.

- **MovieAssetParticleMaterial**: Material that uses a movie clip asset as a source. This is the only material that can be made interactive.

Before we go through the three types of material and apply them to particles, we will first create a template class that makes it easy for you to follow along with the examples.

A template class for all the examples

Because the examples have a lot in common, we will first create a template class (based on the `BookTemplateExample`), which we can reuse as a starting point for each example.

The template class for this chapter looks like this:

```
package {

    import flash.events.Event;
    import org.papervision3d.view.BasicView;
    import org.papervision3d.core.geom.Particles;
    import org.papervision3d.core.geom.renderables.Particle;

    public class ParticleTemplate extends BasicView
    {
        private var numberOfParticles:uint;

        private var easeOut:Number = 0.3
        private var reachX:Number = 0.1
        private var reachY:Number = 0.1
```

```
        private var reachZ:Number = 0.5;

        public function ParticleTemplate()
        {
                super(stage.stageWidth,stage.stageHeight);
                stage.frameRate = 40;

                init();
                startRendering();
        }

        private function init():void
        {
                //code to be added

                numberOfParticles = 1000;

                for(var i:uint = 0; i < numberOfParticles; i++)
                {
                        //code to be added

                }
        }

        private function randPos():Number
        {
                returnMath.random() * 4000 -2000;
        }

        override protected function onRenderTick(e:Event=null):void
        {
                var xDist:Number = mouseX - stage.stageWidth * 0.5;
                var yDist:Number = mouseY - stage.stageHeight * 0.5;

                camera.x += (xDist - camera.x * reachX) * easeOut;
                camera.y += (yDist - camera.y * reachY) * easeOut;
                camera.z += (-mouseY * 2 - camera.z ) * reachZ;

                super.onRenderTick();
        }

    }
}
```

Basically, we took the `BookExampleTemplate` class and added the following few things:

- We imported the `Particle` class, as well as the `Particles` class, as you need both to create particles.

- In the `init()` method we defined the number of particles we want to create—`1,000` in our examples. In some of the examples we need to access the value of `numberOfParticles` outside the `init()` method, so we made it a class property.

- Still in the `init()` method, we created a `for` loop, which is still empty. However, it will be used to instantiate particles, give them a material, and add them to the `Particles` instance.

- We added a `randPos()` method that returns random positions between `2,000` and `-2,000`.

- Inside the `onRenderTick()` method we added some code that makes the camera position respond to the position of the mouse. In order to make this work, we also added some class properties.

Let's put this template into practice and start with the first particle material class— `ParticleMaterial`.

When you work in Flex Builder or Flash Builder, you may want to change the background color of the project to black, in order to see the particles more clearly.

ParticleMaterial

In this example named `ParticleMaterialExample`, we will apply the most basic type of particle material. Take the template we just created as a starting point, and change the class definition and the constructor name. To use `ParticleMaterial` we first need to import it.

```
import org.papervision3d.materials.special.ParticleMaterial;
```

Now add this code at the top of the `init()` method.

```
var particles:Particles = new Particles();
scene.addChild(particles);
```

You just instantiated the `Particles` class and added it to the scene. This instance will display the particles we're about to create inside the `for` loop.

Inside the loop, add the following:

```
var particleMaterial:ParticleMaterial = new ParticleMaterial(Math.
            random()*0xFFFFFF,1,ParticleMaterial.SHAPE_CIRCLE);
```

We define the material inside the `for` loop and not before the loop starts, as we want to apply a separate material to each particle. In this example, we give each particle its own color. While instantiating the material we pass two required parameters to the `ParticleMaterial` constructor. Let's sum up all available parameters:

	Parameter	Data type	Default value	Description
1	color	Number	–	Defines the color.
2	alpha	Number	–	Sets the transparency of the particle.
3	shape	int	0	You can choose between two shapes, a square or a circle, by passing `ParticleMaterial.SHAPE_CIRCLE` or `ParticleMaterial.SHAPE_SQUARE`. The default value of 0 equals the square shape.
4	scale	Number	1	Scales the material and with that the particle.

In our example, we pass a random, hexadecimal color, leave the transparency to its default value, and choose the circle shape. After the material instantiation, but still inside the loop, we create a particle at each iteration and add it to the `Particle` instance using the `addParticle()` method.

```
var particle:Particle = new Particle(particleMaterial,5,
            randPos(),randPos(),randPos());
particles.addParticle(particle);
```

The `Particle` constructor takes one required and four optional parameters:

	Parameter	Data type	Default value	Description
1	material	ParticleMaterial	–	The material that we apply to the particle.
2	size	Number	1	Defines the size of the particle.

	Parameter	Data type	Default value	Description
3	x	Number	0	The x coordinate of the particle
4	y	Number	0	The y coordinate of the particle
5	z	Number	0	The z coordinate of the particle

In our example, we give a random position to each particle by calling the `randPos()` method.

Apparently we have two ways to affect how big the particle looks — the `scale` parameter of `ParticleMaterial` and the `size` parameter of the `Particle` class. In our example, we use only the second one, setting it to a value of `5`.

Publishing the file should show what we have asked for — 1000 circular particles of different colors. The following screenshot shows part of the viewport:

{Ex.} ParticleMaterialExample {Ex.}

BitmapParticleMaterial

The `BitmapParticleMaterial` class lets you use a bitmap as particle material. The bitmap can be created in two ways:

- A dynamically drawn bitmap
- A loaded bitmap

The next two sections will show an example for each of them. Let's start with a drawn bitmap.

Using a dynamically drawn bitmap as BitmapParticleMaterial

Again we will use the `ParticleTemplate` class as our starting point. In this example named `BitmapParticleMaterialShapeExample`, we need to import the `BitmapParticleMaterial` class.

```
import org.papervision3d.materials.special.BitmapParticleMaterial;
```

Add the following code at the top of the `init()` method to instantiate the `Particles` class and add it to the scene:

```
var particles:Particles = new Particles();
scene.addChild(particles);
```

Add the following inside the `for` loop:

```
var triangle:Shape = new Shape();
triangle.graphics.beginFill(Math.random() * 0xFFFFFF);
triangle.graphics.moveTo(0,0);
triangle.graphics.lineTo(20,20);
triangle.graphics.lineTo(40,0);

var bitmapData:BitmapData = new BitmapData(40,20);
bitmapData.draw(triangle);

var material:BitmapParticleMaterial = new BitmapParticleMaterial
                                    (bitmapData);

material.smooth = true;

var particle:Particle = new Particle(material,1,randPos(),
                    randPos(),randPos());

particles.addParticle(particle);
```

The code in the loop looks a lot like the code we have used in the previous section, where we applied `ParticleMaterial` and had to choose between a circle and a square shape for our particles. However, this time you can choose any kind of shape by drawing it dynamically. We draw a randomly-colored triangle inside a `Shape` instance using the Flash drawing API. The triangle has a width of 40 and a height of 20.

We instantiate a `BitmapData` object and pass the width and height of the triangle shape. The third parameter of `BitmapData` defines whether the background of the object is transparent. However, we leave it untouched as it is set to `true` by default. We then draw the triangle shape onto the bitmap image.

Next, we instantiate the material and pass the `BitmapData` object, which is a required parameter. The `BitmapParticleMaterial` constructor has four parameters available as shown next:

	Parameter	Data type	Default value	Description
1	bitmap	*	—	The `BitmapData` or `ParticleBitmap` object to make the material from.
2	scale	Number	1	The scale of the object.
3	offsetx	Number	0	The x position relative to the registration point of the particle.
4	offsety	Number	0	The y position relative to the registration point of the particle.

Note that the first parameter can also be of the `ParticleBitmap` type. We will take a look at how that works in a bit.

Both `offsetx` and `offsety` are numbers and default to 0. The registration point is at the top left. If you want to place the `bitmapData` object at the center, pass `bitmap.bitmapData.width * -0.5` and `bitmap.bitmapData.height * -0.5` as the third and fourth parameters respectively.

After we set the material to smooth, we instantiate the particle while passing the material, the scale, and the coordinates, similar to what we did in the `ParticleMaterial` example.

Publishing the file again shows 1000 randomly positioned and colored particles, but this time their shape is triangular.

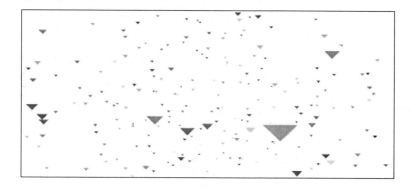

(Ex.) BitmapParticleMaterialShapeExample (Ex.)

Passing a ParticleBitmap instance to the BitmapParticleMaterial constructor

Although the Papervision3D documentation says that the first parameter in the `BitmapParticleMaterial` constructor should be of the `BitmapData` type, you can also pass an instance of `ParticleBitmap`. Using this Papervision3D class allows bitmaps to be created automatically from display objects, meaning we can simply pass the triangle shape to the constructor of `ParticleBitmap`.

```
var particleBitmap:ParticleBitmap = new ParticleBitmap(triangle);
```

Now we can instantiate our material and pass the `ParticleBitmap` instance.

```
var material:BitmapParticleMaterial = new BitmapParticleMaterial
                                      (particleBitmap);
```

Working with `ParticleBitmap` removes the need to create a `BitmapData` object and draw the shape onto it, allowing for a shorter notation. The previous two lines of code can be replaced with the following line:

```
var material:BitmapParticleMaterial = new BitmapParticleMaterial
                                      (new ParticleBitmap(triangle));
```

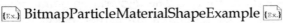 BitmapParticleMaterialShapeExample

Using a loaded bitmap as BitmapParticleMaterial

The alternative to drawing a bitmap dynamically is to load one. Let's see how that goes in an example named `BitmapParticleMaterialImageExample`.

We can use the particles template class for this example, however we need to change it a little. Loading the image will be done inside the `init()` method, and we will create the particles and their material in the event handler that is associated with the load complete event listener.

Inside the `init()` method we will use the `Loader` class to load the image, so don't forget to do the necessary imports for that. The code assumes that the bitmap is in a folder called `assets`, inside the `src` folder. You can find the bitmap in the similarly named example in the download section. The `init()` method should look like:

```
private function init():void
{
    var imgLoader:Loader = new Loader();
    imgLoader.contentLoaderInfo.addEventListener(Event.
                              COMPLETE, loadComplete);
    imgLoader.load(new URLRequest("assets/glassBall.png"));
}
```

We move the `for` loop to the event handler, which looks like the following:

```
private function loadComplete(e:Event):void
{
    var bitmap:Bitmap = e.target.content as Bitmap;

    var material:BitmapParticleMaterial = new BitmapParticleMaterial
                                        (bitmap.bitmapData);
    material.smooth = true;

    numberOfParticles = 1000;

    var particles:Particles = new Particles();
    scene.addChild(particles);

    for(var i:uint = 0; i < numberOfParticles; i++)
    {
            var particle:Particle = new Particle(material,1,randPos(),
                                    randPos(),randPos());
            particles.addParticle(particle);
    }
}
```

When the bitmap is loaded, we assign it to a local variable `bitmap`. We then instantiate the material and pass the bitmap data to it. Notice that this time you can do this *before* instead of *inside* the `for` loop, as each particle will have the same bitmap data applied to it. We also instantiate the `Particles` class before the loop, as we did in the previous two examples. Inside the loop, we instantiate the particles and add them to the `Particles` instance.

When you publish the file, you should see 1000 particles, all having the bitmap as material applied to them. Notice that the bitmap is transparent. You can look through a particle and see the particles behind it. The bitmap is a 24-bit PNG and the ball was already made partly transparent in a graphics-editing program. The following screenshot shows part of the viewport of this example:

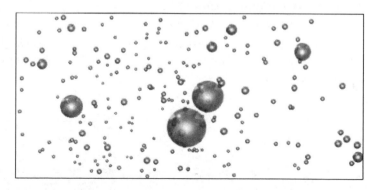

[Ex.] BitmapParticleMaterialImageExample [Ex.]

MovieAssetParticleMaterial

The third and last particle material that Papervision3D has in store is
`MovieAssetParticleMaterial`. The name is a bit misleading as it suggests that this
material works only with movie clip assets as a source. However, in Flex Builder and
Flash Builder, you can also directly use a bitmap, without putting it into a movie clip
first. We will see how that works later in this section.

In Chapter 4, we discussed `BitmapAssetMaterial` and
`MovieAssetMaterial`, which are classes that work with movie
clip and bitmap assets respectively. However, these classes do not
allow for embedding a bitmap in Flex Builder or Flash Builder,
like `MovieAssetParticleMaterial` does.

Compared to `BitmapParticleMaterial`, the `MovieAssetParticleMaterial` class
enables you to do two more things:

- Use (animated) movie clips as the source for the material
- Add interactivity to particles

Flash takes another approach than Flex Builder and Flash Builder in handling this
material. In the following example, both authoring tools will be addressed. We will
create an example that involves adding interactivity to particles. Moreover, the
particles will have an animated movie clip as the source for their material.

Creating an animated movie clip for Flash, Flex Builder, and Flash Builder

Let's start by creating an animated movie clip that we can use in Flash, as well as in
Flex Builder and Flash Builder.

1. Open Flash and save a new document as
    `MovieAssetParticleMaterialExample.fla`.

2. Create a movie clip with a timeline animation. You can also use the one
    provided in the example in the download section, of which the following
    screenshot has been taken:

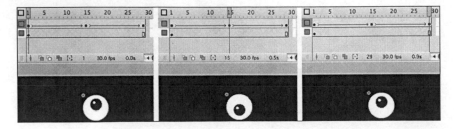

The movie clip in the example is a simple animation of an eye that looks up and down, using a motion tween. There are no stops added so the tween will loop continuously. The movie clip that contains these frames has the size of the white eyeball background, which is 50 by 50 pixels. The movie clip should not be on the stage, only in the library.

3. In the **Linkage** properties of the clip, select the **Export for ActionScript** checkbox, set the class to `AnimatedParticle` and the base class to `flash.display.MovieClip`. This linkage process is similar to what we have seen in working with `MovieAssetMaterial` in Chapter 4.

Now you have an animated clip inside Flash. If you want to continue working in Flash this will do for now. If you want to use the clip in Flex Builder or Flash Builder, you can export it as an SWC.

Exporting the animated clip as an SWC for Flex Builder and Flash Builder to use

In order to use the animated movie clip in Flex Builder and Flash Builder, we will export it from Flash as an SWC. Let's see how it works:

1. Open the library in Flash if it is not open yet.
2. Right-click on the movie clip symbol in the library and select **Export SWC File...**. We haven't yet created the project in Flex Builder or Flash Builder, so save the SWC somewhere on your computer and remember the location for later use.
3. Save it under a name that you will recognize. It does not have to be the same as the class name you used in the linkage properties.

Creating the document class for Flash, Flex Builder, and Flash Builder

The document class looks pretty much the same in the three authoring tools, except for the way you create the material, which we will see in a bit. Let's continue by creating the example for both authoring tools with the `ParticleTemplate` as the starting point.

In this example we won't just randomly spread the particles all over the scene. You will build something similar to what we have done before in Chapter 3 where we created a sphere. At the position of each vertex, we positioned another smaller sphere. In our current example we will position a particle on each vertex of a sphere. These are the imports that we need to carry out.

```
import org.papervision3d.materials.special.MovieAssetParticleMaterial;
import org.papervision3d.objects.DisplayObject3D;
import org.papervision3d.objects.primitives.Sphere;
```

First, we create the sphere. Because we want to have access to it outside the init() method, we assign a Sphere instance to a class property.

```
private var sphere:Sphere;
```

Add the following code at the top of the init() method to instantiate the sphere. We don't add it to the scene.

```
sphere = new Sphere(null,500,10,10);
```

Next, we create an empty array that will be used to hold the particles when we instantiate them. This way we can access the particles separately, which is necessary when we want to add interactivity for each particle. Add the following line to create a class property that holds this array:

```
private var particlesArray:Array = [];
```

Right after instantiating the sphere in the init() method, we create the material. The line of code to achieve this is slightly different for Flash, as compared to Flex Builder and Flash Builder.

When you work in Flash, add the following line:

```
var material:MovieAssetParticleMaterial = new
                MovieAssetParticleMaterial("AnimatedParticle");
```

And add this when you work in Flex Builder or Flash Builder:

```
var material:MovieAssetParticleMaterial = new
                MovieAssetParticleMaterial(AnimatedParticle);
```

Notice the difference. In Flash, the material argument is set as a string within quotes, just like you would use a library symbol in any other situation in Flash. In Flex Builder and Flash Builder it is passed without the quotes, as the class.

You saved the SWC in a folder somewhere on your computer. Now you need to set the library path to this folder. See *Setting the path to the SWC in Flex and Flash Builder* section in Chapter 1 for instructions on how to do this. Follow the instructions, but this time browse to the folder in which you have stored the SWC we just exported from Flash. Both Flex Builder and Flash Builder can now access the SWC, which refers to the AnimatedParticle class that we specified earlier in the **Linkage properties**.

We have just walked through the only difference in this example between Flash on one hand and Flex Builder and Flash Builder on the other. Let's continue for both authoring tools again, by smoothing the material and, in order to see the animation in the movie clip, setting the animated property to true.

```
material.smooth = true;
material.animated = true;
```

Before we run the for loop, we have to set the number of particles. This time it does not equal 1000, but the number of vertices of the sphere.

```
numberOfParticles = sphere.geometry.vertices.length;
```

Now let's add some code inside the for loop, which is still empty.

```
var particles:Particles = new Particles();
var particle:Particle = new Particle(material,1);

particles.addParticle(particle);
scene.addChild(particles);

particlesArray.push(particles);
```

In previous examples, we created only one Particles instance, before the for loop. Now that we plan to add interactivity to each particle, we want to add an event listener to each particle. But as a particle is not a do3D, we cannot add a listener directly to it. Therefore, we need to add the listener to the Particles instance that displays the particle, which we will do in a bit.

We also want to access each particle separately outside the init() method. To achieve this, we add the Particles instances to the array.

After the loop, but still inside the init() method, add the following line:

```
positionParticlesOnSphere();
```

To map the particles to the coordinates of the sphere's vertices, add the following method:

```
private function positionParticlesOnSphere():void
{
    for(var i:uint = 0; i < numberOfParticles;i++)
    {
            Tweener.addTween(particlesArray[i],{
                    x:sphere.geometry.vertices[i].x,
                    y:sphere.geometry.vertices[i].y,
                    z:sphere.geometry.vertices[i].z,
                    time:1,
                    transition:"easeOutBack"});

    }
}
```

The method contains a `for` loop, which again iterates as many times as there are vertices on the sphere. Inside the loop, we tween each `Particles` instance to the position of a vertex of the sphere. Don't forget to import `Tweener`.

When you publish the file, you should see an imaginary sphere consisting of particles as shown in the following screenshot. Make sure that you set the background color of the stage to black in order to see the result clearly.

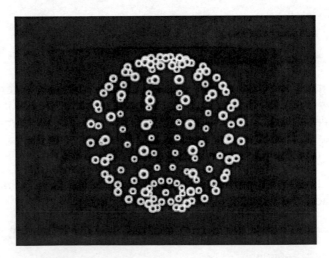

The eyeball particles should be animated. In other words, they should "look up and down" continuously. Let's continue by adding some user interactivity to this example.

Adding interactivity to MovieAssetParticleMaterial

The interactivity that we will implement in the example looks like this: When you click with the mouse on a particle, all particles will tween to a random position. When you click one of the particles again, all of them will tween back and reform the shape of the imaginary sphere.

First, we create an interactive viewport by setting the fourth parameter of the `super()` call to true.

```
super(stage.stageWidth,stage.stageHeight,true,true);
```

We also make the material interactive. Add the following line inside the `init()` method, right after the instantiation of the material:

```
material.interactive = true;
```

As said, we will add an event listener to the `Particles` instances. We can add this listener anywhere inside the `for` loop in the `init()` method, as long as it is after the instantiation of the `Particles` instances.

```
particles.addEventListener(InteractiveScene3DEvent.OBJECT_CLICK,
onParticleClickHandler);
```

The accompanying handler method looks like this:

```
private function onParticleClickHandler(e:InteractiveScene3DEvent):
void
{
    if(randomMode)
    {
        positionParticlesOnSphere();
        randomMode = false;
    }
    else
    {
        positionParticlesRandomly();
        randomMode = true;
    }
}
```

The moment you click on a particle, the method checks whether the particles are randomly positioned or whether they form the shape of a sphere. Based on that information a method is being called. When the particles form a sphere, their position should randomize and vice versa. We use a `Boolean` to check the state of the particles, so add the following line as a class property:

```
private var randomMode:Boolean;
```

The `positionParticlesRandomly()` method looks like this:

```
private function positionParticlesRandomly():void
{
    for(var i:uint = 0; i < numberOfParticles; i++)
    {
        Tweener.addTween(particlesArray[i],{
                x:randPos(),
                y:randPos(),
                z:randPos(),
                time:3,
                transition:"easeInOutElastic"});
    }
}
```

Similarly to the `positionParticlesOnSphere()` method, Tweener is being used inside a loop. However, this time the `Particle` instances are tweened to a random position. The following screenshot shows part of the viewport after this method has been called:

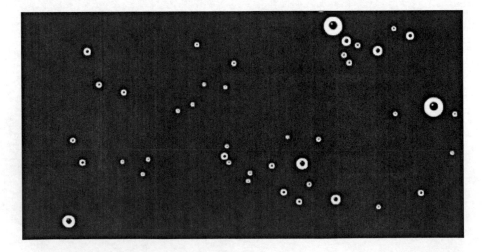

{Ex.} MovieAssetParticleMaterialExample {Ex.}

Embedding a bitmap in Flex Builder and Flash Builder as the source of MovieAssetParticleMaterial

In the previous example we used a movie clip as the source for our particle material. But what if we want interactive particles that use a bitmap as material? We cannot use the `BitmapParticleMaterial` as it does not allow for interactivity. However, for this purpose we can also use `MovieAssetParticleMaterial`, which is the only particle material that can be made interactive. In Flash you can just put a bitmap (instead of the timeline animation) inside the movie clip we created and that will work. In Flex builder and Flash Builder you could also use an SWC. However, there is an easier way—you can simply embed a bitmap.

Let's stay with the `MovieAssetParticleMaterialExample` file and walk through the process of embedding a bitmap and using it as the source for your particles.

Add the following two lines where you defined your class properties. It is important that they have this order.

```
[Embed(source="assets/glassBall.png")]
public var GlassBall:Class;
```

The code embeds a bitmap named `glassBall.png` and assumes that it is stored in an `assets` folder inside your `src` folder. We have used this bitmap before in the `BitmapParticleImageExample`.

Replace the line that instantiates the previously used material with this one:

```
var material:MovieAssetParticleMaterial = new
                        MovieAssetParticleMaterial(GlassBall);
```

While instantiating the material, we pass the class object that we defined after embedding the bitmap. Also, we no longer need the `animated` property of the material set to `true`, so remove that line.

That's it, publishing the file should now show particles with the bitmap material. The particles should be interactive and clicking one of them should tween their positions randomly. The following two screenshots show part of the viewports for the two modes in this example:

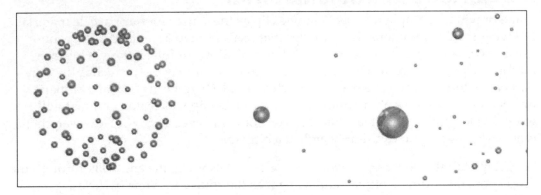

In our examples of the three types of particle material, we added our own code to randomize the coordinates of the particles. However, Papervision3D provides a class that enables you to create a field of randomly positioned particles.

{Ex.} MovieAssetParticleMaterialExample {Ex.}

Creating particle fields with the ParticleField class

The `ParticleField` class lets you create a field of particles in an easy way. The particles are positioned randomly within limits that you set. The following lines demonstrate how you can instantiate a particle field and add it to the scene:

```
var particleField:ParticleField = new ParticleField(material,1000,5,
                             1800,1800,1800);
scene.addChild(particleField);
```

When you create a particle field, you don't have to instantiate the `Particles` or `Particle` classes—the `ParticleField` class takes care of this.

The `ParticleField` constructor has one required and five optional parameters as shown in the next table:

	Parameter	Data type	Default value	Description
1	mat	ParticleMaterial	–	The material to apply to the particles. This can be any of the three types we have discussed.
2	quantity	int	200	Sets the number of particles.
3	particleSize	Number	4	Defines the size (that is, scale) of the particles.
4	fieldWidth	Number	2000	Sets the width of the particle field.
5	fieldHeight	Number	2000	Sets the height of the particle field.
6	fieldDepth	Number	2000	Sets the depth of the particle field.

Think of the `ParticleField` class as a utility that allows you to quickly generate a lot of particles, for instance resulting in a galaxy of stars.

[Ex.] ParticleFieldExample [Ex.]

Particles don't have to be tiny—a billboard example

The examples we saw have one thing in common—they all consisted of a large number of relatively small particles. Also, even though generating many small particles in a scene is a widespread technique, it is not the only way particles can be used.

Here is another scenario. At the beginning of this chapter we introduced particles by briefly discussing two examples—one referred to adding trees to your scene and the other to shiny balls. Let's take a closer look at the tree example. The point that was made is that loading a tree model, which is exported from a 3D modeling tool would take up a lot of polygons. Instead, using a particle with a 2D graphic of a tree as material, would massively cut down the number of polygons.

What you could do, and what actually happens a lot in 3D applications is create a scene with partly 3D objects and partly particles that suggest 3D objects, such as the tree example. You could even build a whole scene made of relatively large sized particles. Keep in mind though that the use of particles can reduce the degree of realism of your scene.

To illustrate this concept, a demo is included in the download section named `BillboardingDemo`. It shows the model of the mill that we have loaded earlier in Chapter 8. This time we added some foliage. Each piece of foliage is a particle with `BitmapParticleMaterial` applied to it. The following screenshot was taken from the demo:

The Flint particle system

Although you can create particles in Papervision3D, it does not include an elaborate particle system. A Flash particle system that can be used in conjunction with Papervision3D is **Flint**, which was developed by Richard Lord. Flint is a well-structured open source library, which allows you to create all kinds of effects such as explosions, fountains, fireworks, and falling snow.

The next section will show you how to download Flint and how to create a fountain of Papervision3D particles.

Downloading the Flint particle system

The home of Flint offers information, examples, and tutorials, and can be found at `http://flintparticles.org/`.

Similar to Papervion3D, you can download an SWC with the compiled code or a ZIP with the source code. You can also download the code through SVN. The SVN repository is at: `http://code.google.com/p/flint-particle-system/source/checkout`.

To work with the ZIP or SWC, go to the **Downloads** section and download the featured version of either one of them. Setting the path to Flint is done exactly the same way as setting the path to the Papervision3D SWC or `src` folder. This process has been described comprehensively in Chapter 1.

 The example in this section was made with Flint version 2.1.0

Creating a fountain of shiny balls with Flint

We will use the Flint particle system to create a fountain of shiny balls. The balls are Papervision3D particles, but they are instantiated by the Flint engine. The following example by no means pretends to cover the Flint engine comprehensively. More tutorials, examples, and information can be found on the Flint home page.

We will build the example with `ParticleTemplate` as our starting point. To make the Flint particle system work, we need several, easy-to-instantiate objects as listed next:

- An emitter—creates the particles for us
- A counter—defines the number of particles
- A zone—a defined area in 3D space where the particles are shot to
- Initializers—set properties of the particles once at initialization
- Actions—set properties of the particles continuously after initialization
- A renderer—draws the particles on the screen

To use these objects we need quite a few imports, so let's start with that. All the imported classes will be discussed in a bit.

```
import org.flintparticles.common.counters.Steady;
import org.flintparticles.common.initializers.Lifetime;
import org.flintparticles.common.actions.Age;
import org.flintparticles.threeD.actions.Accelerate;
import org.flintparticles.threeD.actions.Move;
import org.flintparticles.threeD.geom.Vector3D;
import org.flintparticles.threeD.geom.Point3D;
import org.flintparticles.threeD.initializers.Velocity;
import org.flintparticles.threeD.papervision3d.PV3DParticleRenderer;
import org.flintparticles.threeD.papervision3d.initializers.
                                        PV3DObjectClass;
import org.flintparticles.threeD.zones.DiscZone;
import org.flintparticles.threeD.emitters.Emitter3D;
```

We don't need the `numberOfParticles` class property from the template class. Replace it with the following four:

```
private var emitter:Emitter3D;
private var flintRenderer:PV3DParticleRenderer;
private var particles:Particles;
private var material:BitmapParticleMaterial;
```

As in the `BitmapParticleImageExample`, we use the `init()` method to load the `glassBall.png` and the associated complete handler to set the material we want to apply to the particles. Make sure you have an `assets` folder in the `src` folder, which contains the bitmap.

```
private function init():void
{
    var imgLoader:Loader = new Loader();
    imgLoader.contentLoaderInfo.addEventListener(Event.
                                COMPLETE,loadComplete);
    imgLoader.load(new URLRequest("assets/glassBall.png"));
}

private function loadComplete(e:Event):void
{
    var bitmap:Bitmap = e.target.content as Bitmap;
    material = new BitmapParticleMaterial(bitmap.bitmapData);

    initParticles();
    initEmitter();
    initFlintRenderer();
}
```

As you can see, we also call three methods from the event handler. The first is solely meant to create and add a Papervision3D `Particles` instance.

```
private function initParticles():void
{
    particles = new Particles();
    scene.addChild(particles);
}
```

You don't have to create `Particle` instances because the Flint emitter will do that for you.

The emitter

The emitter creates particles and sets their initial attributes. Let's first write an empty `initEmitter()` method.

```
private function initEmitter():void
{
    //code to be added here
}
```

Inside this method, we will create the emitter. We will add a counter, initializers, and actions, and then start the emitter. Instantiating the emitter looks like this:

```
emitter = new Emitter3D();
```

The counter

Flint has a set of counter classes. Counters tell the emitter how many particles to emit. To create particles continuously and at a steady rate, we use the `Steady` counter.

```
emitter.counter = new Steady(80);
```

This will cause the emitter to create 80 particles per second.

Initializers

As the emitter is responsible for creating particles, it needs to know about their characteristics such as appearance, position, and velocity. Flint provides all sorts of initializers for this job, which are added to the emitter using the `addInitializer()` method.

We will continue by instantiating and adding an initializer called `PV3DObjectClass`.

```
var pv3dObjectClass:PV3DObjectClass = new PV3DObjectClass(Particle,
                                        material,0.1);
emitter.addInitializer(pv3dObjectClass);
```

As said, we don't have to create particles ourselves as the emitter does that for us. The `PV3DObjectClass` initializer tells the emitter which Papervision3D class to use to draw the particles. The first parameter stands for the class to use when creating the particles. In our example this is simply the `Particle` class.

You can (or should when required) add more parameters. The parameters are the same as those that you would use when instantiating the class that you passed as the first parameter. Therefore, when you pass `Particle` as the first parameter, the parameters that follow are those that you would use when instantiating `Particle`—material and scale in our example.

To set the velocity of the particles we add another initializer. We do this by creating a zone. A **zone** in Flint is a defined 3D region of the particle system. Flint has a set of classes to define several kinds of zone shapes such as a spherical or a cylindrical shape. You may wonder why we use a zone to set the velocity. By passing the zone to the `Velocity` initializer, you tell the initializer to move the particles to a random point within that zone in one second.

In our example we create a `DiscZone`, which defines a 3D area in the shape of a disc. Each emitted particle will reach a point on the disc in one second, meaning that the velocity of the particle is defined by the position and shape of the disc. Let's instantiate the zone and pass it to an instance of `Velocity` by adding the following code in the `initEmitter()` method:

```
var discZone:DiscZone = new DiscZone(new Point3D(0,500,0),
                        new Vector3D(0,1,0),200,0);
var velocity:Velocity = new Velocity(discZone);
emitter.addInitializer(velocity);
```

The `DiscZone` constructor takes four parameters, which are listed below:

	Parameter	Data type	Default value	Description
1	center	Point3D	null	A 3D point that defines where the center of the disc is. In our example the center is right above the origin of the emitter, with a y position of 500.
2	normal	Vector3D	null	A 3D vector that defines the normal, which is a vector perpendicular to the center of the disc. Normals have been discussed in Chapter 7.
3	outerRadius	Number	0	Defines the outer radius of the disc.
4	innerRadius	Number	0	Defines the inner radius of the disc. Setting it higher than 0 creates a donut shape.

You can use the `normal` parameter to set the rotation of the disc and thus the direction of the particles. We set only the y value so that the normal will run upward and parallel to the y-axis of the world scene. As we keep both the x and z value of the normal to 0, it doesn't matter how high we set the y value.

`Lifetime` is the last initializer that we add. It sets the lifetime of the particle — 3 . 6 seconds in the following example:

```
var lifetime:Lifetime = new Lifetime(3.6);
emitter.addInitializer(lifetime);
```

To destroy the particle when its lifetime is over, we need to add an action. Let's see what actions are.

Actions

An initializer does what its name promises — it modifies properties of the particles at initialization. But that's not enough to see particles in action. We need actions to continuously modify the properties after they have been created.

First, let's get back to the lifetime of the particle. To destroy the particle at the end of its lifetime we combine it with the `Age` action that ages the particle over its lifetime. Add the following in the `initEmitter()` method:

```
var ager:Age = new Age();
emitter.addAction(ager);
```

The `Move` action updates the position of each particle every frame, based on its velocity.

```
var mover:Move = new Move();
emitter.addAction(mover);
```

Only using the `Move` action would just shoot the particles from the origin straight to a point of the imaginary disc. But we want some gravity as well and use the `Accelerator` to accomplish this.

```
var accelerator:Accelerate = new Accelerate(new Vector3D(0,-300,0));
emitter.addAction(accelerator);
```

The `Accelerator` adjusts the velocity of the particle by a constant acceleration and is defined by a 3D vector perpendicular to the origin of the emitter. Think of the end point of the vector as a magnet that pulls on the particles. In order to simulate gravity, we set the y value to -300. The lower you set this value, the sooner the particles will start falling down.

To finish the `initEmitter()` method, we start the emitter.

```
emitter.start();
```

We now have created the emitter and told it what the particles should look like and what their behavior should be. Let's finish the example by creating a renderer.

The renderer

The emitter needs a renderer, which keeps track of each particle's properties at every frame so that Papervision3D can draw the particles according to their current state. Flint has several types of renderers. We use the renderer that was developed to render Papervision3D particles and, at instantiation, we pass the Papervision3D `Particles` instance to its constructor. We then add the emitter, so it will render the emitter's particles.

```
private function initFlintRenderer():void
{
    flintRenderer = new PV3DParticleRenderer(particles);
    flintRenderer.addEmitter(emitter);
}
```

The following screenshot shows what you should see when you publish the file—a fountain-like effect where particles are being launched upwards and then fall down because of the acceleration we added:

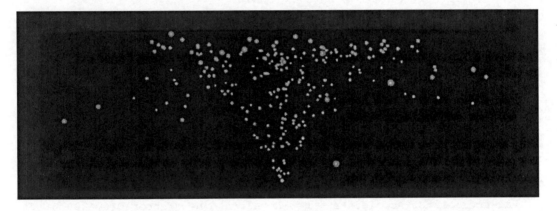

{Ex.} FlintExample {Ex.}

Particles are not the only Papervision3D objects that Flint can deal with. The following are three types of renderers that are specifically used in conjunction with Papervision3D objects:

- The `PV3DParticleRenderer` renders particles
- The `PV3DPixelRenderer` renders 3D pixels
- The `PV3DRenderer` renders other Papervision3D objects such as primitives

To see examples of Flint with pixels and other do3Ds, visit `http://code.google.com/p/flint-particle-system/downloads/list` and download the examples ZIP.

The Flint PV3DPixelRenderer renders pixels, which always have the size of one pixel, and hence are very lightweight. Papervision3D also includes classes that allow you to render pixels in 3D space. The Papervision3D classes that deal with pixels are Pixels and Pixel3D. However, they will not be discussed in this book. Visit http://blog.zupko.info/?p=82 for further reading on how to create 3D pixels.

Summary

Particles are 2D graphics that always face the camera. Being lightweight makes them interesting to work with in a web-based engine such as Papervision3D. Two ways of using them are:

- Billboarding, the technique of using a texture instead of high-poly geometry to cut down on the vertices
- Creating organic effects, with the help of a particle system

We walked through some examples to demonstrate how to create particles and how to apply the available materials. MovieAssetParticleMaterial is the only material that you can add interactivity to.

A demo was presented to illustrate that particles don't have to be small. Using BitmapParticleMaterial, we added some billboards representing foliage to the mill model.

We discussed the Flint particle system. Flint is a Flash-based particle system, which also can be used in combination with Papervision3D. It is able to generate, render, and manage particles, pixels, and other do3Ds.

The next chapter will discuss how to add all kinds of effects to your scenes — from simple transparency, to glows, blurs, blend modes, and even fire.

11
Filters and Effects

When applied with care, filters and effects can enhance your applications quite a lot. Think of adding not only blurs and glows, but also creating fire and smooth vapor-like trails. There are several ways to apply all sorts of effects in Papervision3D, which will be discussed comprehensively.

This chapter covers the following topics:

- Applying Flash filters to 3D objects
- Setting transparency and blend modes of 3D objects
- Applying Flash filters to the entire viewport
- Applying built-in Papervision3D effects to 3D objects
- Adding fog to your scene
- Adding reflection to 3D objects
- Creating the illusion of depth by applying different levels of blur

First, we will look at Flash filters, along with how to add them to viewport layers that contain objects. We will then examine the built-in Papervision3D effects. Next, we will discuss some extra classes that allow you to create a fog-like effect and add reflections. At the end of the chapter, a basic example will demonstrate how to create the illusion of depth of field, which is the region of your view that is focused, whereas the rest is blurred.

What are filters and effects?

While discussing effects in Papervision3D, they are usually mentioned in the same breath with filters. But how do they relate to one another? They seem to be somewhat semantically blended, so let's start by clarifying what we mean when we speak of filters and effects.

Filters refer to the Flash filter classes that reside in the `flash.filters` package such as `BlurFilter`, which applies a blur effect on a display object. Basically, filters are hidden calculations that you use to create visual effects.

In addition to the Flash filters that we can apply, Papervision3D has a set of classes that make it easy for you to create some special effects. For instance, they allow you to set an object "on fire". Most of the built-in effects make use of Flash filters. Therefore, in Papervision3D, effects can refer to effects in general and also to the built-in effects, which are located in a package named `org.papervision3d.core.effects`.

Using Flash filters to create effects

If you have worked with Flash filters before, you probably have added them to 2D objects such as sprites and movie clips. In Papervision3D, applying filters to a do3D goes pretty much the same. However, not all filters may be appropriate for all sorts of 3D objects.

Imagine for instance, a sphere that has real-time shading and at the same time a bevel filter applied to it. Bevel filters add a three-dimensional look to objects by adding a "light and shadow" effect. But the sphere is already three-dimensional and shaded, so adding a bevel may lead to undesired results. Of course, this is a matter of taste and as all filters can be applied to all 3D objects, you may find pretty exciting results by experimenting. In this section, we limit ourselves to three of the most used filters:

- `BlurFilter`: Applies a blur
- `DropShadowFilter`: Applies a drop shadow
- `GlowFilter`: Applies a glow

To demonstrate filters in Papervision3D, we create an example with three cubes. Each cube will have one of the above listed filters applied to it. We use the following class as a starting point:

```
package {
    import flash.events.Event;
    import flash.filters.BlurFilter;
    import flash.filters.DropShadowFilter;
    import flash.filters.GlowFilter;
    import flash.filters.BitmapFilterQuality;

    import org.papervision3d.lights.PointLight3D;
    import org.papervision3d.materials.ColorMaterial;
    import org.papervision3d.materials.shadematerials.CellMaterial;
    import org.papervision3d.materials.utils.MaterialsList;
    import org.papervision3d.objects.primitives.Cube;
```

```
import org.papervision3d.view.BasicView;
import org.papervision3d.view.layer.ViewportLayer;
public class FiltersExample extends BasicView
{
        private var cubesLayers:Array = [];
        private var easeOut:Number = 0.1;
        private var rotX:Number = 0.1;
        private var rotY:Number = 0.05;
        private var camPitch:Number = 90;
        private var camYaw:Number = 270;
        public function FiltersExample()
        {
                super(stage.stageWidth,stage.stageHeight,true,true);
                stage.frameRate = 40;
                init();
                startRendering();
        }
        private function init():void
        {
                var material:CellMaterial = new CellMaterial
                        (new PointLight3D(),0x00FFCC,0x000000,6);
                var cubeMaterials:MaterialsList = new
                                                MaterialsList();
                cubeMaterials.addMaterial(material,"all");

                var numberOfCubes :int = 3;
                var dist:int = 300;
                for(var i:uint = 0; i < numberOfCubes; i++)
                {
                var cube:Cube = new Cube(cubeMaterials,100,200,
                        100,4);
                cube.x = ((i + 0.5)* dist) - ((numberOfCubes * dist)
                                                * 0.5);
                cube.localRotationY = 30;
                var cubeLayer:ViewportLayer = viewport.
                                        getChildLayer(cube);
                cubesLayers.push(cubeLayer);
                scene.addChild(cube);
                }
                //code to be added here
        }
        override protected function onRenderTick(e:Event=null):void
        {
                var xDist:Number = mouseX - stage.stageWidth * 0.5;
                var yDist:Number = mouseY - stage.stageHeight * 0.5;
```

```
                          camPitch += ((yDist * rotX) - camPitch + 90)
                                       * easeOut ;
                          camYaw += ((xDist * rotY) - camYaw + 270) * easeOut ;
                          camera.orbit(camPitch, camYaw);
                          super.onRenderTick();
                      }
                  }
              }
```

The relevant part can be found in the init() method, where we create a cell material and apply it to three cubes. The x positions of the cubes are equally divided over the x-axis of the scene.

You do not apply a filter to a do3D directly, but to the viewport layer it's in. As we have seen in Chapter 9, one way to create a viewport layer is by using the getChildLayer() method. For each cube we create a layer, which we put in an array to have easy access to it.

Applying BlurFilter, DropShadowFilter, and GlowFilter to a 3D object

Now that we have created some cubes and put them in a layer, we can apply a filter to each of them. Let's start by adding a blur to the first cube. You simply create a new blur filter and then apply it to the cube's layer.

Applying a Flash filter to a display object is done by instantiating a filter and then adding it to the filters property of the display object, which is an array. For example, adding a blur filter to a display object would look like this:

```
var blur:BlurFilter = new BlurFilter(7,7,
                          BitmapFilterQuality.LOW);
displayObject.filters = [blur];
```

The first two parameters define the horizontal and vertical blur respectively, and the third parameter defines the quality.

The type, number, and quality of filters you apply to objects may affect the performance of your application. The more filters you apply, the heavier the workload will be for the Flash player to correctly display the effects. More information on Flash filters and their parameters can be found in the ActionScript 3.0 documentation: http://livedocs. adobe.com/flash/9.0/ActionScriptLangRefV3/flash/ filters/package-detail.html.

Remember that we have put the layers in an array, so we can access the layer of the first cube in the array using `cubesLayers[0]`. Add this to the `init()` method.

```
var blur:BlurFilter = new BlurFilter(4,4,BitmapFilterQuality.LOW);
cubesLayers[0].filters = [blur];
```

You can also use a shorthand notation.

```
cubesLayers[0].filters = [new BlurFilter(4,4,
                         BitmapFilterQuality.LOW)];
```

The amount of blur, both horizontally and vertically, is set to 4, and the quality is set to low. For example, a blur can be used to give the illusion of mist or to suggest that the object is out of focus.

Applying a drop shadow filter is done the same way:

```
cubesLayers[1].filters = [new DropShadowFilter(6,45,0,1,6,6,0.6,
                         BitmapFilterQuality.LOW)];
```

A drop shadow will not always lead to realistic results when applied in a 3D scene, whereas a blur can be used in many situations. It adds the shadow right behind the object, so you should use it only when you want your viewers to believe that there is a flat surface behind the object.

Finally, adding a glow filter goes like this:

```
cubesLayers[2].filters = [new GlowFilter(0x000000,1,5,5,20,
                         BitmapFilterQuality.LOW)];
```

The glow filter can be used to add a glow, but it can also serve as a way to create a border around an object. In Chapter 7 we have discussed cell shading and the absence of silhouette rendering in Papervision3D. The previous line of code demonstrates how you can still have a border to simulate silhouette rendering for example. The following screenshot shows a cube with a glow filter:

You can add multiple filters to a do3D's layer the same way you add them to a 2D Flash object—by simply adding them to the filters array. Adding a blur filter and a drop shadow to the layer of the first cube, both with their parameters set to default can be done as follows:

```
cubesLayers[0].filters = [new BlurFilter(),new DropShadowFilter()];
```

We have discussed three filters, but as said before, any of the Flash filters can be applied to 3D objects. There is more, as you can also set the transparency and blend mode of your objects.

Setting the transparency and blend mode of a viewport layer

In Chapter 4, we saw how you can set the transparency of a do3D's wireframe material and color material, resulting in an object that looks transparent. Similar results can be achieved by adding the do3D to a viewport layer and adding transparency to that layer. When working with layers, you can also change its **blend mode**.

Similar to filters, blend mode and transparency are Flash features, which we can set as soon as we put a do3D in a viewport layer. As you undoubtedly know, the transparency of a sprite is defined by its `alpha` property, but let's take a closer look at what blend mode does.

The Flash `BlendMode` class provides a number of constant values such as `BlendMode.LIGHTEN` and `BlendMode.SCREEN`. The blend mode affects the appearance of a sprite or movie clip when it is in a layer above another object. Therefore, when we put a 3D object in a layer, we can set the blend mode for that object and affect how it looks when it is in front of other objects.

When using blend modes, Flash player compares the color of each pixel to the corresponding color of the pixel in the background. It then uses that information to change the color of the pixel, depending on the selected blend mode. For more information on blend modes and an overview of the different types, see: `http://livedocs.adobe.com/flash/9.0/ActionScriptLangRefV3/flash/display/DisplayObject.html#blendMode`.

To demonstrate transparency and blend mode, we will add a plane to the scene and place it in front of the cubes.

```
plane = new Plane(new ColorMaterial(0x0000FF),400,300);
plane.z = -300;
scene.addChild(plane);
```

At the top of the class, we create a class property for the viewport layer to which the plane will be added:

```
private var planeLayer:ViewportLayer;
```

We instantiate it at the end of the `init()` method, and then set the transparency of the layer along with the blend mode.

```
planeLayer = viewport.getChildLayer(plane,true);
planeLayer.alpha = 0.6;
planeLayer.blendMode = BlendMode.MULTIPLY;
```

We also import the `BlendMode` class.

```
import flash.display.BlendMode;
```

The published example shows a partly transparent plane in front of the cubes, as shown in the screenshot:

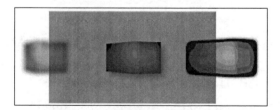

To see the difference between the available blend modes, just change the blend mode property of the plane layer. For instance, `BlendMode.ADD` results in a lightened effect. You may need to change the background color of your application to clearly see the different blend modes.

 FiltersExample

Changing filters, alpha, and blend mode dynamically

We added filters to the cubes and set the transparency and blend mode of the plane. Changing filters, transparency, and blend mode dynamically is fairly simple. Let's first make the plane interactive and add an event listener to it:

```
plane.material.interactive = true;
plane.addEventListener(InteractiveScene3DEvent.OBJECT_CLICK,
onClickHandler);
```

Also, set the interactivity of the viewport to `true`. By clicking the plane we will update its blend mode and at the same time change the amount of blur applied to the cube on the left. This is the associative handler:

```
private function onClickHandler(e:InteractiveScene3DEvent):
void
{
  if(planeLayer.blendMode == "overlay")
  {
    planeLayer.blendMode = BlendMode.MULTIPLY;
    cubesLayers[0].filters = [new BlurFilter(20,0,3)];
  }
  else
  {
    planeLayer.blendMode = BlendMode.OVERLAY;
    cubesLayers[0].filters = [new BlurFilter(0,20,3)];
  }
}
```

We evaluate the current blend mode of the plane layer and change the blend mode type. Also, we overwrite the `BlurFilter` on the layer of the first cube by creating a new one.

Applying filters on viewport level

So far we have discussed applying filters on viewport layers. You can also apply a filter to the entire viewport. This can be done in two ways:

- Directly applying a filter to the viewport, resulting in basic filter effects.
- Using the `BitmapViewport3D` class to create a bitmap viewport of the rendered scene and apply filters to the data (pixels) of this bitmap. This allows you to create more advanced filter effects, for instance effects that can be best described as "trails".

For example, a trail is the illusion of vapor or smoke, as demonstrated in the following screenshot. It shows a particle moving upward, leaving a vapor or comet trail behind:

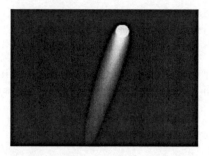

{Ex.} BitmapViewportExample {Ex.}

Directly apply filters to the entire viewport

Applying a filter directly to the entire viewport is easy and goes as follows:

```
var blur:BlurFilter = new BlurFilter(8,8,BitmapFilterQuality.LOW);
viewport.filters = [blur];
```

The previous two lines of code will blur the whole viewport, so every object in it will have the same blurry look. You can add multiple filters to the `filters` array.

Apply filters on viewport level with BitmapViewport3D

Another way to add Flash filters to an entire viewport is through the `BitmapViewport3D` class, which turns every render into a `Bitmap` object. So the result is a viewport, which is a bitmap version of the rendered scene, allowing you to manipulate pixels of the bitmap data. Working with `BitmapViewport3D` gives you more control over the visual result of the filters than adding them directly to the regular viewport and allows you, for instance, to create the aforementioned trails.

We will build an example that consists of one particle drifting in 3D space and leaving a vapor trail. We use only one particle in this example to keep the code short, but based on what you have learned in the previous chapter, it shouldn't be too hard to add more particles.

As the basis of this example, we will use the `BookExampleTemplate` class. Let's start by doing some imports. To create one or more particles you need to import `Particles`, `Particle`, and `ParticleMaterial`.

```
import org.papervision3d.core.geom.Particles;
import org.papervision3d.core.geom.renderables.Particle;
import org.papervision3d.materials.special.ParticleMaterial;
```

We will apply a glow filter to the viewport, so we need to import `GlowFilter`. We also import two other Flash classes: `ColorTransform` and `Point`.

```
import flash.filters.GlowFilter;
import flash.geom.ColorTransform;
import flash.geom.Point;
```

And last but not least, import the class that this example is all about—`BitmapViewport3D`:

```
import org.papervision3d.view.BitmapViewport3D
```

Next we add all the class properties we are going to need:

```
private var container:DisplayObject3D;
private var bitmapViewport:BitmapViewport3D;
private var glow:GlowFilter;
private var colTransform:ColorTransform;
private var destinationPoint:Point = new Point(0,0);
private var particle:Particle;
private var angle:Number = 0;
```

Some of the properties will look familiar; the others will be explained in a bit.

We have taken care of the imports and added class properties, so let's continue by adding code to the `init()` method. We start by creating a do3D, which will hold the particle, so we can move around the particle more freely later on:

```
container = new DisplayObject3D();
scene.addChild(container);
```

We then create an instance of `BitmapViewport3D`:

```
bitmapViewport = new BitmapViewport3D(viewport.width,viewport.
height,true,true);
```

The constructor takes the following parameters:

	Parameter	Data type	Default value	Description
1	viewportWidth	Number	640	The width of the bitmap viewport.
2	viewportHeight	Number	480	The height of the bitmap viewport.
3	autoScaleToStage	Boolean	false	Defines whether the bitmap viewport should automatically scale on resizing the stage.
4	bitmapTransparent	Boolean	false	Defines whether the bitmap viewport will be transparent or not.
5	bgColor	int	0x000000	Defines the background color of the bitmap viewport.
6	interactive	Boolean	false	Defines whether the bitmap viewport should be interactive.
7	autoCulling	Boolean	true	Defines whether auto culling should be applied.

In our example, we pass the width and height of our regular viewport so that both viewports are the same size. We intend to apply a glow filter to the bitmap viewport, and hence we need to set its transparency (the fourth parameter) to `true`.

Now add the following lines:

```
bitmapViewport.fillBeforeRender = false;
addChild(bitmapViewport);
```

The `fillBeforeRender` property is important. When set to `false`, the screen will not be cleared before rendering the next frame. This results in pixels staying on the screen and will give us the vapor trail. The second line adds the bitmap viewport to the stage.

Next, we create a particle and add it to the container do3D:

```
var particles:Particles = new Particles();
var material:ParticleMaterial = new ParticleMaterial(0xFFFFFF,0.6,
                          ParticleMaterial.SHAPE_CIRCLE,10);
particle = new Particle(material,4);
particles.addParticle(particle);
container.addChild(particles);
```

We then instantiate the glow filter:

```
glow = new GlowFilter(0xFFFFFF,1,12,12,0.1);
```

The glow has a white color and an alpha of 1. Both blurX and blurY are set to 12 and the strength of the glow is 0.1.

The last line within the init() method is the following:

```
colTransform = new ColorTransform(1,1,1,1,1,1,1,-6);
```

The Flash ColorTransform class lets you adjust the color values of a display object by applying color transformations to the four color channels—red, green, blue, and transparency. We will not discuss each parameter of ColorTransform, you can look them up in the ActionScript 3.0 documentation. The first seven parameters are set to 1, which is their default value. The parameter we want to set in our example is the eighth one, alphaOffset, which is a number from -255 to 255 that is added to the transparency channel value. We will use an alphaOffset of -6 in the render method to gradually fade out the pixels left on the screen from previous frames. This will give us the desired vapor trail. Let's see how that works by moving on to the render method.

In the onRenderTick() method we first apply the glow filter to the bitmap viewport, or to be precise, to its bitmapData property:

```
bitmapViewport.bitmapData.applyFilter(bitmapViewport.bitmapData,
bitmapViewport.bitmapData.rect,destinationPoint,glow);
```

 Because we don't clear the screen before each render, applying a filter in the render method will result in a trail-like effect when the particle is moving. This is something that cannot be done when using the regular viewport.

The applyFilter() method that we call is inherited from the Flash BitmapData class, which takes a source image and a filter and then creates the filtered destination image. In our example, the source image is the rendered bitmap viewport. Let's briefly walk through the parameters that you pass to applyFilter().

	Parameter	Data type	Default value	Description
1	sourceBitmapData	BitmapData	—	The input bitmap image to use, in our example is the bitmap data of the bitmap viewport.
2	sourceRect	Rectangle	—	A rectangle that defines the area of the source image to use as input. In our example, this is defined by the size of the bitmap viewport.
3	destPoint	Point	—	The point in the destination image that corresponds to the upper-left corner of the source rectangle.
4	filter	BitmapFilter	—	The filter object that you use to perform the filtering operation.

We have set the destination point to (0,0) when we assigned the Point class to the variable destinationPoint. Also note that each type of filter has certain requirements. A requirement for the glow filter is that the destination image is transparent. This is why we have set the transparency of the bitmap viewport to true.

In the init() method we already instantiated a ColorTransform object. Let's put it to work in the render method:

```
bitmapViewport.bitmapData.colorTransform(bitmapViewport.
                              bitmapData.rect,colTransform);
```

We pass two arguments to the colorTranform() method of the bitmapData property. The first argument defines the area of the image in which the transformation is applied and in this example, it is the rectangle that represents the bitmap viewport. The second argument is the earlier created ColorTransform instance with the alphaOffset set to -6, which affects the color values of the bitmap viewport. This will slowly fade out the trail that follows the particle.

The particle will not do much yet, so let's create some motion by adding the following inside the render method:

```
particle.x = Math.cos(angle) * 400 ;
particle.y = Math.sin(angle) * 400 ;
angle += 0.03;
container.pitch(1);
```

What happens here is that the particle will move in circles and the container that holds the particle will rotate around its z-axis, resulting in a random-like movement of the particle.

Finally, we need to tell the renderer that it should render the bitmap viewport:

```
renderer.renderScene(scene,camera,bitmapViewport);
```

The render method still contains the `super.onRenderTick()` call, which refers to the renderer as implemented in `BasicView` and renders the scene to the regular viewport. In this example, the regular viewport is hard to see, so you might as well remove the call, resulting in a slightly better performance. By removing it you only render to the bitmap viewport.

As we have created a white particle with a white glow, the result is best viewed on a dark background. Here is a sequence of screenshots showing the result, a particle with a trail effect caused by a glow filter:

{Ex.} BitmapViewportExample {Ex.}

Built-in Papervision3D effects

So far we have used the generic Flash filters and applied them to objects and to the entire viewport. However, Papervision3D also offers a set of classes that make it easy for developers to apply more advanced effects. Internally, most of these classes make use of Flash filters.

This enables you to create the following built-in Papervision3D effects:

- **BitmapColorEffect**
- **BitmapFireEffect**
- **BitmapMotionEffect**
- **BitmapPixelateEffect**

The `org.papervision3d.core.effects` package that stores these classes also includes a `BitmapLayerEffect` class (not to be confused with `BitmapEffectLayer`!), which offers another way to apply Flash filters to objects. We will see how that works after we have examined the effects listed previously.

All the effects will be demonstrated within one class. We will create a simple scene containing one cube. Let's take the next class as a starting point:

```
package
{
  import flash.events.Event;
  import flash.filters.BlurFilter;
  import flash.display.BlendMode;
  import flash.geom.ColorTransform;
  import flash.geom.Point;

  import org.papervision3d.core.effects.BitmapColorEffect;
  import org.papervision3d.core.effects.BitmapFireEffect;
  import org.papervision3d.core.effects.BitmapLayerEffect;
  import org.papervision3d.core.effects.BitmapMotionEffect;
  import org.papervision3d.core.effects.BitmapPixelateEffect;
  import org.papervision3d.core.effects.utils.BitmapClearMode;
  import org.papervision3d.core.effects.utils.BitmapDrawCommand;
  import org.papervision3d.lights.PointLight3D;
  import org.papervision3d.materials.shadematerials.GouraudMaterial;
  import org.papervision3d.materials.utils.MaterialsList;
  import org.papervision3d.objects.primitives.Cube;
  import org.papervision3d.view.BasicView;
  import org.papervision3d.view.layer.BitmapEffectLayer;

  public class EffectsExample extends BasicView
  {
    private var cube:Cube;
    private var angle:Number = 0;

    public function EffectsExample()
    {
      stage.frameRate = 40;
      init();
      startRendering();
    }

    private function init():void
    {
      var material:PhongMaterial = new PhongMaterial
      (new PointLight3D(),0xEEEEFF,0xCCCCCC,3);
      cube   = new Cube(newMaterialsList({all:material})
                     ,100,100,100,8,8,8);
      scene.addChild(cube);
      camera.z = -300;

      //code to be added here
    }

    override protected function onRenderTick(e:Event=null):void
    {
      cube.x = Math.cos(angle) * 200;
      angle +=0.01;
```

```
        cube.yaw(1.5);
        cube.roll(0.3);
        super.onRenderTick();
    }


  }
}
```

In this class, we made quite a few imports and added two class properties. We create a cube with Phong shading applied to it and set the camera closer to the cube. Inside the render method, we tell the cube to rotate and continuously move from right to left and back, which will give us a good view of the effects we are about to apply.

To apply effects from the Papervision3D effects package we need to create a bitmap effect layer. Let's see what that is and how to create it.

Creating an effect layer

A bitmap effect layer is a viewport layer rendered into a bitmap, and thus allows you to make use of bitmap data, similar to BitmapViewport3D.

In the BitmapEffectLayer class, a sprite is created—the draw layer which holds all the rendered content. Also, a bitmap is created. The draw layer serves as the source that is drawn onto the bitmap image each frame.

A bitmap effect layer is created with the BitmapEffectLayer class. Add the following line in the init() method to instantiate the layer:

```
var bitmapEffectLayer:BitmapEffectLayer = new BitmapEffectLayer
                 (viewport,viewport.width,viewport.height,
                  true,0,BitmapClearMode.CLEAR_PRE,true,false);
```

The constructor takes nine parameters:

	Parameter	Data type	Default value	Description
1	viewport	Viewport3D	—	The viewport that you want to render into a bitmap.
2	width	int	640	The width of the bitmap data to which the image will be drawn.

	Parameter	Data type	Default value	Description
3	height	int	480	The height of the bitmap data to which the image will be drawn.
4	transparent	Boolean	true	Defines the transparency of the bitmap data. Set it to true when you still want to see other objects in your scene.
5	fillColor	int	0	A 32-bit integer that defines the initial fill color of the bitmap data, which is visible when transparent is set to false.
6	clearMode	String	clear_pre	A string that can be defined by a constant from the BitmapClearMode class, which specifies when to clear the draw layer.
7	renderAbove	Boolean	true	Defines whether the draw layer should be displayed above or below the bitmap image that it is drawn onto. When set to true, the draw layer is displayed above the bitmap.
8	clearBeforeRender	Boolean	false	Defines whether the bitmap data should be cleared before each render.

Let's take a brief look at the clearMode options. BitmapClearMode holds three constants:

- BitmapClearMode .CLEAR_PRE: The default setting for the BitmapEffectLayer constructor, clearing the draw layer before each render. In this mode, you can see the draw layer.

- BitmapClearMode .CLEAR_POST: The draw layer is cleared after each render. You cannot see the draw layer.

- BitmapClearModeCLEAR_NEVER: The draw layer is never cleared and you always can see it.

We instantiated the layer, but we still need to add it to the container sprite of the viewport.

```
viewport.containerSprite.addLayer(bitmapEffectLayer);
```

Next we add the cube to the effect layer.

```
bitmapEffectLayer.addDisplayObject3D(cube);
```

Before we actually apply effects to the cube, let's examine some methods that affect how the bitmap data are displayed on the screen.

Methods to affect the way the effect is displayed

`BitmapEffectLayer` has three methods that affect the way the bitmap data are displayed. Let's take a look at them:

- `setScroll()`:

  This method calls the `scroll()` method in `BitmapData` and scrolls the bitmap image by a certain number of pixels in each frame. In the following example, the bitmap image scrolls it 3 pixels up:

  ```
  bitmapEffectLayer.setScroll(0,-3);
  ```

  Use the method when you want a trail effect. It not only defines the direction of the trail, but also its speed.

- `setBitmapOffset()`:

  This method defines the offset of the bitmap. In other words, its position relative to the (0,0) coordinate of the screen. The following line will cause the bitmap effect to be applied only on pixels with an x value higher than `400`:

  ```
  bitmapEffectLayer.setBitmapOffset(400,0);
  ```

- `setTracking()`:

  This method defines the offset of the bitmap relative to an object.

  ```
  bitmapEffectLayer.setTracking(cube,new Point(150,150));
  ```

  The object that you pass can be any do3D in your scene. It doesn't have to be added to the effect layer.

We will use `setScroll()` for most of the effects, so add the above line that calls this method to the `init()` method of our example.

When you call the `setTracking()` method, the `BitmapEffectLayer` class makes use of the `screen` property of the passed do3D, which returns the 2D screen coordinates of the object.

In order to save on performance, the calculation of the `screen` property value is optional and not done by default. To make screen work you should set the `autoCalcScreenCoords` property of the do3D to `true`:

```
cube.autoCalcScreenCoords = true;
```

If you don't do this, the screen property will return (0,0).

We have added and discussed quite some code so far. Let's quickly move on to adding the actual effects so that we can see some results.

Adding a color effect with BitmapColorEffect

The bitmap color effect applies a color matrix filter to the object. It takes the red, green, blue, and alpha values as parameters respectively.

```
var bmColorEffect:BitmapColorEffect = new
                              BitmapColorEffect(0.1,0.1,1,0.9);
```

The previous line emphasizes the blue values of each pixel, and sets the alpha value to `0.9`, decreasing the alpha value of each pixel by 10 percent of its current value on each render.

To actually see the effect we add it to the effect layer:

```
bitmapEffectLayer.addEffect(bmColorEffect);
```

The previous code results in a color effect as shown in the screenshot:

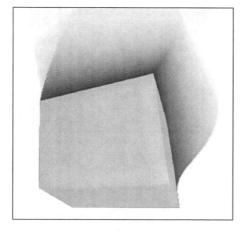

Adding a fire effect with BitmapFireEffect

The bitmap fire effect adds the illusion of fire to an object. BitmapFireEffect has several properties that define how the effect looks:

```
var bmFireEffect:BitmapFireEffect = new BitmapFireEffect();
bmFireEffect.blueFlame = true;
bmFireEffect.fadeRate = 0.5;
bmFireEffect.flameSpread = 0.6;
bmFireEffect.flameHeight = 0.4;
bmFireEffect.distortion = 0.5;
bmFireEffect.distortionScale = 0.4;
bmFireEffect.smoke = 0.1;
```

Let's run through the properties:

Property	Data type	Default value	Description
blueFlame	Boolean	false	Setting this to true results in a blue flame instead of a red one.
fadeRate	Number	0.4	The rate that flames fade out. A value of 0 is slowest, 1 is fastest.
flameSpread	Number	0.3	Defines how much the fire spreads out around the target. A value of 0 is no spread, 1 is a lot of spread.
flameHeight	Number	0.3	Defines how high the flames will burn. A value of 0 is lowest, 1 is the highest.
distortion	Number	0.5	The amount of distortion. A value of 0 is little distortion, 1 results in wilder, more chaotic flames.
distortionScale	Number	0.4	Sets the scale of the distortion. A value of 0 is tiny and chaotic, 1 gives large, smooth flames.
smoke	Number	0	Sets the amount of smoke. A value of 0 gives a small amount, 1 results in lots of smoke.

Different settings of the properties listed in the previous table result in a wide range of results, so play with them to see what they do. And don't forget to add the effect to the layer.

```
bitmapEffectLayer.addEffect(bmFireEffect);
```

The settings used in the example code give the result as shown in the following screenshot, except that the `blueFlame` property is not set, which results in the default red flames. Keep in mind though that the static screenshot does not give a fair presentation of the effect, which is pretty dynamic:

 Although the constructor of `BitmapFireEffect` takes the same parameters as `BitmapColorEffect`, they are not being used in the class at the time of writing. In other words, passing parameters to the constructor when instantiating the class does not have any influence on the effect.

In the fire effect example the `renderAbove` parameter is set to `true`, displaying the draw layer on top of the bitmap image and partially "hiding" the effect. Try setting it to `false` to see how this affects the result.

Adding a pixelating effect with BitmapPixelateEffect

The bitmap pixelate effect gives the object a pixelated look. The constructor of `BitmapPixelateEffect` takes only one parameter that sets the size of the pixels:

```
var bmPixelateEffect:BitmapPixelateEffect = new
BitmapPixelateEffect(5);
bitmapEffectLayer.addEffect(bmPixelateEffect);
```

To get the same result as in the following screenshot, set the `clearBeforeRender` parameter in the `BitmapEffectLayer` to `true`, clearing the bitmap data before each render. Also, comment the line that scrolls the bitmap image.

Adding a motion effect with BitmapMotionEffect

The bitmap motion effect renders the pixels that have changed since the last render, thus showing the motion that takes place. Instantiate the effect and add the instance to the effect layer:

```
var bmMotionEffect:BitmapMotionEffect = new BitmapMotionEffect
                                        (0xFFFF0000);
bitmapEffectLayer.addEffect(bmMotionEffect);
```

The constructor takes an ARGB hexadecimal color value, which in this example a non-transparent red color. The `renderAbove` parameter in the `BitmapEffectLayer` should be set to `false`, showing the effect in front of the draw layer. Also, the line that scrolls the bitmap image is of no use for this effect, so you can comment it if you haven't already. The result shown in the screenshot displays only those pixels that have changed since the last render and gives them the color we passed. Note that the background color also changes to black, which is something that comes with the effect and cannot be altered.

Adding a Flash filter as an effect with BitmapLayerEffect

The final effect is one that takes a generic Flash filter. You first instantiate a filter, which you then simply pass to the constructor of `BitmapLayerEffect`:

```
var blur:BlurFilter = new BlurFilter(7,7);
bmLayerEffect = new BitmapLayerEffect(blur);
bitmapEffectLayer.addEffect(bmLayerEffect);
```

Note that not passing the quality parameter to the filter defaults to low quality. Uncomment the line with the `setScroll()` method. The following screenshot shows the result with the blur filter:

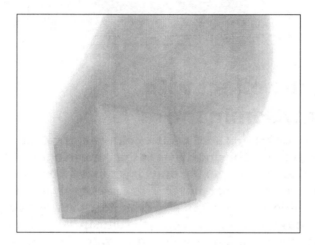

Combining effects

You can add multiple effects to an effect layer—for instance, if you want a more subtle result. To add the color effect and the bitmap layer effect that we just discussed, simply use the following code:

```
bitmapEffectLayer.addEffect(bmColorEffect);
bitmapEffectLayer.addEffect(bmLayerEffect);
```

The next screenshot shows the cube with both the effects applied to it, which results in a blurred, blue trail:

Adjusting the effect with BitmapDrawCommand

As we have seen, `BitmpEffectLayer` creates a draw layer, which is a sprite that holds the rendered content. The draw layer is then drawn onto a bitmap image. We have also seen that you can put the draw layer in front or behind the bitmap image, using the `renderAbove` parameter. This can strongly affect what you see on the screen. But as a little extra, you can also customize the way your effect looks by changing how the draw layer is drawn onto the bitmap. For instance, you can affect the color values and the blend mode of the draw layer.

To accomplish this you can use `drawCommand`, which is a property from `BitmapEffectLayer`. You can assign a `BitmapDrawCommand` object to this property to change the way the draw layer is drawn. Here is an example:

```
bitmapEffectLayer.drawCommand = new BitmapDrawCommand(null,new
                    ColorTransform(0.1,1,0.1,0.6),BlendMode.ADD);
```

Let's see what this example does by looking at the parameters of
`BitmapDrawCommand` **first:**

	Parameter	Data type	Default value	Description
1	`transMat`	`Matrix`	`null`	A transformation matrix to apply to the draw operation.
2	`colorTransform`	`ColorTransform`	`null`	Defines how the color and alpha values of the pixels will be altered when they are drawn onto the bitmap.
3	`blendMode`	`BlendMode`	`null`	Sets the blend mode applied to the pixels in the draw layer when they are drawn onto the bitmap.
4	`smooth`	`Boolean`	`false`	Defines whether or not to smooth the pixels in the draw operation.

In the above example, we change the color and alpha values of the pixels in the
draw layer, emphasizing the green values, and we add a blend mode that brightens
the effect.

As the draw layer is a sprite you can also set its blend mode:

```
bitmapEffectLayer.drawLayer.blendMode = BlendMode.OVERLAY;
```

When you add the previous two lines to the example and apply the bitmap layer effect
(the blur), the result will be a greenish cube with a soft looking blurred green trail.

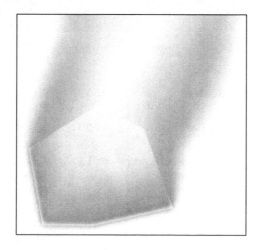

Now that we have covered Flash filters and Papervision3D effects, we will take a look at two more Papervision3D classes. Although they are not part of the built-in effects, they are closely related to the subject of effects.

[Ex.] EffectsExample [Ex.]

Adding fog with FogFilter

The fog filter allows you to create the illusion of objects disappearing gradually in a fog when the distance between the objects and the camera increases. This is a common effect in 3D games, preventing objects from suddenly disappearing behind the far plane, usually somewhere on the horizon. The filter generates a number of viewport layers with alpha transparency distributed over a region that you specify. The transparency of the layers is based on the number of layers you define.

Instantiating the filter is easy:

```
renderer.filter = new FogFilter(new FogMaterial(0xFFFFFF),
                                16,800,2000);
```

It takes the following parameters:

	Parameter	Data type	Default value	Description
1	material	FogMaterial	—	The fog material. The FogMaterial class only takes one parameter, which is a hexadecimal color value.
2	segments	uint	8	Sets the number of layers. The higher this value, the lower the alpha value of the layers will be, and the more gradual the fogging effect. Keep in mind that adding a lot of layers may affect performance.
3	minDepth	Number	200	Sets the distance where the fog filter will start adding layers.
4	maxDepth	Number	4000	Sets the distance where the fog filter will stop adding layers.
5	useViewportLayer	ViewportLayer	null	An optional parameter defining the viewport layer that will contain the fog layers. When no viewport layer is defined, the layers will be added to the viewport directly.

In `FogFilterExample`, you can see the filter at work. It contains a grid of planes that serves as a floor. Also, a rotating sphere is added. For demonstration purposes we use the debug camera. Navigating away from the sphere will make it disappear gradually as if it vanishes into a fog. Moving the camera towards the sphere will make it come out of the fog again. The planes behave the same way. The following sequence of screenshots illustrates the effect:

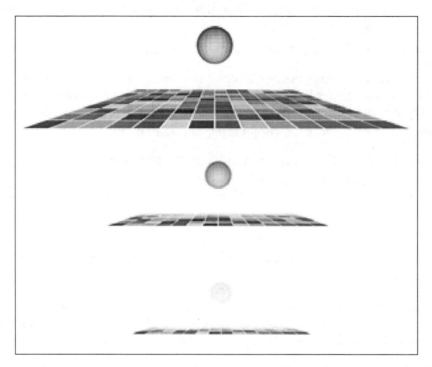

An extra feature of `FogFilter` is the built-in z-depth filter. It automatically prevents all faces that pass the maximum depth from being rendered, resulting in a better performance.

Although `FogFilter` provides an easy way to create the illusion of fog, it also has some limitations. Because the filter adds a number of viewport layers with a certain alpha, you cannot simply add a horizon or background sprite to your scene, as it will always be behind the fog layers. Also, the color that you set for your fog material will be the fill color of your screen.

{Ex.} FogFilterExample {Ex.}

Adding reflection with ReflectionView

Another class included in Papervision3D is `ReflectionView`, which lets you add basic reflections to your scene. The download section of this chapter includes an example in which a carousel of planes is created. The example demonstrates how to work with `ReflectionView`. We will briefly run through the process of adding the reflections:

- Import the `ReflectionView` class. It is located in the `org.papervision3d.core.effects.view` package.

- Extend your document class with `ReflectionView` instead of `BasicView`.

The `ReflectionView` class does not override the `onRenderTick()` method that we have used in all our examples, so we need to change the way we call the rendering process. Replace the `startRendering()` method with the following line:

```
addEventListener(Event.ENTER_FRAME, render);
```

And replace the `onRenderTick()` method with the following:

```
public function render(e:Event):void
{
    singleRender();
}
```

To position the reflection of an object you set the `surfaceHeight` property:

```
surfaceHeight = -20;
```

Because the height of the planes in our example is `-20`, the reflections will be placed right under the planes when using the above setting. If you prefer to add some space between the object and the reflection you should decrease the value.

The following screenshot shows the carousel in the example with `surfaceHeight` set to `-21`:

To add a blur to the reflection, you can simply add it to the filters array of the reflection viewport:

```
viewportReflection.filters = [new BlurFilter(2,2,
                                      BitmapFilterQuality.HIGH)];
```

The class provides a way to add simple, basic reflections. It does not include a fall-off effect, which would make the reflection gradually fade out the further it is from the object. Creating a fall-off effect is not included in Papervision3D.

{Ex.} ReflectionViewExample {Ex.}

Adding objects with no reflection

Suppose you want to add yet another object to the scene, but you prefer not to add a reflection to it. To filter an object from the reflection, use the `viewport.viewportObjectFilter` as follows:

```
viewportReflection.viewportObjectFilter = new ViewportObjectFilter
                               (ViewportObjectFilterMode.EXCLUSIVE);
viewportReflection.viewportObjectFilter.addObject(sphere);
```

The previous code requires the import of two classes, which are located in the `org.papervision3d.core.culling` package: `ViewportObjectFilter` and `ViewportObjectFilterMode`. The latter contains two static constants:

- `ViewportObjectFilterMode.INCLUSIVE`: Includes the objects that are added to the filter and excludes other objects.

- `ViewportObjectFilterMode.EXCLUSIVE`: Excludes the objects that are added to the filter and includes other objects. In the example, we excluded the sphere from the reflection viewport.

We have discussed two classes related to the topic of effects, `FogFilter` and `ReflectionView`. To finish this chapter, we will walk through an example that demonstrates the illusion of depth of field.

Example—creating depth of field

In film and photography **depth of field** is the region in the image that is sharp or in focus. A common trick in portrait photography is to focus on the subject and make the background blurred, drawing the viewer's attention to the subject. A similar effect can be achieved in Papervision3D.

Suppose you have a number of objects in your scene and you want them more in focus the closer they are to the camera. When you put each particle in a viewport layer, you can add a blur filter to each layer. Based on the screen depth of the layer, you can update the strength of the blur at every frame, which will suggest depth of field. Let's apply this idea in a simple example. We create 200 particles with a movie asset particle material and give them a random position. We also add some mouse interaction that makes the camera move. This example assumes that you have an assets folder inside your src folder with the glassBall.png in it, which can be found in the code download.

```
package {

    import flash.events.Event;
    import flash.filters.BlurFilter;
    import flash.display.Bitmap;
    import flash.display.Loader;
    import flash.net.URLRequest;

    import org.papervision3d.core.geom.Particles;
    import org.papervision3d.core.geom.renderables.Particle;
    import org.papervision3d.materials.special.BitmapParticleMaterial;
    import org.papervision3d.view.BasicView;
    import org.papervision3d.view.layer.ViewportLayer;

    public class DepthOfFieldExample extends BasicView
    {

        private var easeOut:Number = 0.9
        private var reachX:Number = 0.4;
        private var reachY:Number = 0.4;
        private var layers:Array=[];

        public function DepthOfFieldExample()
        {
            stage.frameRate = 40;

            init();
            startRendering();
        }

        private function init():void
        {
            var imgLoader:Loader = new Loader();
            imgLoader.contentLoaderInfo.addEventListener
                            (Event.COMPLETE,loadComplete);
            imgLoader.load(new URLRequest("assets/
                            glassBall.png"));
```

```
        }

        private function loadComplete(e:Event):void
        {
                var bitmap:Bitmap = e.target.content as Bitmap;
                var material:BitmapParticleMaterial = new
                        BitmapParticleMaterial(bitmap.bitmapData);
                material.smooth=true;

                for(var i:uint = 0; i < 200; i++)
                {
                        var particles:Particles = new Particles();
                        var particle:Particle = new
                                        Particle(material,1);
                        particles.x = randPos();
                        particles.y= randPos();
                        particles.z = randPos();
                        particles.addParticle(particle);

                        scene.addChild(particles);
                }

        }

        private function randPos():Number
        {
                return Math.random() * 1500 -750;
        }

        override protected function onRenderTick(e:Event=null):void
        {
                var xDist:Number= mouseX - stage.stageWidth * 0.5;
                var yDist:Number = mouseY - stage.stageHeight * 0.5;

                camera.x += (xDist - camera.x * reachX) * easeOut;
                camera.y += (yDist - camera.y * reachY) * easeOut;

                //code to be added here

                super.onRenderTick();
        }

    }
}
```

First we put each particle in a layer so that we can apply a filter to it. At the following code after the last line inside the for loop that is part of the init() method.

```
var layer:ViewportLayer = viewport.getChildLayer(particles);
layers.push(layer);
```

In the render method we dynamically change the strength of the blur of each layer, depending on its distance to the camera:

```
for each(var layer:ViewportLayer in layers)
{
  var blur:Number = Math.round((layer.screenDepth/5000)*30);
  layer.filters = [new BlurFilter(blur,blur)];
}
```

Let's take a look at the line that defines the blur for each layer. Suppose a layer is 1000 units away from the camera. We divide this distance by 5000, which gives us a value of 0.2. Multiplying this value by 30 results in a blur with a strength of 6.

The following screenshot shows part of the viewport. The closer the particles are to the camera, the less blurred they look.

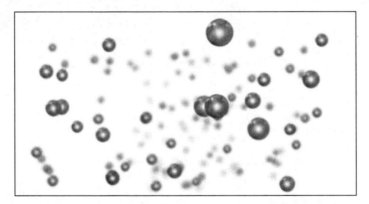

Keep in mind that this example is pretty basic as it takes into account only the distance from the layer to the camera. Another way of creating depth of field would be to specify a certain region in 3D space, which could be somewhere halfway within the frustum, and would keep objects focused within that region. Objects that are closer or farther away than the objects in the defined region would get more blurred.

{Ex.} DepthOfFieldExample {Ex.}

Summary

This chapter discussed filters and effects. By filters we mean the Flash filters such as drop shadow, blur, and glow. The built-in Papervision3D effects allow us to create specific effects such as fire.

You don't apply a filter directly to an object, but to the viewport layer that contains the object. Viewport layers are extended sprites, so you can set their transparency and blend mode.

You can also apply a filter on viewport level, which can be approached in two ways:

- Directly applying a filter to the viewport
- Using the `BitmapViewport3D` class creates a bitmap viewport of the rendered scene. You can then apply filters to this bitmap image

Applying a filter directly to the viewport results in basic Flash filter effects, whereas working with `BitmapViewport3D` allows you to create more advanced filter effects.

Papervision3D has a set of built-in effects:

- A color effect
- A fire effect
- A pixelating effect
- A motion effect
- A layer effect that takes Flash filters

An example has been given for each of the effects, showing you how to create and adjust them.

We discussed two classes that relate to effects: `FogFilter` and `ReflectionView`. The `FogFilter` fades out objects when they move away from the camera. You can set the region in which the object fades in and out. `ReflectionView` enables you to add basic reflections to objects. You can exclude objects from the reflection by using the `viewport.viewportObjectFilter()` method.

Finally, we have discussed an example that shows depth of field, which in film and photography is the region that is in focus. We simulated this by dynamically adding a blur filter to viewport layers, where the strength of the blur was dependent on the screen depth of the layer.

In the next chapter, will take a look at 3D vector graphics and text.

12

3D Vector Drawing and Text

Papervision3D is mainly bitmap based, meaning all that is rendered is converted to bitmaps. Rendering crisp and smooth looking text is quite a challenge when using this approach, as we have seen in the `MovieAssetMaterial` example in Chapter 4. Rendering text directly as vector shapes may offer a good alternative. There are two reasons for this:

- Bitmaps are resolution dependent, and scaling them could lead to a decreasing image quality. Vector shapes are scalable without loss of quality.
- It is hard to wrap text on triangles that are skewed and still make it look good. 3D vector text is not drawn on triangles in order to be rendered.

Papervision3D features a set of classes that allow for drawing vector graphics such as simple shapes and text. The method names that are used for drawing shapes are similar to those of the Flash drawing API such as `lineTo()` and `curveTo()`. Creating 3D text is also fairly simple because of a couple of easy-to-use classes.

The following topics will be discussed:

- Creating 3D vector text
- Creating font files for use in Papervision3D
- Drawing 3D vector shapes and lines
- Adding interactivity to 3D vector text and shapes

The main part of this chapter is dedicated to a library called VectorVision that was incorporated into Papervision3D. After discussing the classes of this library, we will take a look at the `Lines3D` class that also enables you to draw 3D lines. This class was already a part of Papervision3D before VectorVision was incorporated.

VectorVision: 3D vector text and drawing

VectorVision is a library written in ActionScript that allows you to render vector graphics in Papervision3D and add a 3D perspective to them. The project started as a separate library that you could download and use as an add-on. However, it was fully integrated in Papervision3D in June 2008.

Being able to use vector shapes and text theoretically means that you could draw any kind of vector graphic and give it a 3D perspective. This chapter will focus on the features that are implemented in Papervision3D:

- Creating 3D vector text
- Drawing 3D vector shapes such as lines, circles, and rectangles

Keep in mind that 3D letters can be seen as vector shapes too, just like lines, circles, and rectangles. The above distinction is made based on how VectorVision is implemented in Papervision3D. Some classes specifically deal with creating 3D text, whereas others enable you to create vector shapes.

Creating a template class for the 3D text examples

Because the 3D text examples we are about to see have a lot in common, we will use a template class that looks as follows:

```
package
{
  import flash.events.Event;
  import org.papervision3d.materials.special.Letter3DMaterial;
  import org.papervision3d.typography.Font3D;
  import org.papervision3d.typography.Text3D;
  import org.papervision3d.typography.fonts.HelveticaBold;
  import org.papervision3d.view.BasicView;

  public class Text3DTemplate extends BasicView
  {
    private var material:Letter3DMaterial;
    private var font3D:Font3D;
    private var text3D:Text3D;

    private var easeOut:Number = 0.6;
    private var reachX:Number = 0.5;
    private var reachY:Number = 0.5;
    private var reachZ:Number = 0.5;
```

```
public function Text3DTemplate()
{
  stage.frameRate = 40;
  init();
  startRendering();
}

private function init():void
{
  //code to be added
}

override protected function onRenderTick(event:Event = null):void
{
  var xDist:Number = mouseX - stage.stageWidth * 0.5;
  var yDist:Number = mouseY - stage.stageHeight * 0.5;

  camera.x += (xDist - camera.x * reachX) * easeOut;
  camera.y += (yDist - camera.y * reachY) * easeOut;
  camera.z += (-mouseY * 2 - camera.z ) * reachZ;

  super.onRenderTick();
}
}
}
```

We added some class properties that are used in the render method, where we added code to move the camera when the mouse moves. Also, we imported four classes and added three class properties that will enable us to create 3D text.

How to create and add 3D text

Let's see how we can create 3D vector text that looks crisp and clear. The general process of creating and displaying 3D text looks as follows:

1. Create material with Letter3DMaterial.
2. Create a Font3D instance.
3. Create a Text3D instance, passing the text, font, and material to it, and add it to the scene or to another do3D.

We will create an example that demonstrates several features of Text3D:

* Multiline
* Alignment
* Outlines

All the following code should be added inside the `init()` method. Before we instantiate the classes that we need in order to display 3D text, we assign a text string to a local variable.

```
var text:String = "Multiline 3D text\nwith letter spacing,\nline
spacing,\nand alignment ;-)";
```

Now, let's create a text material, font, and text. First we instantiate `Letter3DMaterial`, which resides in the `org.papervision3d.materials.special` package:

```
material = new Letter3DMaterial(0x000000);
```

The constructor of this class takes two optional parameters:

	Parameter	Data type	Default value	Description
1	fillColor	uint	0xFF00FF	Defines the material color with a 24-bit hexadecimal value, which in turn defines the color of the text.
2	fillAlpha	Number	1	Sets the transparency of the material.

In our example, we created black text material with no transparency.

Next, we choose the font of our liking by instantiating one of the font classes. Papervision3D has four classes that represent the following fonts:

- HelveticaBold
- HelveticaLight
- HelveticaMedium
- HelveticaRoman

The classes have the same name as the font and are subclasses of `Font3D`. Later we will look at how we can use fonts other than these four, but for now we will pick `HelveticaBold`. The `Font3D` constructor does not have any parameters.

```
font3D = new HelveticaBold();
```

We then create a `Text3D` instance:

```
text3D = new Text3D(text,font3D,material);
```

Text3D has four parameters available, of which only the last one is optional.

	Parameter	Data type	Default value	Description
1	text	String	—	Defines the text you want to display.
2	font	Font3D	—	Sets the font of the text.
3	material	Letter3DMaterial	—	Sets the text material.
4	name	String	null	An optional name for the Text3D instance.

Text3D is inherited from DisplayObject3D, so we can position, rotate, and scale the instance.

```
text3D.x = 800;
text3D.y = 400;
text3D.localRotationY = -30;
text3D.scale = 2;
```

But Text3D has more to offer, as it has the following properties that format the text:

- align
- letterSpacing
- lineSpacing

The align property aligns the text to the left (default), right, or center, and takes a string:

- "left"
- "right"
- "center"

The following code aligns the text to the right:

```
text3D.align = "right";
```

To set the amount of space that is distributed between all characters, you can set letterSpacing.

```
text3D.letterSpacing = -3;
```

Notice that we didn't import any classes from the flash.text package. Although these properties are named after Flash TextField properties, they are actually created and set in Text3D.

The `lineSpacing` property is the equivalent of `leading` in Flash's `TextFormat` class and defines the amount of vertical space between lines:

```
text3D.lineSpacing = -30;
```

Creating multiline text requires only a regular line break — \n — to go to a new line.

You can also add an outline to the text. The outline is defined by three properties of the material such as line thickness, line alpha, and line color:

```
text3D.material.lineThickness = 2;
text3D.material.lineAlpha = 1;
text3D.material.lineColor = 0xFF0000;
```

Finally, we add the `text3D` instance to the scene:

```
scene.addChild(text3D);
```

Publishing this example should show you the text that we have passed, multilined, aligned to the right, and last but not least, in 3D:

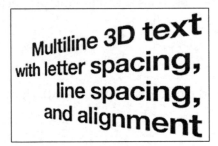

The classes that we have described make it quite simple to get 3D text onto your screen. But what if we do not want to limit ourselves to the four font types that Papervision3D has incorporated?

Font creation

In order to use other fonts in Papervision3D, we need to create our own custom `Font3D` classes. Although this may sound pretty daunting, it is not hard at all, thanks to a tool by Mathieu Badimon, the developer of Five3D.

 Five3D is a 3D engine written in ActionScript 3.0 that lets you create interactive vector-based 3D animations. See `http://five3d.mathieu-badimon.com`

In short, downloading the tool and placing in it the correct folder will create a new panel inside the Flash IDE. When the panel is opened, you can choose a font and the tool will generate an ActionScript class file that contains vector data about the font. The following screenshot shows the panel:

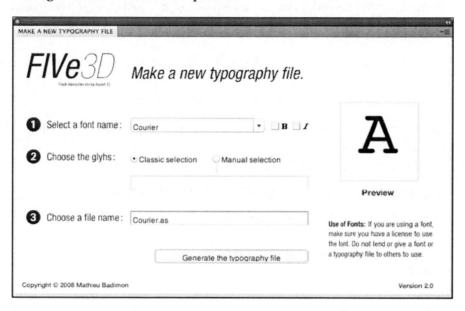

Go to `http://code.google.com/p/five3d/downloads/list` and download the latest release, which was `FIVe3D_make_typography_v2.0.zip` at the time of writing.

Inside the ZIP file you will find a SWF and a PDF file. The PDF contains instructions on where to place the SWF and how to create a font file. Read these instructions carefully and create a file with the font of your choice.

In the instructions, a `WindowSWF` folder is mentioned. The path to this folder is as follows:

On Windows:

```
C:\Program Files\Adobe\Adobe Flash CS4\en\First Run\
WindowSWF\
```

On Mac OS X:

```
\Users\Username\Library\Application Support\Adobe\
FlashCS4\en\Configuration\WindowSWF\
```

Where it says FlashCS4 in the path, it can also be FlashCS3, depending on the version you use. Note that on Mac OS X the generated font file does not end up in the folder where you saved your FLA, but in the root drive **Macintosh HD**

When you have created a font file, which contains an ActionScript class, there are a few things to be done before we can use it. Let's assume we have exported a font file that contains data of the **Courier** font and thus is called `Courier.as`:

- Create a folder named `five3D` inside your `src` folder. Inside the `five3D` folder, create a folder named `typography`. Save the font file in the `typography` folder.

- Open the font file and add the following import to the first line of the class it contains:

  ```
  import org.papervision3d.typography.Font3D;
  ```

- Extend the font class with the `Font3D` class, so that the first line of the class definition looks like this:

  ```
  public class Courier extends Font3D{
  ```

- Add the following three methods to the class definition:

  ```
  override public function get motifs():Object
  {
      if(!__initialized)initialize();
      return __motifs;
  }

  override public function get widths():Object
  {
      if(!__initialized)initialize();
      return __widths;
  }

  override public function get height():Number
  {
      if(!__initialized)initialize();
      return __heights;
  }
  ```

The class is now compatible with Papervision3D. Let's return to our previous example where we instantiated the `HelveticaBold` font and see how we can get this new font working. First we import the font class:

```
import five3D.typography.Courier;
```

Then, all you have to do is alter the line that instantiates the font:

```
font3D = new Courier();
```

Publishing the file should now show you the font that you exported with the tool, in our example `Courier`.

 For further reading about font creation, VectorVision, and Papervision3D, visit `http://code.google.com/p/vectorvision/wiki/FontCreation`

Text3DExample

Adding interactivity to 3D vector text and shapes

Adding interactivity to 3D vector objects basically works the same as adding interactivity to any other 3D object. You can use the `InteractiveScene3DEvent` similar to what we have done in previous chapters. However, to increase the accuracy you should import `VectorShapeHitTest`, which is located in the `org.papervision3d.core.render.command` package, and add the following line at the top of your `init()` method:

```
VectorShapeHitTest.instance.assignViewport(viewport);
```

Another aspect worth taking a look at, is adding interactivity to 3D text. If you would try to add an event listener to a `Text3D` instance directly, you are out of luck. Adding interactivity is done by adding listeners to the letters of the text. Let's see how that works.

Adding interactivity to 3D text

Again, we will take the Text3DTemplate as our starting point. We will create a simple example with some 3D text and make it interactive. When the mouse hovers a letter, it will turn red and the color of all the other letters will change randomly. When the mouse leaves the letter, then the color of all letters will change randomly. First, we create some 3D text in the init() method.

```
var text:String = "Interactive Text3D";
material = new Letter3DMaterial(0xFFFFFF);
material.interactive = true;
font3D = new HelveticaBold();
text3D = new Text3D(text,font3D,material);
text3D.scale = 2;
scene.addChild(text3D);
```

Set the interactive property of the material to true to enable interactivity. Also, let the BasicView class know that you want to make the viewport interactive, by adding the super() call in the constructor and setting the fourth parameter to true.

```
super(stage.stageWidth,stage.stageHeight,true,true);
```

Before we add listeners and their associated methods, add the line we discussed in the previous section at the top of the init() method for more precise interactivity:

```
VectorShapeHitTest.instance.assignViewport(viewport);
```

Now, let's add a listener to each letter of the Text3D instance:

```
for each(var letter:VectorLetter3D in text3D.letters)
{
  letter.addEventListener(InteractiveScene3DEvent.
                          OBJECT_OVER,overLetterListener);
  letter.addEventListener(InteractiveScene3DEvent.
                          OBJECT_OUT,outLetterListener);
}
```

We use a for each loop to add an event listener to each letter. Letters in a Text3D instance are of the VectorLetter3D type, so you need to import this class, which can be found in the org.papervision3d.typography package. Text3D has a letters property, which is an array that holds the letters of the text.

The event handler that is associated with the OBJECT_OVER event looks like this:

```
private function overLetterListener(e:InteractiveScene3DEvent):void
{
  for each(var letter:VectorLetter3D in text3D.letters)
  {
```

```
    if(letter != e.target)
    {
      letter.material = new Letter3DMaterial(Math.random()
      * 0xFFFFFF);
      letter.material.interactive = true;
    }
    else
    {
      e.target.material.fillColor = 0xFF0000;
    }
  }
}
```

Again we use a `for each` loop. Inside the loop, an `if-else` statement evaluates for each letter whether it is the one that has been hovered. If it is not, we assign a new material to the letter with a random color. If it is the letter that has been hovered over, then we change the `fillColor` property of its material to red. Notice that we also set the `interactive` property to `true` when we apply new material to the letters that haven't been hovered over.

If you only add `target.material.fillColor = 0xFF0000;` in the handler, the whole text would turn red on hovering a letter. This makes sense because all letters have the same material. That is why we applied a new material to the letters that haven't been hovered.

In the handler method that accompanies the `OBJECT_OUT` event, we give each letter a random color:

```
private function outLetterListener(e:InteractiveScene3DEvent):void
{
  for each(var letter:VectorLetter3D in text3D.letters)
  {
    letter.material = new Letter3DMaterial(Math.random() * 0xFFFFFF);
    letter.material.interactive = true;
  }
}
```

The following screenshot shows what you should see when publishing this example. The letter the mouse is over should be red, the other letters should be randomly colored.

{Ex.} InteractiveText3DExample {Ex.}

Drawing vector shapes—lines, circles, and rectangles

The integrated VectorVision library not only lets you create 3D text, it also provides a VectorShape3D class that allows drawing basic vector shapes such as lines, circles, and rectangles. The shapes are initially drawn in 2D and then projected in 3D space.

Working with vector shapes requires two classes, VectorShapeMaterial — located in the org.papervision3d.materials.special package — and VectorShape3D - located in the org.papervision3d.objects.special package. To create a vector shape material, use the VectorShapeMaterial class.

```
var material:VectorShapeMaterial = new VectorShapeMaterial();
```

The constructor of this class does not take any parameters.

When you want to draw a shape, you must instantiate VectorShape3D. The following code draws a line:

```
var line:VectorShape3D = new VectorShape3D(material);
line.graphics.lineStyle(2,0x00CCFF);
line.graphics.beginFill(0x666699)
line.graphics.moveTo(-300,-300);
line.graphics.lineTo(300,-300);
scene.addChild(line);
```

The first line of code instantiates the VectorShape3D class, passing the material we just created. The code that then follows illustrates that vector drawing in Papervision3D is very similar to 2D drawing in Flash. The last line adds the vector shape to the scene.

In the VectorShape3D class, an instance of the Graphics3D class is created, which is the 3D equivalent of the Flash Graphics class. We can call the methods in the Graphics3D class the same way we call methods in the Graphics class. When you create an instance of VectorShape3D, you can draw lines, circles, ellipses, and rectangles using methods such as drawRect() and lineTo(). Compared to the Graphics class, Graphics3D is a little less elaborate because it does not provide methods to draw gradient lines or fills.

This is how you would draw a rounded rectangle:

```
var roundedRect:VectorShape3D = new VectorShape3D(material);
scene.addChild(roundedRect);
roundedRect.graphics.lineStyle(3,0xff0000);
roundedRect.graphics.beginFill(0x666699)
roundedRect.graphics.drawRoundRect(-100,-100,200,200,20,20);
```

You can also draw curved lines.

```
var curvedLine:VectorShape3D = new VectorShape3D(material);
scene.addChild(curvedLine);
curvedLine.graphics.lineStyle(2,0x00CCFF);
curvedLine.graphics.moveTo(-300,-300);
curvedLine.graphics.curveTo(0,-600,300,-300);
```

The following screenshots show a circle, a filled rounded rectangle, a line, and a curved line. The screenshot at the left shows a frontal view. In the screenshot at the right, the objects are rotated, offering a 3D perspective.

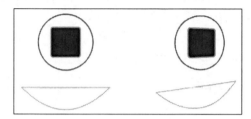

{Ex.} VectorShape3DExample {Ex.}

Drawing lines with Lines3D

Before VectorVision was integrated, Papervision3D already had a `Lines3D` class for drawing 3D lines. Two differences between drawing lines with `VectorShape3D` and `Lines3D` are:

- Whereas `VectorShape3D` enables you to easily draw rectangles, circles, and ellipses, `Lines3D` does not have built-in methods to do such things.
- `Lines3D` creates lines with a `Vertex3D` as the start and end point, resulting in 3D projection of the vertices that make the line. On the other hand, `VectorShape3D` lets you draw a 2D shape, which you then can rotate in order to achieve a 3D perspective.

Let's take a look at how to create straight as well as curved lines with `Lines3D`, and how to add interactivity. The following class will serve as a template for the `Lines3D` examples to come:

```
package
{
   import flash.events.Event;
   import org.papervision3d.core.geom.Lines3D;
   import org.papervision3d.core.geom.renderables.Line3D;
   import org.papervision3d.core.geom.renderables.Vertex3D;
   import org.papervision3d.materials.special.LineMaterial;
   import org.papervision3d.view.BasicView;
```

```
public class Lines3DTemplate extends BasicView
{
  private var lines:Lines3D;
  private var easeOut:Number = 0.6;
  private var reachX:Number = 0.5
  private var reachY:Number = 0.5
  private var reachZ:Number = 0.5;

  public function Lines3DTemplate ()
  {
    super(stage.stageWidth,stage.stageHeight);
    stage.frameRate = 40;
    init();
    startRendering();
  }

  private function init():void
  {
    //code to be added
  }

  override protected function onRenderTick(e:Event=null):void
  {
    var xDist:Number = mouseX - stage.stageWidth * 0.5;
    var yDist:Number = mouseY - stage.stageHeight * 0.5;

    camera.x += (xDist - camera.x * reachX) * easeOut;
    camera.y += (yDist - camera.y * reachY) * easeOut;
    camera.z += (-mouseY * 2 - camera.z ) * reachZ;

    super.onRenderTick();
  }
 }
}
```

Let's first examine what happens when we draw a line using the Lines3D class.

How drawing with Lines3D works

Each line is defined by a start and an end point, both being 3D vertices. The vertices are converted into 2D space coordinates. The lineTo() method of the Flash drawing API is then used to render the line.

The way we create lines with Lines3D has a lot in common with how we created particles in Chapter 10. To create a line with the Lines3D class, we need to take these steps in the following order:

- Create line material with the LineMaterial class. The material defines the look of the line.

- Create a Lines3D instance, which is a do3D that will be used to store and render the lines.

- Use the `Line3D` class to instantiate a line.
- Add the line to the `Lines3D` instance with the `addLine()` method.

Equivalent to how `Particle` instances need to be added in `Particles` using the `addParticle()` method, we add `Line3D` instances to a `Lines3D` instance in order to render them.

`Lines3D` has the following three methods to add `Line3D` instances:

- `addLine()`
- `addNewLine()`
- `addNewSegmentedLine()`

Let's have a look at what they do and create some lines.

Straight lines

All the following code should be added inside the `init()` method. First we create line material.

```
var blueMaterial:LineMaterial = new LineMaterial(0x0000FF);
```

You can pass two optional parameters as shown in the next table:

	Parameter	Data type	Default value	Description
1	color	Number	0xFF0000	Defines the color of the line material using a 24 bit hexadecimal color value.
2	alpha	Number	1	Sets the transparency of the material.

We passed blue as the color and and added no transparency.

Next, we instantiate a `Lines3D` object that will contain and render the lines to be created. The `Lines3D` class inherits from `DisplayObject3D`, so we can add the instance to the scene:

```
lines = new Lines3D();
scene.addChild(lines);
```

Each line is defined by two 3D vertices, which refer to the start point and the end point.

```
var v0:Vertex3D = new Vertex3D(-300,0,0);
var v1:Vertex3D = new Vertex3D(-300,300,0);
```

Now we create a line by instantiating `Line3D`.

```
var blueLine:Line3D = new Line3D(lines,blueMaterial,3,v0,v1);
```

We passed five parameters to the `Line3D` constructor, all of them required.

	Parameter	Data type	Default value	Description
1	instance	Lines3D	—	The Lines3D instance that will hold and render this line.
2	material	LineMaterial	—	The material for the line.
3	size	Number	—	The weight (thickness) of the line.
4	vertex0	Vertex3D	—	The start vertex, which is the 3D coordinate where the line starts.
5	vertex1	Vertex3D	—	The end vertex, which is the 3D coordinate where the line ends.

Finally, we add the blue line to the `Lines3D` instance so that it will be rendered:

```
lines.addLine(blueLine);
```

Actually this is quite a lot of code to draw just one line. Let's draw another line, this time using a much shorter, inline notation.

```
var redLine:Line3D = new
Line3D(lines,new LineMaterial(0xFF0000,1),3,new Vertex3D(0,0,0),
new Vertex3D(-300,0,0))
lines.addLine(redLine);
```

We have just seen how to draw a straight line. Let's make it curved.

Curved lines

To make a line curved, you add a control vertex using the `addControlVertex()` method. You can only add one control vertex because the curve is defined by a quadratic Bezier. Let's curve the red line we just created.

```
redLine.addControlVertex(-150,-300,0);
```

Just like the 3D vertices that define the start and end point of the line, the control vertex is converted into 2D space and rendered using the Flash drawing API, this time using the `curveTo()` method. The following screenshot shows both—the straight and the curved line:

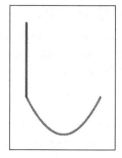

Adding lines with addNewLine()

When you call the addNewLine() method, you don't have to create a Line3D instance before you add a new line:

```
lines.addNewLine(5,0,0,0,300,0,300);
```

The material that has been passed to the Lines3D constructor defines the color and the transparency of the line. If no material has been passed, the line will use the default material color 0xFF0000 and the default alpha value of 1. The seven parameters required are:

	Parameter	Data type	Default value	Description
1	size	Number	—	The weight of the line.
2	x0	Number	—	The line's start x position.
3	y0	Number	—	The line's start y position.
4	z0	Number	—	The line's start z position.
5	x1	Number	—	The line's end x position.
6	y1	Number	—	The line's end y position.
7	z1	Number	—	The line's end z position.

The addNewLine() method returns the created Line3D instance, enabling you to create a line first and then modify it.

```
var line:Line3D = lines.addNewLine(5,0,0,0,300,0,300);
line.size = 2;
```

Or we can create and modify a line within one line of code, in the following example a curved line:

```
lines.addNewLine(5,0,0,0,300,0,300).addControlVertex(150,150,150);
```

Creating segmented lines

Dividing a line in multiple segments can help you when z-fighting takes place between the line and another object. The `addNewSegmentedLine()` method adds a line that is made of two or more segments:

```
lines.addNewSegmentedLine(3,8,300,0,300,600,0,0);
```

The parameters of `addNewSegmentedLine()` are identical to those in `addNewLine()`, except that you also need to pass the number of segments.

	Parameter	Data type	Default value	Description
1	size	Number	—	The weight of the line
2	segments	Number	—	The number of segments that make up the line
3	x0	Number	—	The line's start x position
4	y0	Number	—	The line's start y position
5	z0	Number	—	The line's start z position
6	x1	Number	—	The line's end x position
7	y1	Number	—	The line's end y position
8	z1	Number	—	The line's end z position

The next screenshot shows a line made of 8 segments. Setting the transparency to 1 will show a fluent line, but here the transparency of the material is set to 0.6, resulting in a clear view of the segments:

The `addNewSegmentedLine()` method returns an array, which contains the `Line3D` instances that make up the segmented line and can be manipulated. The following code creates a segmented line and curves the third line in the array:

```
var segLine:Array = lines.addNewSegmentedLine(3,10,300,0,300,0,0,500);
segLine[3].addControlVertex(-10,-30,0);
```

Note that when you trace the length of the array, the number it returns is one higher than the number of lines you specify. The array element with index 0 does not refer to a visual line. In this example `segLine[3]` corresponds with the third line.

As said, working with segmented lines can be helpful in avoiding z-sorting problems. When a non-segmented line cuts through a triangle of another object, the whole line will be sorted in front of or behind the triangle. When using a segmented line, the z-sorting process will take into account only the segment that cuts through the triangle. Take a look at the following screenshots. On the left, a non-segmented line runs through a sphere, on the right, a segmented line was used. Both lines are positioned in such a way that they cut right through the center of the sphere. The black line is not segmented and is sorted behind the sphere. The dotted, white line indicates where it should have run. The segmented line does a much better job, giving the desired illusion of cutting through the sphere. Again, the transparency of the segmented line is set to 0.6 to help demonstrate what's happening here.

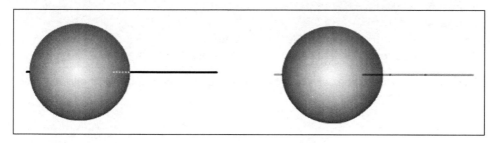

Lines3DExample

Adding interactivity to Lines3D lines

Interactivity can be added through the material instance. Taking `Lines3DTemplate` as a starting point, we will see an example of lines that are interactive.

All of the following code should be added inside the `init()` method. First we create a material and make it interactive:

```
var material:LineMaterial = new LineMaterial(0x000000,0.6);
material.interactive = true;
```

Don't forget to change the `super()` call in the constructor to make the viewport interactive as well.

We then define the number of lines and add some variables that we will use to create a circular shape of lines:

```
var numberOfLines:uint = 80;
var radius:Number = 100;
var angle:Number = (Math.PI*2) / numberOfLines;
```

Next we add a `for` loop:

```
for(var i:uint = 0; i < numberOfLines; i++)
{
  var v0:Vertex3D = new Vertex3D(-300,0,0);
  var v1:Vertex3D = new Vertex3D(300,0,0);

  var lines:Lines3D = new Lines3D();
  var line:Line3D = new Line3D(lines,material,3,v0,v1);

  lines.addLine(line);
  scene.addChild(lines);

  lines.x = (Math.cos(i*angle) * radius);
  lines.y = -300;
  lines.z = Math.sin(i*angle) * radius;
  lines.rotationY  = (-i*angle) * (180/Math.PI) + 270;

  lines.addEventListener(InteractiveScene3DEvent.OBJECT_OVER,
  linesOverListener);

}
```

Inside the `for` loop we create two 3D vertices at each iteration, `v0` and `v1`, that refer to the start and end point of each line. Then we create a `Lines3D` instance that will contain and render the line. We instantiate `Line3D` while passing the `Lines3D` instance, the `material`, a line weight of `3` and the start and end points. Next, we add the line to the `Lines3D` instance, which in turn is added to the scene. The position and rotation of each line are defined by some math, which results in a circular arrangement. Finally, we add an event listener to the `Lines3D` instance, which will trigger the associated handler method when the mouse hovers a line.

The handler method looks as follows:

```
private function linesOverListener(e:InteractiveScene3DEvent):void
{
  Tweener.addTween(e.displayObject3D,{y:200,time:1,transition:
  "easeInOutExpo"});
}
```

Using `Tweener`, the line that has been hovered tweens upwards from its current `y` position of `-300` to a new `y` position of `200`. The following image shows three different states of the example:

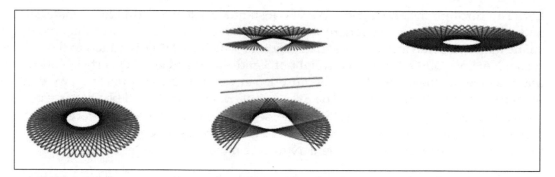

[Ex.] InteractiveLines3DExample [Ex.]

Growing lines example

Although the previous example tweened the position of the lines when they were hovered, the lines themselves were pretty static. Their length and shape stayed the same. The next example shows how to grow a line dynamically . We will create a small sphere and move it around. Out of the sphere a line will grow, which curves depending on how the mouse moves.

We first need to prepare the Lines3DTemplate. Remove all the code in the onRenderTick() method that makes the camera interact with the mouse, but leave the super.onRenderTick(); call. Also remove all the private class properties and put these in their place:

```
private var lines:Lines3D;
private var sphere:Sphere;
private var lineMaterial:LineMaterial;
private var previousVertex:Vertex3D;
```

Now the class is ready for our example. Most of the work will be done in the render method, but first add this in the init() method:

```
sphere = new Sphere(new PhongMaterial(new PointLight3D(),0xFFFFFF,
                                       0x484848,10),100,20,20);
scene.addChild(sphere);

lineMaterial = new LineMaterial(0xFFFFFF);
lines = new Lines3D(lineMaterial);
scene.addChild(lines);

lines.addNewLine(2,0,0,0,0,0,0);
previousVertex = lines.geometry.vertices[1];
camera.target = sphere;
```

Let's run through the above code. We first instantiate a sphere with Phong material and add it to the scene. The sphere will serve as a guide for the dynamic line. We create a line material and a `Lines3D` instance, of which the latter is added to the scene. Next, we add a line with a weight of 3 and a start and end 3D vertex. Notice that we give the line a length of 0, because when we publish the application we don't want to see a line from the start. The `previousVertex` variable will be used in the render method but we initially set it to the coordinates of the second 3D vertex in `Lines3D` instance, which is the end point of the line we just added. Finally, we set the sphere as the target of the camera. Now let's move to the render method.

Inside the render method, we let the sphere rotate depending on the mouse position and we move it forward by 100 units per frame:

```
sphere.localRotationX = -(mouseX/stage.stageWidth) * 360;
sphere.localRotationY = -(mouseY/stage.stageWidth) * 360;
sphere.moveForward(100);
```

The next piece of code, still in the render method, takes care of growing the line dynamically:

```
var new Vertex:Vertex3D = new Vertex3D(sphere.x,sphere.y,sphere.z);
var line:Line3D = new Line3D(lines,lineMaterial,2,previousVertex,
                            newVertex);
lines.addLine(line);
previousVertex = newVertex;
```

At each frame, we create a new 3D vertex with the coordinates of the sphere at that moment. Also, we create a new line and add it. Finally we set `previousVertex` to the new 3D vertex.

So what happens here? In each frame, the start position of the new line is defined by `previousVertex`, which is set to the new 3D vertex after the new line has been added. The end position of every new line is defined by the position of the sphere, which is constantly moving (and rotating if the user moves the mouse). All this results in creating a dynamically growing line that follows the sphere, as shown in the following images:

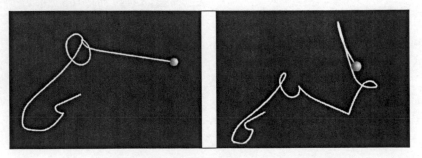

If you don't want to lose sight of the sphere because of its growing distance to the camera, adding the following code to the `onRenderTick()` method copies the position of the sphere to the camera and moves it backward:

```
camera.copyPosition(sphere);
camera.moveBackward(4000);
```

To prevent the line from growing too long, we add the following:

```
if(lines.lines.length > 500)
{
   lines.removeLine(lines.lines[0]);
}
```

`Lines3D` has a `lines` property, which is an array that contains the lines added. If this number exceeds 500, we remove the first line from the array by using the `removeLine()` method.

⌐Ex.⌐ GrowingLines3DExample ⌐Ex.⌐

Summary

Papervision3D offers a set of easy-to-use classes to draw 3D vector shapes such as simple graphics and text. The classes were originally part of VectorVision, a separate project that was developed to create 3D vector text, but was integrated into Papervision3D.

3D vector graphics can be created similar to how the Flash drawing API works, with methods such as `drawCircle()` and `lineTo()`. The graphics, such as lines, circles, rectangles, and ellipses are drawn in 2D and can then be rotated to create a 3D illusion.

The 3D text classes allow you to create crisp looking multiline text with alignment, letter spacing, and line spacing. Although Papervision3D has only four built-in fonts, it is possible to create text with other fonts. An external tool has been discussed, which generates font classes, containing vector information about the font you want to use. These classes can easily be incorporated into your Papervision3D project.

You add interactivity to 3D text as well as other 3D vector shapes, similar to adding interactivity to any other 3D object.

We discussed the `Lines3D` class that also allows you to draw 3D lines. Each line is defined by two 3D vertices, which refer to a start point and an end point. As this class works with 3D vertices, it is possible to set z coordinates, resulting in the illusion of lines with depth. You can also add a control point in order to curve a line. The `Lines3D` and `Line3D` classes were already part of Papervision3D before VectorVision was incorporated. In several examples, we have seen how to create lines with these classes, add interactivity to them, and make them grow dynamically.

The next and final chapter examines how you can make your Papervision3D applications perform better.

13
Optimizing Performance

In the final chapter of this book, we will have a look at how to make your Papervision3D applications perform better. Papervision3D is a cutting edge technology, which may ask for a lot of the CPU to render all the content. This chapter discusses how to reduce the hit on the CPU, so your applications will run faster.

Some optimizations have already been mentioned in previous chapters. We will summarize them here and discuss more performance optimizations.

This chapter will cover the following topics:

- Measuring performance
- Basic optimization strategies
- Optimizing materials
- Optimizing objects
- Optimizing shading
- Optimizing rendering

Before we take a look at the different optimization techniques, we first need to define what performance is in a Papervision3D context and how we can measure it.

Measuring performance

When we speak of performance in a Papervision3D context, we mean everything that relates to how fast Papervision3D can render a scene. Each do3D that is placed somewhere in a scene needs to be calculated. Even when objects are not within the view frustum of a camera, they have a small footprint on the CPU. During each render, Papervsion3D has to decide which triangles are within the view frustum and which triangles are not. Camera-facing surfaces that are placed inside the view frustum have the highest CPU footprint. They need to be projected and then drawn on the screen. Drawing the faces with materials is the most CPU-intensive task.

In order to optimize performance, we first need to know how to measure it. One way to do this is looking at the Activity Monitor on the Mac, or at the processes tab in the Task Manager on Windows. In both utilities, you can look for Flash or the browser used for publishing with Flex Builder or Flash Builder. However, most of the time you can't tell what the performance is based purely on CPU usage. When you set the frame rate of your Flash movies to a relatively high value (like we did in all the examples of this book) chances are that your Flash player won't be able to keep up with the defined frame rate, resulting in using maximum CPU. This doesn't necessarily mean your application isn't performing well. In other words, CPU usage is not the best way to measure performance.

Frame rate is a better indicator to see how your application is performing. The Papervision3D library includes a class, which—if added as an instance to the stage—shows you the currently achieved frame rate. Besides showing the current frame rate, it also displays information such as the memory that is being used and how many triangles were rendered during the last render. A complete list will be shown and explained in a bit. First, let's see how we add these stats to the stage.

The class that we use for these measurements is called `StatsView` and can be imported from the `org.papervision3d.view.stats.StatsView` package. Just add this import to a project of your choice to see how it works.

Instantiating and adding this class to the stage is simple. It is an extended movie clip with just one parameter, which refers to the render engine as follows:

```
var stats:StatsView = new StatsView(renderer);
addChild(stats);
```

That's all. You create an instance and add it to the stage. Publish the project and you'll see the following **stats view** at the top left corner:

The statistics that show up are important indicator, which tell you what is happening behind the scenes and whether your application is performing well. The stats view contains quite a few abbreviations. Take a look at what they stand for:

- **FPS**: Frames Per Second.
  Frames per second is based on the time it took to perform the last render. The highest possible outcome of this value is the defined frame rate of the movie. Defined frame rate is not always accomplished. Frames Per Second is also known as frame rate.

- **Tri**: Triangles.
  The number of triangles that were rendered during the last render.

- **Sha**: Shaders.
  The number of shaded triangles that were rendered during the last render. Triangles that are shaded won't be counted in the **Tri** field.

- **Lin**: Lines.
  The number of lines that were rendered during the last render.

- **Par**: Particles.
  The number of particles that were rendered during the last render.

- **Ren**: Rendered.
  At the time of writing, this value was not in use.

- **RT**: Render Time.
  The time that it took to perform the last render, measured in milliseconds.

- **PT:** Projection Time.
  The time that it took to project the last render, measured in milliseconds.

- **COb**: Culled Objects.
  The number of objects that were culled during the last render. At the time of writing the statistics returned twice as much objects as are actually culled. You should divide this value by two to get the correct number of culled objects.

- **CTr**: Culled Triangles.
  The number of triangles that were culled during the last render.

- **CPa** : Culled Particles.
  The number of particles that were culled during the last render.

- **FOb**: Filtered Objects.
  The number of objects that were added to the `viewportObjectFilter` property of the viewport.

- **Mem**: Memory.
  The memory that is in use by the Flash player and browser.

- **Poly count**: Polygon Count.
  The number of triangles present in a scene. This will only be updated when you call the `updatePolyCount()` method on the stats view. For example:

  ```
  stats.updatePolyCount(scene);
  ```

  Although the name suggests that the number of polygons are being counted, this stat displays the number of triangles. Papervision3D doesn't know polygons, so the names of this label and method are a bit misleading.

When tuning performance you should realize that the frame rate and render time depend heavily on the computer that is running the application. The faster the computer is, the higher the FPS will be. It is most likely that users of your application have a slower computer than you have as a developer. Also, take into account that a standalone Flash player is always faster than a Flash player that runs in a browser. If the Flash IDE is your authoring tool, then you should test the performance of your applications in a browser frequently.

[Having a steady frame rate is often more important than having a fluctuating frame rate with a lot of drops. To accomplish this, the frame rate of the Flash movie should sometimes be set to a lower, average value.]

Basic optimization strategies

When you optimize your application, many factors should be taken into consideration. Performance optimization isn't solely related to optimizing the way you use Papervision3D. In the end, it's all about optimizing performance in Flash. Let's first examine some optimization techniques that are not specific to Papervision3D.

Stage quality

Changing the **stage quality** to low is the easiest way to gain a lot of performance. This might sound odd, as you want to create applications that look good. But decreasing stage quality doesn't necessarily mean that you decrease the quality of what you see on screen. First, take a look at the quality settings that you can set and the effect this will have on your application:

- StageQuality.BEST: Graphics are anti-aliased using a 4 by 4 pixel grid. This always smoothens bitmaps.

- StageQuality.HIGH : Graphics are anti-aliased using a 4 by 4 pixel grid. This smoothes out bitmaps if the movie is static. By default, the quality of the stage is set to high.

- StageQuality.MEDIUM: Graphics are anti-aliased using a 2 by 2 pixel grid. This does not smooth out bitmaps and has little effect on the readability of text that is optimized for animation.

- StageQuality.LOW: Graphics are not anti-aliased and bitmaps are not smoothed. This affects the look of texts optimized for animation dramatically.

Anything lower than high may affect your application visually. Especially, text that is not optimized for readability can look less readable, which is something to take into account and could be optimized. Aim at developing at least medium stage quality and only set the low stage quality when really necessary.

A common trick is to use medium or even high stage quality when there is a static view of the scene and set the stage quality to low during animations. Let's see what happens if you do this. When an animation is playing, it is hard to see what the quality of the textures is, because of the motion. So we might as well set the quality to low. On the other hand, when the view is static and the quality is set to high, you will be able to see the high quality of the renders, because of the absence of motion.

Another common trick is to base the stage quality on the frame rate achieved on the user's computer, while playing the movie. If the frame rate drops below a certain value, your application can detect this and set the stage quality to medium or low. This way a user with a fast computer will see the best graphics and have an application that is performing well, while users with a slow computer can still view the content at a reasonable frame rate.

In order to change the quality of your stage, you need to import the `StageQuality` class, which will give you access to the static constants that define the quality. The class can be found at: `flash.display.StageQuality`. By changing the `quality` property of your stage, you can change the quality at any time:

```
stage.quality = StageQuality.LOW;
```

A problem that might occur when changing the stage quality is that it changes the quality of text that isn't optimized for readability and isn't part of a Papervision3D render—for example, the labels used on the buttons of your 2D interface. What you could do in such situations is create a snapshot of the elements that cause the problems and show the snapshot instead. The following code illustrates how this can be achieved for a fictive button:

```
var bmpData:BitmapData = new BitmapData(button.width,button.height);
bmpData.draw(button);
var bmpButton:Bitmap = new Bitmap(bmpData);
bmpButton.x = button.x;
bmpButton.y = button.y;
addChild(bmpButton);
removeChild(button);
```

Try setting the stage quality in previous examples. For example, set the quality of the animated mill to medium and see how your frame rate increases; it is guaranteed to boost performance.

Other general Flash optimizations

In general, you should always try to write optimal code. Clean up your event listeners when you do not need them anymore. Don't create lots of enter frame event listeners or timers. Aim at never declaring variables inside a loop. This will make your applications in general perform better and so will your Papervision3D applications.

When you finish your project and publish the version that your users will see, you can do this in two ways. During development in Flex Builder and Flash Builder you probably publish a debug build by default, and so does Flash when the permit debugging option in the Publish Settings is selected. However, you can also publish a release build, which performs much better than debug builds.

Destroy unwanted objects

As part of clean programming, you should always clear references to objects that you no longer need. This way the object can be removed from memory as soon as the garbage collector runs its cycle.

Because Papervision3D makes use of a lot of bitmap data objects, it is very important to clean up your objects correctly when you no longer need them. So, when you remove a child from the scene and you no longer need access to it, be sure to delete its reference as well as its material. Once you can completely remove an object from memory, you need to execute the following three lines of code:

```
scene.removeChild(do3d);
do3d.material.destroy();
do3d = null;
```

The first line removes the object from the scene. The second removes all references to the material used by the object. The third line sets the reference to this object to null. Make sure that you also remove other references to the object in your code. Memory can only be cleared when all references are removed.

Viewport size

The bigger the size of your viewport, the more that is revealed of the scene and needs to be rendered. Keeping the total amount of pixels that need to be rendered as low as possible, will have a positive effect on performance. Although applications that make use of the entire available screen are often very impressive, it is not always a good idea to run your Papervision3D applications in this mode. Carefully consider which viewport size fits your needs and the limitations of Papervision3D.

Camera frustum and field of view

A camera can see everything that happens in the scene. The more it sees at the same time, the heavier the workload for the Flash player. Therefore, you can try tweaking the camera a bit so that it sees less objects simultaneously. If your project needs every possible optimization, you can try narrowing the view a bit by using the `fov`, `zoom` and `focus` camera properties. As this technique probably does not strongly affect the amount of rendered triangles, the impact on the performance may be small. Although setting more extreme values will save more on performance, it will also result in unnatural looking renders.

Culling

In Chapter 5, which is about cameras, we saw what culling is and how to use it. Culling is the process of identifying what is located totally or partially inside a camera's view frustum and getting rid of what is not inside. Frustum culling is a performance optimization, which you can set as a camera's property. This would look like this.

```
camera.useCulling = true;
```

With `useCulling` set to `true`, all objects outside the view frustum will be ignored, which is a performance saver.

Creative thinking

Optimizing performance requires a creative approach. Every application is different and may require other performance optimizations than those mentioned in this chapter. If you have an idea about how to increase the performance of your application (which has not been mentioned here), then try it out and see if it works for you.

Optimizations can often be found in faking 3D. Although faking might have negative connotations, it is actually a very good thing to do. At the beginning of a project, you always need to ask yourself which elements you could fake—for example, by using billboard particles.

Optimizing materials

When materials are not used optimally, they can give Papervision3D a hard time rendering them. In Chapter 4 about materials, you have already seen some techniques to keep them as lightweight as possible. In this section, we will discuss these techniques one by one and introduce more optimization strategies.

Transparency

Transparency can set on instances of MovieMaterial or classes that inherit from MovieMaterial. By default, transparency of movie materials is turned off. Whenever you can, you should keep it this way. Transparent images are 32-bit and non-transparent images are 24-bit. The latter are much faster to render.

Tiled

Always try setting the tiled property of a material to true. Depending on your situation this will slightly increase the performance due to the presence of a performance bug in the Flash player.

Power of two textures

Power of two textures enable mipmapping, which allows you to set smoothing on materials to true without losing any performance. Chapter 4 about materials describes extensively how this works.

Some situations just won't let you use power of two dimensions In order to still benefit from the advantages of mipmapping, you can set the static BitmapMaterial property AUTO_MIP_MAPPING to true.

```
BitmapMaterial.AUTO_MIP_MAPPING = true;
```

When you set this, Papervision3D corrects all newly created bitmap materials. The drawback is that it takes a bit more memory than it would take when set to false.

Material size

In the modeling chapter, you already saw that you should keep the width and height of your materials as small as possible. For example, when you have a model of a car and you want to texture the wheels, it would be wise to texture them as small as possible. The wheels will probably not appear full screen, so using a texture of 1024 by 1024 pixels wouldn't make any sense. Use small power of two textures instead, like a 64 by 64 pixels image.

Animated materials

An animated material is a pretty tough material type for the Flash player to deal with. Every time we render an object that uses an animated material, the player creates a new snapshot of the current state of the movie clip. The snapshot is then used as a regular bitmap material and from there it is transformed into 3D perspective and drawn on the screen.

Creating this snapshot is very CPU intensive, therefore the `animated` property should only be set to `true` when the material is animating. When you no longer need the animation, set this property to `false`. By default, it is set to `false` on all materials that inherit from `MovieMaterial` with the exception of `VideoStreamMaterial`, which obviously has to be animated.

As animations on a material are CPU intensive, you should always try to use as few simultaneously animated materials as possible.

A trick to gain performance while using animated materials, is to store each frame of the animation as a snapshot in memory. Each time the movie hits a frame, which has already been shown, you can show the cached snapshot from memory instead of recreating a new snapshot of the frame.

Unfortunately, this feature is not implemented in Papervision3D. However, Andy Zupko, one of Papervision3D's core team members has posted an article on his blog, where he introduced a material type that stores each frame in memory and offers this class as a download. Check it out here: `http://blog.zupko.info/?p=248`.

There are a few things that you need to take into account while implementing this caching mechanism:

- As all snapshots are stored in memory as bitmap data, this can take up quite some memory. The more frames you'll use or the higher the resolution of the movie clip, the more memory is needed.

- This works only for static movie clips, which play the same animation over and over again.

- As each frame is stored as bitmap data, you won't be able to have material interactivity.

When using multiple animated materials at the same time, caching frames is an absolute performance booster.

Optimizing objects

The more complex your objects are, the more triangles need to be drawn. It's been said before that you should always try to keep the triangle count as low as possible. When modeling with external tools, it's better to make a very low poly model first and then add more polygons or triangles afterwards if necessary. Doing it vice versa, by removing triangles from an advanced model, will be a lot more work.

But there are more techniques available to optimize objects. We will have a look at these in the following sections.

Remove objects that are behind other objects

It sounds easy: Just remove your objects when you know they won't be visible. This does not refer to objects that are positioned outside the camera's view frustum or back facing surfaces of 3D objects, as Papervision3D will detect these automatically for us. The title of this section refers to objects that are located in the view frustum, but are positioned behind other objects from certain points of view.

Because Papervision3D uses the painter's algorithm by default, it draws all objects from the furthest to the nearest. So, when one object is in front of another object both of them will be drawn on your screen. When the object in front entirely obscures the object that is behind, it would be a waste of capacity to draw both of them.

Let's imagine the situation where you make a 3D environment made of two rooms—a bathroom and bedroom. A wall divides the rooms and you can walk around. When you click the door, you enter the other room. Let's say you are looking in the direction of the door, which will give you access to the bathroom. Because of the painter's algorithm, this will result in drawing the bathroom first, with a big wall in front preventing you from seeing the bathroom. By simply removing the bathroom from the scene, you could solve a lot of performance issues.

Isn't this what the far plane of a camera is for, you might think? Well, that is partly true for this example. The far plane can save you from rendering objects that are too far away to be seen at all, but it doesn't save you from rendering the bathroom while heading towards that direction. When the camera comes close to the door, the far plane wouldn't be of any use.

Removing objects that are behind other objects can be helpful whenever you know that you will not be able to see them. Remove objects when you know they are out of sight and you will gain some performance, especially when it concerns objects with a high triangle count.

Coding this could be a lot of work to achieve. When you are planning your project and already know that it will balance on the edge of what is possible in Papervision3D, the idea of removing hidden objects may be worthwhile considering.

Level of detail

Level of detail (also known as **LOD**) is about decreasing the complexity of 3D objects, based on their distance to the camera. Let's say you have a do3D that is positioned very close to the camera. The do3D appears big on your screen and you can see all the details. However, when that same object is positioned somewhere in the background, it is not necessary to see all its details, as it is rendered so small on your screen that you can hardly see it anyway. This is where LOD comes in, which can be used to show a low or high triangle count version of an object, based on the distance to the camera. If we wanted to make this work even better, the triangles of two models should be interpolated, so you don't get sudden changes from one version of the do3D to the other. This slightly changes the look of the do3D by adding more interpolated triangles.

Papervision3D has built-in support for LOD, but it doesn't support interpolation between do3Ds. Without this interpolating feature this technique is called **simple level of detail**, or **SLOD**.

The class that provides the built-in SLOD support is `SimpleLevelOfDetail`, which can be imported from `org.papervision3d.objects.special.SimpleLevelOfDetail`. Have a look at how we can put this class to work:

```
private var slod:SimpleLevelOfDetail;

private function init():void
{
  var stats:StatsView = new StatsView(renderer);
  addChild(stats);
  var mat:WireframeMaterial = new WireframeMaterial
                              (Math.random()*0xFFFFFF);
  var sphere1:Sphere = new Sphere(mat,200,12,12);
  var sphere2:Sphere = new Sphere(mat,200,6,6);
  var sphere3:Sphere = new Sphere(mat,200,3,3);
  var spheres:Array = [sphere1,sphere2,sphere3];
  slod = new SimpleLevelOfDetail(spheres,600,2000);
  scene.addChild(slod);
}

override protected function onRenderTick(e:Event=null):void
{
  slod.z += 5;
  super.onRenderTick();
}
```

First, we instantiate three spheres and we put them in an array. The array is passed as the first parameter for the SimpleLevelOfDetail class. You add objects to the array with different degrees of detail, starting with the closest and most detailed object and ending with the furthest and simplest object.

Instantiation of the SimpleLevelOfDetail class takes four parameters:

	Parameter	Data type	Default value	Description
1	object	Array	—	An array of 3D objects. The first element in the array stands for the closest and most detailed version. The last element is the furthest and most simple version of the 3D object.
2	minDepth	Number	1000	Defines from what distance the closest and most detailed objects should be used.
3	maxDepth	Number	10000	Defines from what distance the furthest and less detailed objects should be used.
4	distances	Array	null	An array of integers used to define the depth value per object in the object array. This is set to null by default. When an array is provided, this array will replace the minDepth and maxDepth parameter, as these values are provided in the array by the first and last element.

Once the SimpleLevelOfDetail class has been instantiated, we add the instance to the scene, which is possible because this class inherits from DisplayObject3D.

In each onRenderTick call the SLOD spheres will be moved a little bit farther away from the camera, which clearly demonstrates how the object changes.

After publishing, you will see a movie that looks like the following sequence of images:

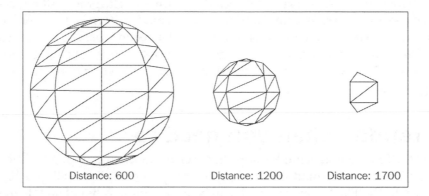

Because a `StatsView` instance has been added to the stage, you'll also be able to see the number of rendered triangles decreasing in the top left corner.

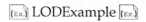 LODExample

Optimizing shading

Real-time shading is an enormous performance hit on your CPU. Real-time shading should always be limited to just a few objects, especially when you apply Phong shading. Wherever possible, you should use baked textures that contain the shading information instead. However, when your project requires real-time bitmap-based shading, a small performance optimization is possible.

A good trick is to add the object that needs to be shaded to the scene twice. The first object has the regular bitmap material applied to it, which is the material you want to be shaded. The other object uses a color-based shader as material, for instance `PhongMaterial`. The ambient color of this shader should be black to make this trick work. Each object should be added to a sublayer of an index sorted viewport layer. This renders the second object with a color based shader as the top layer. By using the `BlendMode.MULTIPLY` as the blend mode of the top layer, you can create an illusion of shading on the underlying objects. This technique saves a bit of performance, but it will not boost it. An example named `BlendModeShading` can be found in the book downloads.

Optimizing rendering

When a new render is called for every enter frame, a new render cycle starts. Within this cycle, Papervision3D will run through the process of clipping, culling, z-sorting triangles, projecting vertices, and drawing transformed materials. In other words, everything that results in an image on our screen has been a part of the rendering pipeline. The best way to increase performance is not to render at all. Of course this isn't an option. However, with some creativity you can also win performance in the rendering process.

Only render when you need to

As long as the 3D scene is static because the user is interacting with other elements in your application, you could pause the rendering process. This will give back some performance to the Flash player, which can be of benefit to other elements in your application and the experience of the user.

When working with the `BasicView` class, the renderer can be stopped by calling the `stopRendering()` method. As soon as you want to start rendering again you can call the `startRendering()` method.

Selective rendering

Selective rendering is a smart concept to save a lot of render time. In situations where your camera and objects have the same position and orientation as the previous render, you can decide not to render at all. What if the whole scene is exactly the same, except for one animated object or animated material? Executing a whole new render on each enter frame is far from efficient. A way to render only certain objects is using viewport layers, as these can be selectively rendered.

Instead of rendering your scene the regular way, you render an array, which contains the layers that you want to be rendered. The syntax is very similar to rendering a scene the way we have learned in Chapter 2, when we did not extend `BasicView`.

```
renderer.renderLayers(scene,camera,viewport,[layerReference]);
```

The only difference with a regular render is in the name of the method and the fourth parameter, which is an array holding all the viewport layers that need to be rendered. A basic example has been included in the book downloads of this chapter under the name `SelectiveRendering`.

At the time of writing there is an issue with selective rendering and nested objects. This problem introduces more performance problems than it solves. Nested objects will increase the amount of triangles that are used dramatically. So never use nested objects in combination with selective rendering. Especially when you are working with external models, this might be a huge challenge to meet.

Viewport scaling

In order to save on performance, but maintain a screen filling view you could use a smaller viewport and scale it up so that it will match the previous viewport size. Depending on how much you scale up the viewport, this will result in pixelated renders.

Suppose your scene contains an object, of which the rendering quality doesn't matter so much. For example, the terrain in a game, which is generally accepted to be a blurry surface. Rendering the terrain to a special viewport type called `BitmapViewport3D` can achieve the scaling. This viewport type has previously been discussed in Chapter 11 about filters and effects. A regular viewport can be used to render all the other objects that you want to be sharp. This means that we need to create two viewports and add them both to the stage. In a way, this is the manual equivalent of layering viewport layers. Only this time, you use viewports instead of viewport layers. A regular viewport cannot be used is because you cannot properly scale up your viewport to create pixelated renders and gain performance. The renders will always stay sharp.

An example of how this works is included in the book downloads under the name `ViewportScaling`. The example contains the animated mill with the green colored floor, which we've used in earlier examples. The scaling of the floor as illustrated in this example isn't that beneficial, as it is just a composite material of a wireframe and a color. Using a bitmap texture instead would be more appropriate, but the idea should be clear.

Summary

In this final chapter we discussed a number of ideas on how to get the best possible performance, giving you the tool to make your applications perform as good as possible.

We have examined:

- What performance is and how we can measure it
- How to change the stage quality for faster rendering
- Basic performance optimizations for Flash, materials, and objects
- What power of two textures are and how they can help increase performance for smooth rendering
- Caching snapshots of animated materials
- How to use level of detail in your applications
- How to fake shading by using viewport layers
- What selective rendering is and how to use it
- How to scale a bitmap version of the viewport for faster rendering special objects

Performance optimizations are definitely not limited to what has been discussed here. Optimizing performance requires creative thinking in order to come up with ideas on how to win CPU power.

Index

size 386
tiled 386
transparency 386
materials list 67
material property 61
materials parameter, cube 68
material type, interactivity
  about 112
  buttonMode parameter, using 112
  event listeners, defining 113
Memory (Mem) 381
mipmapping 120
model
  exporting, from Google's 3D Warehouse
    258, 259
  importing, into Papervision3D 260, 261
modeling, for Papervision3D
  about 240
  best practices 240-243
  object, positioning 243
  quality and performance balance,
    determining 243
  recognizable names for materials, using 243
  recognizable names for objects, using 243
  size, maintaining 243
  textures, baking 242
models
  creating, Blender used 261
  creating, SketchUp used 257
  loading, Blender used 261
  loading, SketchUp used 257
modelLoaded() method 251, 267
moveBackward() method 145
moveDown() method 145
moveForward() method 145
moveLeft() method 145
moveRight() method 145
moveUp() method 145
movieAsset parameter 99
MovieAssetParticleMaterial
  about 302
  animated movie clip, exporting
    fromSWC 303
  animated movie clip, using in Flex
    Builder 303

animated movie clip for Flash, creating 302
animated movie clip for Flash Builder,
  creating 302
animated movie clip for Flex Builder,
  creating 302
bitmap as source, embedding in Flash
  Builder 309
bitmap as source, embedding in Flex
  Builder 309
comparing, with BitmapParticleMaterial
  302
document class, creating for Flash 303-306
document class, creating for Flash Builder
  303-306
document class, creating for Flex Builder
  303-306
interactivity, adding 307, 308
movie clip, using
  MovieAssetMaterial class 99-106
  MovieAssetMaterial class, instantiating 103
  MovieAssetMaterial class, parameters
    used 102
  MovieMaterial class 99
  MovieMaterial class, instantiating 99-101
  MovieMaterial class, parameters used 99
  problems, causes 104
  ways, as material 98, 102
myName property 30

N

name parameter 255
nesting
  about 72, 73
  addChild() method, using 73
  benefits 72
  DisplayObject3D 73
  pivot point creation, DisplayObject3D
    used 75, 76
  Scene3D 73
  world space versus local space 74, 75
non-compiled source
  downloading, in ZIP file 17
  downloading, on Mac OS X 14-17
  downloading, on Windows 12-14

downloading
  compiled source 18
  Flint 312, 313
  Papervision3D 8
  Tweener 180, 181
dynamically drawn bitmap
  ParticleBitmap instance, passing to Bitmap-
    ParticleMaterial constructor 300
  using, as BitmapParticleMaterial 298, 299
dynamic animation 162

E

effects
  about 322
  creating, Flash filters used 322
  displaying ways, methods 338
emitter 292
EnvMapShader 231
Euler angles 165, 166
ExampleClass function 30
excludeFaces parameter, cube 68
exported animations 256

F

faces. See triangles, 3D object
far property 134
fill BeforeRender property 331
Filtered Objects (FOb) 381
filters
  about 322
  applyFilter() method, destPoint
    parameter 333
  applyFilter() method, filter parameter 333
  applyFilter() method, sourceBitmapData
    parameter 333
  applyFilter() method, sourceRect
    parameter 333
  applying, BitmapViewport3D used 329-332
  applying, directly on viewport level 329
  applying, on viewport level 328, 329
  BlurFilter 322
  BlurFilter, applying 325, 326
  demonstrating 322
  DropShadowFilter 322

DropShadowFilter, applying 324-326
GlowFilter 322
GlowFilter, applying 325, 326
fisheye lens 132
Five3D tool
  about 360
  downloading 361
Flash
  animation 161
  applications, Flash ways 163
Flash, configuring
  example, running 22
  in CS3 20
  in CS4 19
  path, setting to compiled source 21
  path, setting to non-compiled source 19, 20
  ways 19
Flash Builder, configuring. See Flex
    Builder, configuring
Flash filter
  adding, BitmapLayerEffect used 343
  effect adjustment, BitmapDrawCommand
    used 344-346
  effects, combining 343, 344
  using, to create effects 322, 324
Flash IDE
  document class 35
FlatShadeMaterial
  about 218
  ambientColor parameter 219
  lightColor parameter 218
  light parameter 218
  parameters 218
  specularLevel parameter 219
FlatShadeMaterial, for color-based
    shading 217
FlatShader, for bitmap-based
    shading 220, 221
flat shading
  about 215, 216
  FlatShadeMaterial, for color-based
    shading 217
  FlatShader, for bitmap-based shading 220
  usage 216

getChildLayer, recurse parameter 280
getChildLayer, using 280
useOwnContainer, using 278-280
do3d parameter 281
instantiating 281
isDynamic parameter 281
viewport parameter 281
viewport layers
blend mode, setting 326
transparency, setting 326
using 275
viewportWidth parameter 51

W

width parameter, cube 68
width parameter, plane 59
wireframe materials, basic materials
alpha parameter 86
color parameter 86
creating, manually 85, 86
thickness parameter 86

X

X, plane 122
X property 77, 78

Y

yaw() method 164

Z

z-sorting
about 271
defining 272
diagramatic representation 272
painter's algorithm 272
triangles, sorting 273, 275
triangles, subdividing 274, 275

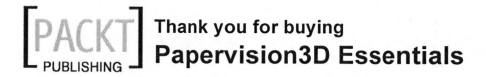

Packt Open Source Project Royalties

When we sell a book written on an Open Source project, we pay a royalty directly to that project. Therefore by purchasing Papervision3D Essentials, Packt will have given some of the money received to the Papervision project.

In the long term, we see ourselves and you—customers and readers of our books—as part of the Open Source ecosystem, providing sustainable revenue for the projects we publish on. Our aim at Packt is to establish publishing royalties as an essential part of the service and support a business model that sustains Open Source.

If you're working with an Open Source project that you would like us to publish on, and subsequently pay royalties to, please get in touch with us.

Writing for Packt

We welcome all inquiries from people who are interested in authoring. Book proposals should be sent to author@packtpub.com. If your book idea is still at an early stage and you would like to discuss it first before writing a formal book proposal, contact us; one of our commissioning editors will get in touch with you.

We're not just looking for published authors; if you have strong technical skills but no writing experience, our experienced editors can help you develop a writing career, or simply get some additional reward for your expertise.

About Packt Publishing

Packt, pronounced 'packed', published its first book "Mastering phpMyAdmin for Effective MySQL Management" in April 2004 and subsequently continued to specialize in publishing highly focused books on specific technologies and solutions.

Our books and publications share the experiences of your fellow IT professionals in adapting and customizing today's systems, applications, and frameworks. Our solution-based books give you the knowledge and power to customize the software and technologies you're using to get the job done. Packt books are more specific and less general than the IT books you have seen in the past. Our unique business model allows us to bring you more focused information, giving you more of what you need to know, and less of what you don't.

Packt is a modern, yet unique publishing company, which focuses on producing quality, cutting-edge books for communities of developers, administrators, and newbies alike. For more information, please visit our website: www.PacktPub.com.

PACKT PUBLISHING

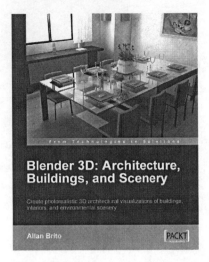

Blender 3D Architecture, Buildings, and Scenery

ISBN: 978-1-847193-67-4   Paperback: 332 pages

Create photorealistic 3D architectural visualizations of buildings, interiors, and environmental scenery

1. Turn your architectural plans into a model

2. Study modeling, materials, textures, and light basics in Blender

3. Create photo-realistic images in detail

4. Create realistic virtual tours of buildings and scenes

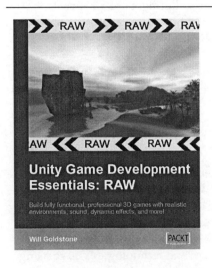

Unity Game Development Essentials [RAW]

ISBN: 978-1-847198-18-1   Paperback: 300 pages

Build fully functional, professional 3D games with realistic environments, sound, dynamic effects, and more!

1. Kick start game development, and build ready-to-play 3D games with ease

2. Understand key concepts in game design including scripting, physics, instantiation, particle effects, and more

3. Test & optimize your game to perfection with essential tips-and-tricks

4. Written in clear, plain English, this book is packed with working examples and innovative ideas

Please check **www.PacktPub.com** for information on our titles

ImageMagick Tricks

ISBN: 978-1-904811-86-2   Paperback: 232 pages

Unleash the power of ImageMagick with this fast, friendly tutorial and tips guide

1. Complete tutorial and a gallery of tricks and techniques

2. Create impressive image manipulations and animations on-the-fly from the command line or within your programs

3. Complete PHP-based sample applications show how to use ImageMagick to add pizzazz your web site

---

Drupal Multimedia

ISBN: 978-1-847194-60-2   Paperback: 264 pages

Create media-rich Drupal sites by learning to embed and manipulate images, video, and audio

1. Learn to integrate multimedia in your Drupal websites

2. Find your way round contributed modules for adding media to Drupal sites

3. Tackle media problems from all points of views: content editors, administrators, and developers

Please check **www.PacktPub.com** for information on our titles

Lightning Source UK Ltd.
Milton Keynes UK
UKOW011502230513

211099UK00002B/55/P